Paving the Way
in
Reading and Writing

Paving the Way

in

Reading and Writing

Strategies and Activities to Support Struggling Students in Grades 6–12

Larry Lewin

JOSSEY-BASS
A Wiley Imprint
www.josseybass.com

Published by Jossey-Bass
A Wiley Imprint
989 Market Street, San Francisco, CA 94103-1741   www.josseybass.com

Jossey-Bass books and products are available through most bookstores. To contact Jossey-Bass directly call our Customer Care Department within the U.S. at 800-956-7739, outside the U.S. at 317-572-3986 or fax 317-572-4002.

Jossey-Bass also publishes its books in a variety of electronic formats. Some content that appears in print may not be available in electronic books.

Library of Congress Cataloging-in-Publication Data
Lewin, Larry, 1949-
  Paving the way in reading and writing : strategies and activities to
support struggling students in grades 6-12 / Larry Lewin.— 1st ed.
    p. cm. — (The Jossey-Bass education series)
Includes bibliographical references and index.
  ISBN 0-7879-6414-X (alk. paper)
  1. Language arts (Secondary) 2. Reading—Remedial teaching. I.
Title. II. Series.
  LB1631.L417 2003
  428'.0071'2—dc21

                                        2002155636

Printed in the United States of America
FIRST EDITION
PB Printing   10 9 8 7 6 5 4 3 2 1

The Jossey-Bass Education Series

Dedicated to Colin,
my three-year-old grandson

and

to his parents Donald and Frédérique,

his cousin Mia,

and his lovely Nana

Contents

Preface

Paving the way. Why would a secondary teacher need to "pave the way" for students to read or write in class?

The answers to this question may be profound, troubling, or even elaborately researched and hotly debated.

But for the purpose of this book the answer is quite simple: We have no choice.

For whatever reasons, the number of students in our middle schools, junior highs, and high schools who struggle in class with basic reading and writing skills is increasing. Any teacher in any state will confirm this. The number of strugglers and rate of increase in that number can be alarming in many districts.

Some of these students struggle so mightily they qualify for special education services. Others are low-skilled, but not low enough to qualify for special ed. And some I call the "in-betweeners." Some days they can handle the reading and writing assignments, and some days they cannot.

In all cases, these are the kids who sit in our classes needing their teachers to pave the way for them. Their road to reading comprehension is so strewn with obstacles that they swerve out of control. And the road to composing interesting, coherent written expression is likewise so littered with potholes, roadblocks, and dangerous curves that they get thrown off track.

Obviously, these obstacles occur in any classroom. So paving the way must occur in any classroom. This opposes the proposition that reading and writing instruction is the exclusive domain of the English and language arts class. No, this instruction must take place in all classrooms, including the "content areas" of math, science, social studies, the arts, health, business . . . *all* classes. You will hear me say, "It takes a village to help students learn to read and write."

We, the teachers of all subjects, can help pave the way for all our students by providing four critical pieces of instruction:

- A *framework* for teaching reading and writing. This book presents a general four-step process approach that helps students solve the problems that inevitably come up in reading or writing.

- A set of *strategies* for effective application of that four-step process. The process approach is not enough in itself—it is the explicit application of key strategies at key moments that makes the difference in reading and writing.

- A strong *linkage* of reading to writing, what I call the two sides of the literacy coin, the twin pillars of literacy. Writing and reading serve at the heart of education, and it is up to each of us, every single teacher of any grade and any subject, to teach them and teach them well.

- A *variety* of new, different, surprising, and maybe even fun reading and writing activities that will grab student attention and provide motivation and energy to read and write. Teachers need something new and different to replace what students perceive as the "same ole, same ole."

These four components provide the foundation of this book. They will give you the specifics for paving the way, for removing obstacles to literacy—for downfield blocking, if you will indulge a sports metaphor, for students who routinely take the big hits from reading and writing assignments.

By paving the way we are not only supporting our students' literacy growth, we are increasing their ability to learn the content information we are teaching them. And if we do not pave the way for them, too many of our students will only partially understand—or completely not understand—the key concepts we teach. Reading and writing serve content learning, so we must help them read and write.

All of this book's suggested activities, assignments, and actions come from secondary classrooms. You will read about actual kids in actual schools across the country whose teachers are paving the way for them.

Many of the activities come from my own classes—I taught junior high, high school, and middle school for twenty-four years before retiring from the classroom to work with teachers. Others come from teachers who have picked up ideas from the workshops, seminars, and courses that I have been presenting for the last decade or so. These teachers are gratefully acknowledged on the pages following this Preface.

These teachers have borrowed my ideas and applied them in unique ways to make them work in their own particular teaching situations. So you will also read about modifications, adjustments, and adaptations to the recommended activities. And you will be urged to do the same, to feel free to tweak whatever ideas you encounter in this book to make them even better for your students.

WHO SHOULD READ THIS BOOK?

If you are a content area teacher and you are assigning reading in your classes, then this book is for you. Because if you are assigning reading, then you are, by definition, a teacher of reading. You really are—even if you are not trained in reading instruction, and even if you have no interest in teaching reading.

And this book is for you if you are assigning writing in your classes, or would like to assign more in order to help your students process what you are presenting to them, but you do not really know how to proceed.

And you know why: Too many of your students struggle with basic reading and writing. Their gap in reading and writing skills interferes with their ability to learn what you are teaching. They need you, and all the rest of their teachers, to help them gain proficiency in these two most important aspects of schooling.

This book is for you.

And this book is for English/language arts teachers, as well, who do know about teaching reading and writing, but who want something new to offer their resistant readers and writers. This book provides a fresh look at the twin pillars of literacy—reading and writing—by presenting many new ideas, activities, and assignments.

This book is also written for pre-service teachers. If you have not yet been hired to teach and you are now studying how to become a teacher, this book can speed up your learning process by providing you the wisdom of dozens of your veteran colleagues who have wrestled with finding ways to reach their strugglers.

This book was also written for administrators who desire to be instructional leaders in their buildings, to bring teaching methodologies to the teachers, to be helpful to those on the front lines of education. Take this book, select your favorite techniques, and give them to your staff as gifts.

Finally, parents should read this book. If you have a son or daughter who, for whatever reason, is struggling with basic skills in school, check out what I have to say about reading and writing. You, too, can take ideas from this book and teach your child how to use them. (And please feel free to share them with your child's teachers!)

OUR GAME PLAN

I have organized this book into seven chapters, each with a distinct focus on teaching literacy skills to struggling adolescents. The first chapter serves as an introduction to my approach to this endeavor. I acknowledge the challenge of the situation, and I provide you with a bit of historical context to the solutions I will be offering, including a generic problem-solving process approach that works for both writing and reading in any classroom.

The next two chapters address the role of reading informational text for solid understanding in a content area class. I divide my suggestions for teaching students how to read better into a set of problem-solving strategies early in the reading process (Chapter Two) and later in process (Chapter Three). I am especially proud of the activities that serve to strengthen visualization skills. If you're an English/language arts teacher, resist the temptation to skip these two chapters. Many of the techniques presented here, you will find, are appropriate for reading literature, too.

Chapter Four addresses reading strategies in English/language arts classrooms. It brings my proposed reading process into focus by offering many literature "tracking devices" for each stage of the process. This chapter concludes with a detailed sample literature lesson plan worth considering for adaptation or modification. Content area teachers, a suggestion: Read this chapter. I predict you will like many of the techniques offered, and that you will see ways of adapting them to your needs.

The next three chapters focus on writing instruction. Chapter Five provides teachers of all subjects with a set of new writing assignments designed to stimulate interest and energy in your students. I will share with you how they work to motivate writing among the nonmotivated, whether writing about history, science, literature, or math. This chapter ends with the very best student-friendly editing technique I have ever used, the Sentence Opening Sheet.

Chapter Six continues with the focus on writing by providing additional concrete examples of assignments, ones that will prove more challenging for students. The same structure presented in Chapter Five is repeated here, but now with the more advanced exercises: study guides, chapter review booklets, persuasive letters, brochures, and essays.

The final chapter examines the nitty-gritty of writing instruction, namely classroom management, editing and rewriting, use of computers, and the always-popular topics of spelling and grammar. This chapter ends with a set of suggestions for student research on the Internet and how to teach students to evaluate Web site information and to avoid the temptation of digital plagiarism.

I close with a brief Epilogue that muses on the necessity for providing students the type of assignments and support outlined in this book, reinforced by figures from the National Assessment of Educational Progress (NAEP). Following the Epilogue, the Appendix lists outstanding Web site resources and the Bibliography lists the sources that went into the creation of this book, which may well prove useful as you develop your own assignments and exercises.

PAVING THE WAY

The purpose of this book is to provide you with a chance. A fighting chance to surprise your students with a different approach to reading and writing. A chance to gain their attention. A chance to engage them. A chance to teach them.

ACKNOWLEDGMENTS

"It takes a village to write a book."

No one person can write a book. I am the author, but I had help. Lots of help. I want to acknowledge the following people for their contributions:

First to Christie Hakim, associate editor in the Education Series at Jossey-Bass, for initiating a meeting with me to discuss this book and for committing to help me write it. Her support and guidance were invaluable.

Also, deep thanks to the people at Jossey-Bass for their contributions to this book: Elisa Rassen, editorial assistant, for her hard work on assisting me in preparing the manuscript. Pam Berkman, senior production editor, Education Series, masterful coordinator of the many facets of book production, Sachie Jones, marketing assistant, for ideas on steering this book to teachers, and to Hilary Powers, text editor and copyeditor extraordinaire, masterful wordsmith, the most careful of readers, for massaging the manuscript into a book that I am proud of. You rock.

To Linda Barber, my wife, my business partner, and my sounding board, for her help steering me to success.

To my colleagues in the Eugene, Oregon School District for their professional support, great ideas, and friendship: Betty Jean Shoemaker, curriculum coordinator, beacon of energy, and collaborator; Dorothy Syfert, former teaching partner and inspiration; master teacher and new friend Eliza Sher; and new colleague Jud Landis.

To Frank Koontz, assistant executive director of the Bureau of Education and Research (BER), for helping me develop my seminar on this topic, "Practical Strategies for Achieving Success with Struggling Readers and Writers," which became the foundation for this book.

To Herb Hrebic, cofounder and publisher of Stack the Deck Writing Program, who encouraged me to write, with coauthor Tanis Knight, my first book, *Open the Deck,* and whose ideas helped me become a teacher of writing.

Eugene, Oregon   Larry Lewin
February 2003

Teacher Acknowledgments

Here are the teachers who have worked with me and are mentioned in these pages—only a fraction of the many whose ideas I have borrowed or enriched (or both) over the years.

Greg Barnett, sixth-grade science teacher, Joseph Lane Jr. High, Roseburg, Oregon.

John Bonar, theology, psychology, and math teacher, Ramona Convent Secondary School, Alhambra, California.

Sue Borkon, sixth-grade teacher, Shorewood School District, Shorewood, Wisconsin.

Carrie Brooks, literature teacher, Schoharie Central School, New York.

Jim Burke, author and English teacher, Burlingame High School, Burlingame, California.

Tom Cantwell, author and seventh-grade connections teacher, Cal Young Middle School, Eugene, Oregon.

Herb Felsenfeld, special day class teacher, and instructional associate Lucy Lopez, Woodside High School, Woodside, California.

Amy Gallagher, reading teacher, Marple Newton High School, Newton Square, Pennsylvania.

Leslie Green, teacher, Benjamin Franklin Middle School, Rocky Mount, Virginia.

Grace Herr, West Linn High School, Oregon.

Vicky Hoag, English and Advancement Via Individual Determination (AVID) teacher, Sierra High School, Tollhouse, California.

Betty Kasow, fifth-grade teacher, Guy Lee Elementary School, Springfield, Oregon.

Ruth King, sixth-grade teacher, Brookside School, Cranford, New Jersey.

Jennifer Knutson, St. Joseph's Catholic High School, Kenosha, Wisconsin.

Elizabeth Kolbush, English teacher, Arcadia High School, Oak Hall, Virginia.

Victoria Lamkey, Haysville Alternative High School, Haysville, Kansas; author with Coni Honn of *Another Brick Wall,* Reading Curriculum Ideas for an Alternative High School, Haysville, KS 67060.

Jud Landis, science teacher, Sheldon High School, Eugene, Oregon.

Chris Lessick, English and creative writing teacher, Great Bridge High School, Chesapeake, Virginia.

Mary Mansell, history of art and music teacher, Ramona Convent Secondary School, Alhambra, California.

Rachel Mappes, music teacher, Franklin Township Middle School, Franklin, Indiana.

Adina Marcus, eighth-grade reading and distant learning coordinator, Churchill Junior High School, East Brunswick, New Jersey.

Marge McCormick, language arts and English teacher, Tamaqua Area High School, Tamaqua, Pennsylvania.

Pat McDougald, chemistry teacher, formerly at Harrison High School in Kennesaw, Georgia, now at Glynn Academy in Brunsick, Georgia.

Jeannine Newman, math teacher, Cal Young Middle School, Eugene, Oregon.

Mari Radostitz and Joel Bradford, Cascade Middle School, Bethel School District, Oregon.

Marsha Ruhl, Glide Middle School, Glide, Oregon.

Elizabeth Salhfeld, substitute teacher, Eugene, Oregon.

Angela Andréa Hernandez Sepulveda, Instituto Tecnologico de Estudios Superiores, Monterey, Mexico.

Jason Shea, humanities teacher, Vedder Middle School, Chilliwack, B.C., Canada.

Eliza Sher, English and literature teacher, Sheldon High School, Eugene, Oregon.

Derek Simmons, Colonel Richardson High School, Federalsburg, Maryland.

Chet Skibinski, retired literature teacher, Sunset High School, Beaverton, Oregon.

Sherry Stoddard, special day class, Livermore High School, Livermore, California.

Elizabeth Strehl and Marcia Santos, seventh-grade social studies teachers, Glide Middle School, Glide, Oregon.

Dorothy Syfert, language arts and social studies block, James Monroe Middle School, Eugene, Oregon.

MaryEtta Taylor, special education teacher, Buford High School, Lancaster, South Carolina.

Glenda Vickery, math teacher, Glide Middle School, Glide, Oregon.

About the Author

Larry Lewin spent twenty-four years as a teacher at the elementary, middle, and high school levels in Oregon. Now he consults nationally to school districts on educational topics of interest, including practical strategies for helping struggling readers and writers, integrating the Internet into instruction, and classroom-based performance assessment.

Larry is coauthor with Tanis Knight of three writing process textbooks for Stack the Deck Writing Program, coauthor with Betty Shoemaker of *Great Performances: Creating Classroom-Based Assessment Tasks* (1999), and author of *Using the Internet to Strengthen Curriculum* (2001). He has published articles in *Educational Leadership, Reading Teacher, Language Arts, Middle Ground,* and *Multimedia Schools.*

He lives in Eugene, Oregon, with his wife, Linda, his niece, Amelia, and their dog, Rudy. When not writing at his desk or on the road presenting workshops, he volunteers in classrooms, typically on Fridays.

He can be reached any day, any time by e-mail: larry@larrylewin.com

Building the Twin Pillars of Literacy

Why are reading and writing such a problem for so many of our students?

In our hearts, teachers of middle school, junior high, and high school know very well of a disturbing trend in our classrooms: Many (many, many) of the students facing us in our classrooms struggle with reading comprehension and writing composition.

And this is not only exposed in English/language arts classes. It is also obvious to teachers of history, health, geography, science, business, economics, math, or any subject.

The problem is that we content teachers often don't really know what to do about this problem. With class sizes too large, with a killer curriculum driven by higher and higher state standards, and with too many courses to prep, helping the struggling readers and writers in any class is tough. And given that many content teachers have limited or no specific training in reading and writing instruction, we often end up doing nothing—and hoping that the English Department is working on it. Meanwhile, the English Department is struggling with the same pressures, and many teachers there have come to doubt the effectiveness of whatever specific training in reading and writing instruction they may have received.

And everyone feels guilty about the situation.

So teachers continue to assign informational text reading, such as textbooks, newspaper articles, photocopied magazine or journal articles, and now Web sites. And how many of the students cannot make head or tail of these sources? Or, more accurately, how many of them can only partially comprehend the ideas expressed in these sources but fail to grasp the information at a level sufficient for really understanding what it is that we are teaching?

In English/language arts classes, we have lots of literature to assign. Same problem: many of our students are behind in their development of reading and writing skills, so they struggle daily.

The same for writing: how many of our students struggle with routine writing assignments? "Write a two-paragraph summary of the videotape we just watched on cell theory" can be a logistical nightmare for some secondary students. "Compare and contrast the writing style of the two authors we are studying" leads to confusion, dread, and eventual incoherence.

If we have an extra moment during the hectic day, we may ponder, "Why is this? Why so many challenged readers and writers in our school district?"

And we may also ponder some hypothesized answers: The TV generation cannot construct mental visualizations from written words. The kids come from non-literary households where written materials don't matter. Cultural distractions may clobber any interest in reading, writing, thinking, or studying. Poor childhood diets restrict mental alertness. Economic stress means families cannot maintain a constant attendance in the neighborhood school. Too much reliance on "whole language" teaching methods (or not enough reliance on "whole language" teaching methods) in the primary grades has left secondary students unable to keep up. . . .

Whatever theory you or I subscribe to, the problem remains obvious: too many students come to class with limited reading and writing skills. Nonetheless, for whatever reasons, we continue to trudge forward assigning them challenging sources to read, and challenging assignments to write, hoping for the best. And they are operating "at a deficit" (Hillocks, 1995, p. 21).

IMPROVING READING AND WRITING IN EVERY CLASSROOM

Face it: Reading comprehension is a very complex activity. So much occurs inside the mind of a reader as the eyes glide over the printed words. Accomplished readers (like most of us) have become so good at it through a lifetime of practice that it's easy to forget how tough it really is, how complicated the comprehension process is.

Consider this quote from the award-winning Italian author Umberto Eco: "Every text is a *lazy machine* asking the reader to do some of its work." (Italics mine.) Here is a noted author admitting that the reader must do some of the work. . . . Reading is difficult—because one must work, one must accomplish multiple things simultaneously. Good readers can afford to forget this because they have become very good at juggling the skills, strategies, and aptitudes required for constructing meaning from text, that is, reading for understanding. But our strugglers have not.

Decoding Skills

The first key skill needed for reading success is *decoding*. Many of our struggling readers find themselves unable to take the first step toward reading comprehension because they lack phonetic awareness of the language—the ability to translate the letters of a word into sounds to produce the word in one's mouth or mind.

Phonetic awareness is developed by learning the sound-symbol relationships of the twenty-six letters, and their various pairings, in the English alphabet. The difficulty, of course, with decoding the sounds that the letters make in the English language is that most letters can make several different sounds, complicating the translation process. English is not a "phonetically correct" language, as all teachers know.

And some secondary students have not, for whatever reasons, mastered in the earlier grades the different sounds that the letters (and letter combinations) make, so they cannot decode individual words—that is, they cannot immediately recognize the letters on the page as words even when those words are part of their speaking vocabulary. This obviously is a fatal roadblock to understanding the meaning of those words in the attempt to understand what the author is trying to communicate.

Likewise, with the arrival of more and more students from other countries with other languages, the number of kids lacking phonetic awareness of English also increases. These "English as Second Language" learners, sometimes called "Limited English Proficiency" learners or just English language learners, need help too.

Unfortunately, this book cannot address the issue of decoding skills. I am not trained in phonics instruction, and like most secondary teachers, I have no experience in teaching remediated decoding to middle or high school students. So if the students you are working with do not understand the sound-symbol relationships, you need help. Notify the administration, the counselor, or the reading specialist in your building that you have a student who appears in need of decoding remediation. Alternatively, if you want to take this on yourself, find a remedial program that you can administer in class to those students. This is a long shot, obviously, given class sizes, curriculum mandates, and hectic schedules. But in case you decide to give it a try, the "Other Instructional Support Sites" section of the Appendix provides three potential resources for the effort.

This book is for teachers of those students who can decode most of the words presented in a reading assignment. These students can figure out how to pronounce the words; their problem is making sense of what the author is trying to say with those words. This book will address strategies for comprehending the meaning of words, the message of words.

Writing Problems, Too

And what about writing? No problem for your students? A piece of cake?

No, writing, like reading, is a tough enterprise. Even the big-time successful authors admit that transposing thoughts to paper in order to share them with readers is very, very difficult work. Ernest Hemingway is reported to have said, "I write with my blood."

As teachers, we know how challenging it is to compose written expression. As writers, we have to juggle so many different concerns.

It, too, is a major problem for many of our students.

What Are We Going to Do?

This book will help us do something about our students' literacy problems. I promise to give you a set of easily implemented teaching strategies that you can use when you are teaching your material through reading and writing assignments. Whether in a content area class or an English/language arts class, these strategies require no master's degree in remedial reading, no special training in writing, and will not compromise your instruction of the content topics you have been hired to teach.

Rather, these strategies will supplement your instruction by aiding your strugglers—and your nonstrugglers, too—in their understanding of what you assign. They are not add-ons to your crowded curriculum, they serve as learning enhancers. These strategies will allow you to pave the way for students who face obstacles in reading and writing.

Additionally, these strategies will serve to motivate those students who struggle. By giving them something new, something different, something that might even surprise them, you can elevate their low energy to an engaged level that offers a chance at teaching them.

In the twenty-four years that I taught middle school, junior high, and high school English/language arts and social studies, science, and math, I came to realize that not only did my struggling students have low reading and writing skills, they also had low energy. You know the kids I am referring to: They trudge into class with the affect of indifference, the posture that says "Who cares?" and sometimes even the stance of suspicion: "What is the teacher going to make me do today that I can't stand?" They are not exactly excited to enter our classrooms. They are "disaffected" (Hillocks, 1995, p. 15).

Low energy, low expectations, low productivity. Mostly due, I theorize, to past failures. If school has been a series of failed assignments, puzzling expectations, and low grades, can we blame students for trudging into class with a less-than-eager attitude? So many obstacles.

But by presenting them something new, different, and maybe even looking like real life instead of school, we can grab their attention, allowing us to coach them into using a set of reading comprehension and writing composition strategies that they can apply when they need help making sense of the assigned text.

And that is exactly what the more skilled readers do: they apply strategies before, during, and after reading that overcome bumps in the comprehension highway. Same with talented writers: they apply key writing strategies at key moments to help them break through writing roadblocks. The more strategies students have, the easier they will find it to comprehend text (reading) or compose it (writing). Strategy acquisition is what separates the successful from the less-than-successful readers and writers. The more strategies, the fewer obstacles.

The trick, of course, is finding the way to get students to learn the strategies and to apply them when reading or writing. That is the purpose of this book: paving the way for improved literacy in both content area classes and English/language arts classes. I urge you—whatever your specialty—to read not only the chapters labeled for your domain (informational text or fiction) but also the others. Many of the suggested activities for literature reading will work for nonfiction reading, and vice versa.

I will begin by linking reading to writing. Merging these "twin pillars of literacy" in every classroom will provide solid learning support for students who desperately need help.

INTEGRATING PROCESS AND VISUALIZATION APPROACHES

A revolution occurred in U.S. education in the early 1970s. It was not just a continuation of the cultural and political revolution from the 1960s. It was *the writing process revolution*.

The Writing Process

I first became aware of the writing process in 1974 in a landmark article written two years earlier by Donald Murray, professor of English education at the University of New Hampshire. Writing in the New England Association of Teachers of English publication *Leaflet,* Murray explained that professional writers, himself included, applied *a problem-solving process approach* to their writing—to help them overcome the inevitable obstacles in composing their thoughts onto paper.

He described this process in three stages: prewriting, writing, and rewriting. From our vantage point, this appears quite obvious to us now. But back then, it was revolution waiting to happen.

Before this writing process began to make its way into schools, writing instruction *for centuries* was virtually the exclusive domain of grammar and mechanics. For those of us who were students in U.S. schools in the 1940s, 1950s, 1960s, and 1970s, think back: How did your English teacher teach you writing? Skill and drill, right? "Open up your English book to page 187, copy sentences 1 to 20 onto your paper, and then underline the subject once and the predicate twice." Some of our senior veteran teachers learned sentence parsing, or "diagramming" as it was later called. (I actually liked this as a student; I grew up to become an English teacher.)

Murray's revelation that the very best writers, the professionals, had developed a process for composing text eventually overturned the old methods. But not immediately. He needed some help.

One of his colleagues at the University of New Hampshire, Donald Graves, took the writing process and brought it into the schools of that state. He showed teachers how to teach their young writers how to imitate what the pros did. He broke the writing process into manageable parts for instruction. And it spread.

Graves's books, along with the books of his disciples Lucy Calkins, Nancie Atwell, and Jane Hansen, showed teachers across the country how writers really wrote. Elementary, middle, and high school teachers of language arts and English understood the benefits of this process approach, and many, many students were taught it in school. And today it is still finding its way into new classrooms.

The Reading Connection

In the early 1980s, some ten years after the introduction of the writing process, researchers revealed a strong connection between writing and reading. In fact, articles appearing in educational journals were touting reading as the natural cousin to writing—two sides of the same coin.

I was influenced by the work of P. David Pearson at the University of Illinois (Pearson and Johnson, 1978), and later Sheila Valencia at the University of Washington, Robert Tierney at Ohio State (Tierney and Pearson, 1983), and Dale Johnson at the University of Wisconsin. Through their writing, these researchers and others helped me see that not only could the teaching of writing be improved by applying a strategy-based process approach, *so could reading.*

Imagine. The instruction of reading comprehension could be reformatted from "read the assignment and answer the questions" to a step-by-step problem-solving process to help readers overcome obstacles inherent in making meaning from written works (text).

As a high school English teacher, and later a junior high and middle school language arts teacher, I found that this approach made immediate sense. Writing and reading could be linked together in a process-oriented instructional approach: writing is the *composing* of one's thoughts onto paper in order to communicate ideas to someone else (the audience), and reading is the *comprehending* of someone else's (the author's) ideas written to communicate to that audience. Two sides of the same literacy coin.

But what about outside the English/language arts class? When I taught social studies, science, math, and computer arts, did reading and writing have a role? Definitely. How could any content teacher teach content without reading; is not reading a primary vehicle for learning new content information in any secondary classroom? What about writing in the content areas? Writing about content helps learners cement newly learned information; it enables them to ponder and apply it, and it allows the teacher to assess their learning.

Reading and writing do not live only in English classrooms. They are the twin pillars of literacy, and it takes every teacher's contributing to student proficiency to make the difference. It "takes a village" to help kids learn how to read and write well.

Comprehension, Expression, and Visualization

Helping challenged readers comprehend and appreciate both nonfiction and literature requires providing them with a structured plan of attack that allows them to use media beyond the written word to absorb and express ideas. Many of the classroom activities discussed in later chapters are designed to tap into student expression in the visual mode.

Visualization is a key reading strategy after a reader can decode. Knowing what the words "say" isn't enough, the student then has to figure out what they mean when strung together in that fashion—to picture the thing the author is describing, grasp the concept the author is trying to convey, see the action of the story play out on the stage of the mind's eye. So visualization is a key to reading comprehension, and students who lack the ability to visualize can be helped to develop it. Likewise, we must remember that writing is not the only mechanism we have to assist our readers. We should provide alternatives such as drawing periodically, and the exercises described in later chapters have proved to be good ones for that.

A FOUR-PART INSTRUCTIONAL FRAMEWORK

Taking Donald Murray's original three-step general writing process of prewriting, writing, and rewriting, other teachers began adapting it. Many added a fourth stage, publishing, because it represents the culmination of the first three—it is the purpose for doing all the work in those three stages. Other teachers decided to subdivide the prewriting stage into exploring a topic and then planning how to organize it. Others took the rewriting stage and split it into editing for content ideas and proofreading for mechanical and grammatical errors. Despite the various versions' differences, they share one critical feature: all offer a process to help student writers overcome the many obstacles inherent in transporting ideas from the head to the page en route to public exposure.

Whatever the details look like, we need to realize what George Hillocks Jr. calls a "general" process. In his research and writing for over thirty years, he has become the beacon of effective writing instruction. He alerts us to understand that a process approach is just that: *a* process, not *the* process. As teachers, we must be aware not to prescribe any version of the process as a lockstep, universal, everybody-must-follow mandate. Rather, we present a process as a framework, as an initial starting point, a beginning for tackling writing. Writers will adapt it to their own needs and invent their own process.

I began playing around with a general process that could also be applied to reading comprehension. Figuring my students needed a beginning support structure for *both* reading and writing, I came up with a generic four-stepper:

- Prepare
- First Dare
- Repair
- Share

Prepare in writing means prewriting, that is, getting ready to write by brainstorming, researching, drawing, interviewing, and the like. In reading, *Prepare* means getting ready to read an assignment by identifying a purpose for reading, by examining the text's structure, or by making a prediction on what is coming up in the reading.

The *First Dare* in writing is the first, or rough, draft (sometimes labeled the "sloppy copy" in elementary classrooms). In reading, the *First Dare* means your initial reading, your first read of new material. I label it a *dare* because for many readers (and writers) it is a dare to dive into something new. For struggling readers and writers it is a great risk to write a draft or to read a chapter. By dare I am not implying a macho taunting or provocation, but rather the recognition that this stage is a tough one for many students. (Plus, "dare" nicely rhymes with the other three stages.)

Repair in writing means rewriting, revising, editing, proofreading—fixing up both your meaning and your mechanics for clearer communication with your readers. *Repair* in the reading process means to revisit the text. It doesn't necessarily mean rereading every word on every page, just reviewing key sections, passages, or paragraphs to boost understanding.

Share in the writing process means publishing—putting your words out in public for an audience to read. *Share* in the reading process means to offer your understanding to others for their consideration—putting your comprehension to use, confirming your understanding and communicating it.

I happen to like this version of the process approach, not only because I invented it but because the four stages rhyme, so that students can memorize it easily. And it works for both reading and writing—for both comprehending an author's text and composing your own text. Plus, the process approach is good news for content area teachers—it's similar to what you're doing already. Math teachers also demonstrate a problem-solving process for their students to succeed at math problem solving, right? And science teachers, too, present a process approach; it is called the "scientific investigative method," and they model it for their students to apply when conducting scientific inquiries. So the process approach is a universal, generic plan of attack useful in any classroom, not just English.

Personalization of the Process

The process approach is not just for the strugglers; better readers and writers also benefit from the reminder. And I've found that the more skilled readers and writers often take liberties with the general structure and modify it to their own liking, to personalize it—which is exactly what we want all students to do.

For example, when I use the process for writing, I constantly link the First Dare stage with the Repair stage: I type my thoughts into the word processor for a while, and then go back and reread what I wrote, pausing to make changes. Then I compose some more, then back to reading and refining. I liken this to woodworking: a hunk of wood is cut into the desired rough shape, which is then refined with smaller tools, and then it is sanded smoother and smoother and smoother until it reaches the point of quality. George Hillocks Jr. refers to this as alternating from the "reading self" to the "writing self" (Hillocks, 1995, p. 7). Nice.

This example points out not only the personalization of a generic process, but also its *recursive* nature: the stages are not necessarily followed in a forward linear order, but in reality may be modified to move forward *and backward* as needed. This looping is determined by the author to solve whatever problems arise. So even though the four steps appear to be linear, they are not in a lockstep order. Hillocks again: "Writing is a *re*cursive process that requires the *re*construction of text already written, so that what we add connects appropriately with what has preceded. That process brings ideas not written into conjunction with what has been *re*constructed, providing endless opportunities to *re*consider ideas and *re*engage the process that gave rise to them in the first place" (Hillocks, 1995, pp. xvii–xviii, italics mine).

A Little Help from the Standards

When I present seminars and workshops on reading strategies to secondary teachers, I often begin by asking this question: "What do good readers do that makes them good readers?" Or, putting it another way, "What skills, aptitudes, and strategies do successful readers have in their comprehension arsenal that they apply when reading?" Or, more simply: "What do good readers do well?"

What do you think? Take a moment now to brainstorm a list of these traits of successful readers.

Many educators have pondered the question of what makes for successful reading. And some have shared their answers.

In Oregon where I taught, the Oregon Department of Education has developed with a committee of teachers the Four Traits of Reading:

1. Comprehension
2. Extends Understanding
3. Reads Critically for Text Analysis
4. Reads Critically for Context Analysis

[Oregon Department of Education; See "Reading and Writing Standards" in the Appendix.]

For a detailed look at this model of reading, see Exhibit 1.1.

A similar but alternative answer to the same question comes from the Northwest Regional Educational Lab (NWREL), whose Web site lists the following "Six Traits of an Effective Reader" (accessed October 2002):

1. Conventions
2. Comprehension
3. Context
4. Interpretation
5. Synthesis
6. Evaluation

Why six traits instead of Oregon's four? I don't know; maybe the level of detail makes more sense to teachers and students; or maybe to match up better with the becoming-famous "Six Traits of Writing" model? For a detailed look at NWREL's model of reading, see Exhibit 1.2. (For more details, see the group's Web site, listed under "Reading and Writing Standards" in the Appendix.)

In Texas, where I have consulted with many districts, they use the Texas Essential Knowledge and Skills (TEKS) model. The Texas list of reading skills is very similar to Oregon's. (For a look at this list, see the Web site listed under "Reading and Writing Standards" in the Appendix.)

What Do Readers Do Well?
The Four Traits of Reading

1. **Comprehension**

   The reader understands both the parts of a selection and the selection as a whole:

   Understands the literal

   Understands the nonliteral—that is, makes inferences

   Understands main ideas

   Understands details

   Uses textual resources such as tables, illustrations, glossary

2. **Extends Understanding**

   The reader makes connections and can see a relationship between this selection and other sources:

   Connects to or reminds of a personal experience

   Connects to or reminds of a friend's or family member's experience

   Connects to or reminds of another text—something read earlier

   Connects to or reminds of TV show, movie, or video

   Connects to or reminds of some issue or event in the community or world

3. **Reads Critically: Text Analysis**

   The reader analyzes and evaluates the author's ideas and writing craft:

   Identifies the author's purpose

   Evaluates the author's use of stylistic devices

   Analyzes the author's use of literary elements

   Critiques author's ideas and writing ability with relevant examples from the text

   Makes reasoned judgments about the author

4. **Reads Critically: Context Analysis**

   The reader analyzes and evaluates the ways in which the author's message or theme may have been influenced by the times in which the author lived:

   Understands the author's life experiences

   Evaluates life experiences that influenced the writing

   Understands the historical, economic, social, political, and cultural issues and events that may have shaped or influenced the author's work

Exhibit 1.1 Oregon Reading Model.

Note: Not all the descriptors must be addressed.

Idea Source: Oregon Department of Education, http://www.ode.state.or.us/asmt/resource/scorguides.

The Traits of an Effective Reader™

Conventions

Decoding words

Decoding symbols

Decoding grammar and punctuation

Reading aloud with sentence fluency

Recognizing genre and mode

Recognizing the organizational framework of the text

Comprehension

Identifying plot

Selecting main ideas

Distinguishing between major and minor characters

Distinguishing between significant and supporting details

Describing turning moments, conflicts, resolutions

Creating a purposeful summary

Context

Finding vocabulary reflective of the context

Describing setting and historical time period

Realizing cultural overtones and social issues

Looking at concepts from multiple perspectives

Interpretation

Locating problems, ambiguities, and gaps in texts

Selecting clues and evidence to analyze problems

Revising interpretations with new information

Connecting interpretations to a bigger picture

Synthesis

Putting information in order

Listing, sorting, outlining information

Comparing and contrasting

Determining cause and effect

Comparing to personal background experience

Using multiple sources to create an "integrated" analysis

Evaluation

Experimenting with ideas

Expressing opinions

Raising questions

Challenging the text

Challenging the author

Noting bias and distortion

Distinguishing between fact and opinion

Exhibit 1.2 NWREL Reading Model.

Source: Northwest Regional Educational Laboratory (NWREL) Assessment Program, 101 SW Main Street, Suite 500, Portland OR 97204. http://www.nwrel.org/. Used with permission.

The state of Washington, too, has developed its own list of benchmarks for students to meet. In reading, this list matches the ones from Oregon and Texas in many ways. (See Web site listed under "Reading and Writing Standards" in the Appendix.)

In fact, any of the forty-eight standard-based states will have a list of reading comprehension skills that is quite similar to any other state's list. Naturally, the similarities will outweigh the differences because educators in all states can agree on what it takes to read well. The same is true for writing standards across the country.

But how do our struggling students react to these state standards? Nervously.

How do we, the teachers of struggling students, react to heightened state standards? Very nervously.

I support high standards in reading, and I support high standards in writing, too. I trust that all teachers believe in high expectations for their students. The problem with standards, though, is that too often they are used for political purposes instead of educational purposes. When a state's legislature enacts a law mandating that all students will achieve at thus-and-so level, this sounds good politically, but if the attendant funding is not part of the law, what are teachers supposed to do? And what do some legislators presume will happen to schools that fail to meet those standards?

Or what about the clear disparity in funding education from state to state, district to district, or even school to school? Guess which schools typically underperform on state tests? No one in education believes that equity in funding exists in the United States—and it certainly does not. And who believes that funding does not matter in education? That "throwing money at a problem won't help solve it"? I believe that *not* adequately funding each and every school will most certainly limit teachers' ability to help each student meet the standards. This applies to both public and privately funded schools.

But standards are here. I will not defend the political propositions behind them, nor will I keep silent about the gross inequities in funding. But I will teach my hardest to help students hit the targets.

That's what I call the state standards—*targets*—to help students understand the standards. These are the skills, I tell them, that are worthy of our time, our attention, and our practice. I, as their teacher-coach, will help them practice at getting better and better at these important skills. I build them into the four-step process so the kids can work with them where they'll make the most difference. Not only to help them perform better on the state tests, which I realize is viewed as very important, but also to become more literate human beings who can read, write, think, analyze, and critique ideas in any subject. I am confident that this is an educationally sound proposition.

CONCLUSION: REMOVING THE OBSTACLES

From the arrival of the writing process in schools to the merger with reading, we have a framework for assisting our students in improving their abilities to read and write. Our states mandate that we do so, and if even the reasons for the mandate are not educationally sound, we must help our kids hit the targets.

By merging reading and writing in our classrooms, we promote student understanding. And by structuring both the reading and the writing and tying both to our students' developing ability to visualize what they read and want to write, we ally ourselves with our students; we work with them for success. We as teachers can pave the way so as to remove the obstacles our students face daily in school.

We can do it.

Our students deserve no less.

Developing the Reader's Confidence

Prepare and First Dare

The problem in any school is the same: Whatever list of state standards a teacher works from, it contains multiple targets for the students to hit. And if a student happens to be a challenged reader—not a very good shot—then the target-shooting event known as *reading content material in school* is going to be difficult, frustrating, or even an aggravating struggle.

As teachers, we join in these students' struggles. We really have no choice. We must help them build confidence that they can, in fact, read and comprehend. Without confidence, they will remain mystified by reading, or worried about reading, or even hostile to reading. This chapter provides you with a structure to build your reading assistance plan.

A STRUCTURED APPROACH TO SUPPORT STRATEGIC READING

English/language arts classes spend a lot of time reading (and struggling with reading), but reading isn't their private province. Whether in a history class reading a textbook chapter, a math class visiting a Web site on fractals, a science class reading a scientific essay, or a consumer ed class reading a photocopied newspaper article, some students will struggle with comprehension of the key content information. All teachers, regardless of grade level, subject matter, and years of experience, know this.

But many of us feel unprepared to deal with this reality. We aren't trained in the teaching of reading, and we are simply swamped trying to teach our content specialty. So, typically, we assign the reading and hope for the best—knowing, of course, that the best won't likely happen for these kids. Instead of the best, the worst occurs: comprehension meltdown, lack of content understanding, failure to learn, and eventually turn-off to school.

Therefore, regardless of our training, or lack of training, it is our job to assist our strugglers. If not us, then who? Our English/language arts colleagues cannot do it alone; the special ed teachers and reading specialist teachers can't do it alone. It takes a village to teach kids to read.

Prepare Before the First Dare

Struggling readers need all the support we can offer them. Chapter One introduced a structure of support, a framework, that has been effective in helping many students reduce comprehension problems: the four-step reading process I call "Prepare, First Dare, Repair, and Share." This chapter focuses on activities that help develop students' confidence by preparing before first daring to read the material. To flesh out these first two steps in the reading process, here is a set of easily implemented classroom activities that teach struggling readers to apply some key comprehension strategies at both the Prepare and First Dare stages.

First, a quick refresher on the label. *Prepare* means "get your brain in gear." Good readers know that before reading, it pays to do a bit of mental preparation, to establish what Madeleine Hunter called the "anticipatory set." Poor readers don't know this; they typically just dive right in and start reading, swim frantically for a few strokes, and then sink fast. Preparation ensures more stamina. In fact, this Prepare stage is a solid strategy for any learning situation. It is the prerequisite for constructing meaning in any subject on any topic.

Prepare Strategies for Reading

When assigned any sort of reading, a smart, active reader prepares for reading by conducting a survey, a preview, of the assigned piece. Namely, a skilled reader would use some or all of the following strategies before diving into the material:

- *Survey:* Take stock of presented information to get an overview.

- *Retrieve:* Tap prior knowledge about the topic or a related topic from memory.

- *Plan:* Determine the parameters of the assignment to allot adequate time, energy, tactics.

- *Forecast:* Anticipate potential learning by predicting or questioning (Shoemaker and Lewin, forthcoming).

For a menu of more specific reading strategies for students to apply at this stage, see Exhibit 2.1.

Of course, it is true that not every good reader applies all of the prereading strategies in Exhibit 2.1 to all assigned readings. Usually, there isn't enough time

---

Menu of Reading Prepare Strategies

- Survey the piece by reading the title.
- Think about the title by converting it into a question.
- Think about the title by making a prediction about what will happen.
- Look over the text structure: notice columns, paragraphs, font size changes, use of italics and boldface type.
- Skim the piece on the look-out for proper names, places, dialogue, illustrations.
- Look at the length of the piece and estimate how long it will take to read it.
- Read the author's name.
- Think about the author by recognizing (or not recognizing) the name.
- Think about the author by recalling other pieces written by the same person.
- Think about the author by reading the short bio, if provided.
- Sample the piece by reading one or two opening paragraphs and a middle paragraph.
- Understand the teacher's reason for assigning this piece, or set your own purpose for reading it.
- Take in all this preview data and recall any prior knowledge that is applicable. Ask, "What do I already know that will help me understand this story or topic?"

Exhibit 2.1 Menu of Reading Prepare Strategies.

to apply them all. Nor do all strategies fit all reading assignments. Good readers know how to pick and choose strategies that are appropriate and timely for a particular reading.

And to save time, a skilled reader can do several strategies simultaneously. Often a quick glance over the material reveals several useful bits of preliminary information. Such readers know the shortcuts for gaining a quick but thorough preview of coming attractions.

Likewise, talented readers most likely would have picked up additional strategies beyond those I've listed. In fact, did you, a veteran reader, think of more strategies to add to my list? For example, perhaps you're still using the good old SQ3R routine: Survey, Question, Read, Recite, Review. If not and you'd like to learn more about it, refer to the University of Arizona and University of St. Thomas Web sites listed under "Other Instructional Support Sites" in the Appendix.

An important aside about the more skilled readers. Many of us teach heterogeneous classes with a spectrum of reading abilities. When we teach Prepare strategies to a mixed-ability class, the better readers may be put off by instruction on what they already know intuitively or have been taught. So we must be careful. We must acknowledge that they already do realize the benefits of preparation, and we can tap into their expertise by perhaps asking them to share what strategies they would apply, and why a certain strategy is preferable for a certain piece of reading.

However, even though some students will think they already know it all, a review of strategies, an introduction of new strategies, and the weighing of relative strengths of a strategy can help even the more skilled readers in any class. We just have to be a little careful so as not to inadvertently insult anyone.

While it is true that good readers know how and when and why to prepare for reading, it is equally true that our less skilled, more challenged, struggling readers possess few or none of the listed prepare-for-reading strategies. They typically do not think about such matters. Rather, when assigned a reading in class, they are thinking, "Oh boy, another headache. What's the fastest way to get this over with?" Not understanding the importance of doing some up-front work, they usually believe that rapid completion is their goal—they try to get through the material as fast as possible even while drowning in the process. They don't try for comprehension and appreciation because that is not their goal.

So we, their reading coaches, must train them how and when to use as many Prepare strategies as we can. And as their seasoned coaches, we know all too well that we cannot simply tell them to use these strategies; we must coach them routinely on how, when, where, and why using them will make a difference. Soon in this chapter, the section "Easily Implemented Classroom Activities" covers a set of specific training mechanisms that teach kids how to become comfortable, confident, and proficient users of the key Prepare reading strategies.

First Dare Strategies for Reading

After a smart reader has conducted a preview of coming attractions, whether it took ten seconds or three minutes and ten seconds, it is now time for the "First Dare." I use this term to describe a reader's initial attempt at comprehension. It is a *dare* to plunge into a new story or a textbook for both understanding and appreciation. It implies taking a chance, taking a risk, by venturing into new territory. The label *first* reminds readers that this stage is a beginning, not necessarily the end of comprehension.

Of course, it is less of a dare now that some preparation has occurred. The reader is not diving into icy uncharted waters without a wetsuit. Preparation makes the plunge far less risky. An analogy with the writing process is apt: It is much easier to write a rough draft after engaging in some prewriting activities than to merely pick up the pencil and hope that ideas will magically begin flowing onto the paper.

So what are some useful First Dare strategies that will facilitate reading? How about these five:

- *Focus strategies:* Selectively attend to significant information.
- *Information-gathering strategies:* Acquire needed new information.
- *Self-regulating strategies:* Monitor one's own construction of meaning (metacognition).
- *Generating strategies:* Produce new information, meanings, ideas, summaries.
- *Organizing strategies:* Track new information, construct and sort meaning, and enhance retention (Shoemaker and Lewin, forthcoming).

These strategies can be presented to students more specifically using the suggestions in Exhibit 2.2.

All these First Dare strategies are designed to help the reader accomplish one thing: *understand the material as best as possible on this first reading.* And just as

Menu of Reading First Dare Strategies

- Ask a question to a character in fiction or a person mentioned in a nonfiction text.
- Ask a question to the author.
- Ask a question to myself.
- Ask a question to my teacher.
- Make a prediction about what will happen next or what the author will tell me next.
- Make a prediction about how a story ends or about the main point a nonfiction author wants me to believe after reading this.
- Revise the prediction based on new information in the piece.
- Visualize what's going on by picturing it in my mind's eye.
- Visualize what's going on by drawing a picture or a set of quick sketches.
- Pause to think by making a summary statement of what I know so far.
- Pause to think by making a request of the piece: What do I need to know to better get what's happening?
- Pause to think by recording a key note I want to remember.
- Pause to think by drawing a quick sketch of a key scene or a key concept.
- Relate to the character or the events by recalling something similar in my own life.
- Relate to the character or the events by recalling something similar from someone I know.
- Relate to the character or the events by recalling something similar from another story.
- Relate to the character or the events by recalling something similar from a movie or TV show.
- Relate to a problem in the piece.
- Compliment the author for something well written.
- Complain to the author about something poorly written or confusing or dumb.
- Slow down my reading rate in a difficult part.
- Speed up my reading rate in easy parts.
- Put on the brakes and stop if I'm really confused.
- Put on the brakes, put it in reverse, and back up and reread a confusing part.

Exhibit 2.2 **Menu of Reading First Dare Strategies.**

with the family of Prepare strategies presented earlier, not all skilled readers apply all of the First Dare strategies all the time. Rather, good readers know when, where, why, and how to select them *as needed* to maximize comprehension.

How do skilled readers acquire these helpful strategies? I bet they get them in two ways: they figure them out themselves from years of reading, or they learn them from someone who shows them new strategies to try out. Either way, they are in business.

Our challenged, less skilled readers also acquire First Dare strategies from their own reading experience. But since their goal is typically to minimize reading time rather than to maximize comprehension, they will apply just one strategy: speeding up their reading rate to skim the material—plunging recklessly through the pages. Not good.

Obviously, we need to expand their repertoire of strategies by training them to use many different ones, like those listed in Exhibit 2.2.

For some Web resources for finding additional strategies, please refer to the "Other Instructional Support Sites" section of the Appendix.

To teach struggling readers how to read better, the strategies are presented, reinforced, and refined. Some teachers keep it up front in students' minds by creating a wall chart delineating the stages. For example, seventh-grade teacher Tom Cantwell has his language arts classes put together large flip charts of recommended strategies, which he displays prominently for the rest of the term as a constant reminder how to proceed. A teacher of any subject is likely to find this exercise time well spent.

SCHEMA THEORY OF READING COMPREHENSION

The Prepare and First Dare stages of the reading process are linked by what researchers call "prior knowledge." Prior knowledge is what readers already know (or think they know) about the incoming topic. This knowledge is critical to comprehension, for comprehension is the *integration* of new information (from an author) into existing information (stored in the reader's memory). This is known as "schema theory" (Anderson and Pearson, 1984).

Schema theory posits four basic assumptions—and they all make sense to me:

- Readers store past knowledge in their memories.
- Past knowledge comes from two basic sources: past direct experience (in life) and secondhand, indirect sources (reading, listening, or viewing).

- Humans are smart, so when they experience firsthand or secondhand events, they do not randomly dump them upstairs; rather they deposit them into their memories in categories, or sets, for easier retrieval. (The categories are called *schemata*.)
- Readers retrieve stored knowledge from their schemata to Prepare for reading and during First Dare reading to assist in understanding (making sense of) the author's message.

From the Bangkok Post Educational Services, here is a fine explanation of schema theory as it relates to everyday life (and specifically to reading comprehension):

Schema theory seeks to explain how we are able to cope with our constantly changing daily environment. Obviously, we do not see each circumstance as unique and unfamiliar. We are quickly able to recognize familiar elements and patterns (schema) in the activities unfolding around us. This enables us to behave correctly in situations as diverse as a history class, a fast food restaurant, or crossing a busy street in a large city in a foreign country.

This remarkable ability to make sense out of our ever-changing surroundings clearly depends on memory. We are somehow able to extract just those elements from our huge store of experiences, facts, smells, tastes—everything we call memory—to allow us to make at least an educated guess as to what is occurring around us. And this memory comes to us not in random bits and pieces, but in an organised form, allowing us to almost immediately distinguish a marriage ceremony from a courtroom trial, or a bus station from a school.

The same process makes reading possible. With remarkably few words, a good writer can evoke vast amounts of stored information from readers' memories, allowing them to make sense of what is written on the page ["A Little Theory," n.d.].

To Prepare for reading, students mentally access their schemata on the incoming reading topic and consider, that is, evoke, *what they already know.* Of course, some students come to class already knowing quite a bit about the topic; perhaps they remember it from an earlier grade, or they watched educational TV shows about it, or they saw a movie that contained the topic, or they recently read something about it. . . . Typically, though, the students who come into our classes possessing prior knowledge are not the strugglers, they are the higher-achieving students.

What about struggling readers? They certainly have memories, they possess vast amounts of prior knowledge, and they can activate it. But do they possess prior knowledge relevant to the incoming school topic? That depends. Sometimes a struggler's prior knowledge is exclusively on topics of interest (friends, music, hobbies, television shows) and not on geometry, American history, or some scientific principle. Quoting again from the Bangkok Post Educational Services: "Of course, this [schema processing] is far from a perfect process as readers may lack the *appropriate* schema or apply a schema *other* than the one intended by the writer" (italics mine).

So as teachers we not only direct our readers to tap prior knowledge, we also pay attention to what was tapped or not tapped. What our students know or do not know should certainly influence our instructional decisions. But how will we know what they know, or don't know, or "kinda" know?

EASILY IMPLEMENTED CLASSROOM ACTIVITIES

Teachers know that it would be naive to assume that all we need to do to help our struggling readers is to simply tell them to "apply *Prepare* strategy of tapping your prior knowledge before you *First Dare* read."

No, telling them won't work; we must show them how. Here is set of activities that will coach kids to apply the key reading comprehension strategies, including tapping prior knowledge, in the context of a reading assignment you give them. And they won't cut into your instructional time; rather, they will fortify your instruction and their learning.

The Folded File Folder

The first is my Folded File Folder (FFF) activity. Give students a sheet of colored paper (color to get their attention) to fold in half leaving a tab on the top—a folded miniature folder.

On the tab have them write the topic of the reading assignment, for example, the causes of the Civil War, or why cells divide, or Elizabethan England, or survival in the Arctic, or whatever topic you are about to teach (or whatever literature selection you are assigning).

Then have them open the Folded File Folder and in the inside top half (between the tab at the top and the fold in the center) apply a key Prepare-for-reading strategy: *tap your prior knowledge.* (Schema theory, right?)

But what about the strugglers who own prior knowledge but aren't aware that it is living somewhere in their memory? Or the ones with prior knowledge on a different but related topic? All this is valuable stuff, and as teachers we need to help the strugglers access it for reading comprehension. That is why I invented the FFF's top half: to aid a struggling reader with this key reading strategy. It serves to remove a key obstacle to comprehension. It helps build confidence. It says, "Hey, I know something already. I'm in the ballpark here."

Two additional tips: Advise the students that if they are not certain that their prior knowledge is accurate, they should write in the top half, "I think that . . ." or "I'm not positive, but maybe. . . . " And point out that if they cannot recall anything even remotely related to the incoming topic, they should not feel embarrassed and leave the top half blank. Rather, they should write, "Presently I know nothing about this topic." And the emphasis is on *presently* because this will change either later in the period or first thing tomorrow when the reading assignment provides new information.

So both strugglers and nonstrugglers alike in the class record whatever they can download from their memories to the top half of the FFF.

Next step: Say, "Generate a prediction about what you think the author will be telling you about our topic." Why a prediction? Because prediction is the engine that drives the comprehension train. (Great metaphor; I use it frequently and wish I remembered where I heard it first.)

Prediction is an excellent way to Prepare for reading; it gets the brain in gear. Anyone have students who come to class with their brains in neutral? Or their brains running in high gear on what just happened in the hallway between classes? We often need a way to help them engage their brains. The FFF does this.

For teachers it is an important reminder that reading for comprehension involves predicting—the *forecasting* of incoming information. Teachers, as strong readers, sometimes forget this because we forecast so automatically and so subconsciously that we don't realize we do it. But we do predict constantly, and this drives comprehension forward. If our prediction comes true, fine. Then we construct a new prediction for the next reading segment. If our prediction doesn't come true, fine. We merely revise it and move forward.

Our struggling readers do not make predictions. First, they do not because they are not sufficiently engaged with the text to generate a prediction about it. And second, even if prompted to make a prediction, they hesitate out of fear of being wrong. So it's important to assure them, "There is no such thing as a wrong prediction."

I say, "Sometimes the author goes the way you thought, and sometimes not. No big deal. It is not the accuracy of the prediction that drives the comprehension train; it is the *act of predicting* that drives it. There is no such thing as a wrong prediction." I have students recite this truism back to me to remove their fear of being wrong.

I also assist strugglers with this making-a-prediction step on the FFF. Instead of generating one out of the blue, I ask them to check out the reading assignment, to look it over, to get a "preview of coming attractions." This can be accomplished quickly by telling the class, "You have one minute and thirty-two seconds to look over the assignment in your book on pages 121–130 and make a prediction about what the author will tell you about environmental issues in the Amazon region."

Then they record their prediction right on the fold in the middle of the FFF. Additionally, students can pair up to compare their predictions. I ask them why I want them to do this: Is it to get into an argument about who is smart and who's dumb? Or to learn another possibility about incoming information? They get the point.

How much time has been invested in the Prepare stage? Four minutes and twenty-seven seconds. . . . Ask yourself: Is this time well spent? Is it dismantling an obstacle to learning? Will it help my students read better?

Last step: Say, "Now that we have prepared, it is time to First Dare, that is, read for initial understanding." To facilitate this, instruct students to use the bottom inside half of the FFF to "jot down newly learned information." It's weird: If you tell them to "take notes" as they read, they complain bitterly, but if you ask them to "jot down newly learned information," they shrug and figure that's not so bad— filling in the bottom half of a piece of paper. . . .

Disguised notetaking. Good idea, yes?

So they read and jot, read and jot, filling in the bottom of the FFF. Of course, if they run out of room at the bottom, they merely turn the FFF over and use the back to continue.

Unless you have a minimalist student. A minimalist reads and jots one or two things on the bottom half, and then raises a hand to proudly announce, "I'm done!"

You can reply, "No you're not, Minimalist. You get to turn your FFF over and draw a picture of the most important point you read. And please add a caption beneath your illustration, so that I can be sure I know what you drew."

Strugglers often appreciate the opportunity to substitute drawing for writing. This FFF reading-tracking device works for students of different reading abilities, and for those of us who teach mixed-ability classes, that is good news.

Many teachers make their own versions of the FFF. Dorothy Syfert, who taught next door to me for many years at James Monroe Middle School in Eugene, Oregon, couldn't do it exactly the way I showed her. Noooo, she had to change it: She instructed her eighth-grade U.S. History students to fold a sheet of 11"x17" paper in half, and then divide it into three columns with a ruler. The three columns were for the three main subtopics of the reading assignment. The world's first "triple-column Folded File Folder" was born.

Greg Barnett, sixth-grade science teacher, modified the FFF into the "folded sun." Instead of distributing regular letter-size paper, he had the students cut bright yellow paper into a circle and then fold it in half to create the "folded sun" to begin a unit on the solar system.

Are my feelings hurt when colleagues take my ideas and modify, adapt, and improve them? No, I am flattered. Trading ideas is what we do as teachers.

Of course, if you choose to use it the way I designed it, that's fine with me, too. Special day class teacher Herb Felsenfeld and his instructional associate Lucy Lopez used it with their high school students when they studied the impact of junk food on the human brain. First, the students used an FFF to get ready to read about this topic. Then they read letters to the editor of the local newspaper and additional information about caffeine, sugar, and bone loss written by a doctor and published on a Web site. After learning about this FFF activity at a workshop I presented, Herb wrote me: "The day after your workshop, we all did the Folded File Folders! It worked! Here are some examples from special day class students. Thanks for all your help." Well, thanks to you, Herb, for sharing them with me, so that I can share them with our colleagues.

As a culminating activity (in the Share stage), Herb's newly informed class decided to challenge their school's position on soft drink vending machines on campus. You can read their persuasive letter to the administration in Exhibit 6.6. (Foreshadow: They convinced the principal to remove the soda machines from campus.)

The Folded File Folder in Social Studies

Last year I was hired to consult with Glide Middle School in Glide, Oregon, on "reading across the curriculum." One morning I worked with Elizabeth Strehl's and Marcia Santos's seventh-grade social studies classes. The topic was a tough one: reading the social studies textbook chapter on Nigeria and comprehending the difficulties the Nigerians are having with intergroup rivalries, the former military dictatorship, and economic "structural adjustment" to comply with the International Monetary Fund (IMF) and World Bank (WB) loans.

Many adults in both the United States and Canada would be hard-pressed to understand these concepts, especially Third World debt as it relates to the IMF and WB funding requirements.

Fortunately for these seventh graders, their teachers had set the stage. Before tackling this challenging informational reading assignment, the students had already

- Created political and physical maps of Africa
- Completed a general survey of the populations, cultures, economies, climate zones, and vegetation of the African continent
- Studied the types, causes, and effects of colonialism and imperialism in Africa
- Read several African folk tales
- Studied the history and present situation in South Africa
- Studied the Sahel region of West and Central Africa
- Studied Kenya

So by the time I entered their classes, they already possessed some important prior knowledge.

To access this critical schema, I distributed colored letter-size paper, told the class to fold it into a mini file folder, and then asked what they could tell me about Africa in general and Nigeria in particular. As I called on volunteers and nonvolunteers to share what they knew, I instructed them to record this prior knowledge on the top half of their FFFs. Students were eager to show what they knew to the teacher. Everyone was at-task.

I decided to vary the FFF's next step. Instead of generating a prediction about what their textbook author would tell them about Nigeria on the fold in the middle, I asked the seventh-grade social scientists to write on the middle fold several key concept vocabulary words that were listed in italics at the beginning of the chapter:

- Structural adjustment programs
- International Monetary Fund
- World Bank

I told them that these terms were very difficult to understand, and that it was likely that not even their parents could easily define the meanings. But, I told them, both their teachers and I figured that this group would be able to handle the challenge.

I asked for predictions on the terms' meanings, and we discussed them. This is an example of conceptual vocabulary instruction, a technique that often does much to help anchor new words in the students' minds.

An Internet Excursion

Then we took a detour away from the textbook and brought in a supplemental resource I found on the Internet. In the week before I was scheduled to visit this middle school, I had Pre-Searched the Web looking for information on these topics.

The *Pre-Search* is a search conducted by a teacher *in advance of student use* of the Web. Instead of sending the class to the computers for a Web search, the teacher does it for them. Why? To save time. Hunting for information on the Web can be a time-consuming event for students, not to mention iffy. So when I incorporate the Web into my instruction, I always begin with the Pre-Search before moving onto the intermediate stage, the We Search, and the final, more independent stage: the Free Search. (For more information on these three stages of Web use, see *Using the Internet to Strengthen Curriculum,* or visit my Web site—the URL is in the first section of the Appendix.)

In my Pre-Search, I located a very helpful Web site, "50 Years Is Enough" from the U.S. Network for Global Economic Justice, which has lots of information in understandable language on the IMF, World Bank, and their conditions for loans—structural adjustment of reducing government spending on social programs, privatization of public services, removing taxes on imports and exports, eliminating barriers to foreign ownership, and large-scale development projects. (See the "General Information" section of the Appendix.)

Instead of signing up for the school's computer lab and taking the class there (my preference), the two teachers decided to speed up the process by providing each student with a printed hard copy of the information for reading in class (a reasonable option).

We spent about fifteen minutes reading and discussing the key concepts and important terms in the printed 'Net article. This supplemental reading assignment certainly helped to *Prepare* them for the upcoming textbook account of the same topic.

For the final step, facilitating their First Dare reading of their text, I modified the bottom half of the FFF by telling the class to split it into two columns: the left column for "Varying Regions" and the right for "Military Leadership." (Note that I stole the columns idea back from my colleague Dorothy Syfert, mentioned earlier.)

When I asked the seventh graders why we would use these particular two labels, many students immediately realized they were the two boldface headers of the chapter's subtopics. I congratulated them by saying, "Yes, good readers notice how the author, editor, or publisher decided to organize the writing. . . . It is called *text structure.*"

I asked the students if the author had done a good job organizing the chapter into a structure that was helpful to their comprehension, and told them that some authors are more considerate of their readers—that is, they do things in their writing that makes understanding their ideas easier, like boldface headers for important topics, or using italics for key vocabulary words, or writing concise intro and summary paragraphs. And some other writers are less considerate of readers; that is, they make comprehension more difficult with confusing organization, over-the-head vocabulary, lack of visuals, and the like. (I'll return to this point at the end of the chapter, but it's worth emphasizing here: Students love the chance to judge their assignments. It gives them a sense of power that is both novel and welcome. And it has a stinger—once they've adopted the concept of considerate and inconsiderate writing, it's relatively simple to widen their view to consideration or the lack thereof in their own work, which opens the door to teaching them effective Writing Repair techniques.)

As they independently read the chapter, the students used the bottom of the FFF to record newly learned information into the two columns. (Disguised note-taking.) No one complained. In fact, several students actually thanked me as I left their classroom. Nice.

Both Elizabeth and Marcia were pleased with their students' work. Everyone gained knowledge on the topic—the good readers, the in-betweeners, and the strugglers. See Figure 2.1. for the top, middle, and bottom of Lindsey's Folded File Folder, showing how one of the in-betweeners made use of the tool.

The class approved of this activity. The following week I received postcards from the students, including this one:

> Dear Mr. Lewin,
>   Yesterday in class I learned that Nigeria is run by the military. I also learned about the World Bank, 50 years is enough, IMF, and WTO. Thank you for making Social Studies fun.
>
> > Sincerely,
> > Jessie Botts

"Social Studies Fun"? I like that. Postcard writing is a good idea. . . . In fact, it's so useful I will revisit it in Chapter Five.

The Venerable K-W-L Sheet

As proud as I am of the FFF, I have a confession to make: I actually stole the idea from another teacher. Yes, it's true. Her name is Donna Ogle, and she's a professor of education at National-Louis University and the past president of the International Reading Association. She is the inventor of the famous *K-W-L*—the grand-mammy of the reading comprehension devices for nonfiction—which I read about in a 1984 article in the *Reading Teacher* journal.

Many teachers also know the K-W-L and use it effectively as a reading comprehension device. The K column stands for "what I already *know* about the topic"; the W column stands for "what I *want* to know about the topic"; and the L column stands for "what I *learned* about the topic." Three great reading strategies are practiced with the K-W-L:

- Tapping prior knowledge
- Generating questions
- Recording newly learned information

The only problem with the K-W-L is that it is so good that it's easy to overuse it. Every time I started to teach a new topic, I instructed my students to take out a

Africa/Nigeria | Lindsey Grimes

Modified FFF

Nigeria is a country in Africa
Nigeria is in the Sahara Desert
Nigeria has big debts they have to pay off
Africa has a lot of wars
Africa still has slaves
Africans do not make much money
The money that Africans make they have to give ???
People in europe are not treating Africa right
Europe has more power than Africa so Europe made the borders of Africa
Lots of Culters and languas

Key Concept Vocabulary Words

World Bank
Structured Ajustment International Monetary Fund (IMF)

Double Column for Two Boldface Sections

Varing Regions

1) Southern Regions may recieve up to 120 inches of rain a year
2) The parched north gets only 20 inches of rain each year
3) These variations affect where people live

Military Leadership

1) Nigeria's governmental problems arose in the early ???
2) As the economy broke down the Military staged a cuop
3) During its structural adjustment, the Nigerian government sold state-run businesses to private companies, fired some government employees

Figure 2.1 The FFF Goes to Africa.

Source: Elizabeth Strehl and Marcia Santos, teachers, Glide Middle School, Oregon.

piece of paper and do a K-W-L. They got tired of it, and once a student even used the b-word in my class: *borrrrrring*. I never want to hear the b-word, so I developed the Folded File Folder as an alternative to the K-W-L. Both devices accomplish the same things, but in different formats. Nod your head if you have students who tire of redundancy and who appreciate variety.

The Folded Time Line

Speaking of variety, how about a third option for assisting struggling readers: the Folded Time Line (FTL). Created by Oregon teacher Elizabeth Salhfeld, it does just what the K-W-L and FFF do: assist struggling readers by integrating key reading comprehension strategies into an easy-to-do activity.

The FTL is a three-column reading-tracking device: past, present, future. (See Exhibit 2.3 for an FTL template.) In the "past" column, before reading, a student records prior knowledge that "I remember from the past." (We know this as "accessing schemata.")

During reading (called the "First Dare") the middle "present" column is used for a place to "record new information about the topic while reading about it." (Disguised notetaking.)

And the right column is "future": after reading, write a summary statement about the main ideas from the reading—an activity explained with something along the lines of "I realize that you probably will not be able to remember every single point the author is making, but you can remember the biggies."

Of course, a teacher could take Elizabeth's Folded Time Line and modify it in any way to better meet the needs of students. Anyone ever borrow an idea from a colleague and change it a bit so that it works better? Yes, we all do, and it's called *staff development.*

Music teacher Rachel Mappes changed the FTL's three columns into "what I know about jazz; what I wonder about jazz; what I learned today about jazz." Her students recorded information in each column during the lesson and then flipped the paper over to illustrate the cover. It must have worked, at least for one lower-ability kid, who now comes into Rachel's class every day and says to her, "This is my favorite class." We like that.

And if you have invented a reading-tracking device that works with your students, please let me know; you can reach me at larry@larrylewin.com.

The Folded Time Line

What I *know* about this topic from the **PAST**	What I am *learning* about this topic in the **PRESENT**	What I expect to *remember* about this topic in the **FUTURE**

Exhibit 2.3 FTL Template.

Source: Adapted from Elizabeth Salhfeld, teacher, Albany, Oregon.

The Open Mind

Speaking of variety, how about the *Open Mind?* I first learned of it probably fifteen years ago from high school teacher Grace Herr. The Open Mind (OM) is the outline of a human head. The student reader uses the OM as a reading tracking device by recording comprehended ideas inside the "mind." These recorded ideas could be "what I, the reader, am thinking about this topic or story as I read it." Or the OM could be used to assist the reader into thinking like the person being read about, say a historical figure, or a scientist, or a character in a story, or anyone else the teacher decides. It facilitates the First Dare reading.

Math teacher Jeannine Newman used the OM with her math students, who were reading a textbook segment about mean, median, and mode. I borrowed the idea when I was teaching a demo math lesson with teacher Glenda Vickery. Her students were learning how to carefully read and comprehend the math textbook. My job was to provide them with a set of strategies for successfully accomplishing this.

First, we examined the text's structure, that is, we looked at how the author (or editor or publisher) decided to organize the information on the pages. The class noticed three sections: A, B, and Think and Write.

Next, I asked if anyone knew the meaning of key words in the lesson: *data, bar graph, bar chart, general statement, average, mean, median, mode.* We reviewed the definitions of these words because of their critical importance in the lesson.

Then we narrowed in on "mean, median, and mode" at the bottom of the page in the "Think and Write" section. Because this part of the lesson bridged new content information with a review of past information, I decided to hit these words hard, that is, teach a mini-lesson at the conceptual vocabulary level. The students all "looked into their heads" to locate prior knowledge about "mean, median, and mode." One of them, Bo, recorded what he already knew about the three math terms inside the Open Mind shown in Figure 2.2. He awarded himself an "A+."

Some students surreptitiously opened their math notebooks to peek at the notes they had taken several periods earlier when Glenda was introducing these terms. I told them they didn't have to hide—referring to notes is not cheating, it's smart student behavior. Some kids decided to fill in their OM from memory and then check their notes for confirmation. Excellent idea. I was impressed. And Glenda was proud.

An Open Mind A+

Mean: Average, add all the scores to find the total, then divide by the number of scores.

Median: List the numbers least to greatest then find the middle number.

Mode: The score/number that happened the most.

Figure 2.2 Bo's Open Mind.

Source: Glenda Vickery, math teacher, Glide Middle School, Glide, Oregon.

Of course, like any other idea in this book, the Open Mind is open to adaptation, modification, and adjustment. For example, consider this formatting change. Instead of an outline of the human head, why not substitute a cartoon thought bubble? You can attach it to a picture of the person (or thing) whose thoughts the kids are imagining in a particular lesson, providing instant variety.

Another quick and easy tracking device is the Circle Version, shown in Exhibit 2.4. I got this one from the staff at Madras High School in Madras, Oregon. Very simple for students to learn, but very helpful. Some teachers have renamed it the "Reader's Bull's-Eye."

KWT Folder

Fifth-grade teacher Betty Kasow invented the KWT folder. This is a manila file folder distributed to each student with the following directions: On the front of the folder do the K (what I already *know* about the topic before we begin); inside the folder later we will do the W (a place for storing *work* safely as the unit progresses); finally, at the end, on the back of the folder is for the T (what I would select to *teach* another student about this topic now that I've studied it).

Betty likes the way this device helps her students accomplish several key Prepare strategies: tap prior knowledge, keep incoming information organized, and then be motivated to Share the new learning. Playing the role of the expert is satisfying for any student.

I've borrowed the KWT idea for use with secondary students, eighth graders in Dorothy Syfert's language arts and social studies block class. Dorothy and I decided to modify the idea by distributing large sheets of colored paper (17"x24") to the students instead of a manila folder. They folded the sheets in half to create a blue paper folder—which is cheaper than the manila ones and also more colorfully engaging to kids.

The topic written on the top tab was a tough one: Dorothy asked me to help her students apply the concept of multiple points of view to the tragic events of September 11.

At first, I was skeptical: Middle schoolers evaluating the horrific attacks from another point of view? How could they possibly move from the emotional reaction to an intellectual stance and consider an alternative perspective, for example Osama bin Laden's opinion of the United States and its foreign policies?

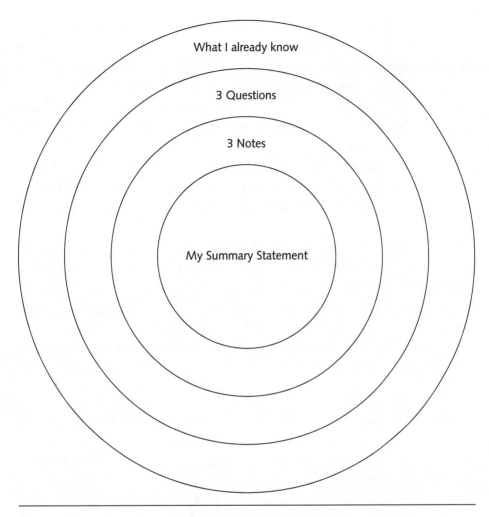

Exhibit 2.4 Circle Version.

Source: Madras High School, Oregon.

Dorothy was optimistic that her students could do this. On the day of the attacks, she had given them class time to write about their feelings—the raw emotional reactions of confusion, fear, anger—in a processing paragraph.

As the days followed, she led them in discussions of the events with an emphasis on respect for different ideas, reactions, and feelings.

Five weeks later she felt it was time to apply what they had learned about point of view in literature to a serious current events issue: the terrorist attacks on New York and Washington.

On the KWT blue folder's cover, the students recorded what they already knew about bin Laden. This downloading of information stored in memory activates schemata, which we know is a powerful and essential element of reading for comprehension.

Next, I provided them with additional information. I Pre-Searched the Web to locate useful supplemental resources for the class, and I found an article from the Pacific News Service written by William O. Beeman and posted on the Alternet Web site on September 12.

In this two-page article, titled "Understanding Osama bin Laden," the author explains bin Laden's resistance to Soviet occupation of Afghanistan in 1979, his resistance to Serbian policy in the former Yugoslavia, his objection to U.S. troops in his native Saudi Arabia, home of the most sacred Islamic religious sites, and his view that the United States unfairly supports Israel over the Palestinians.

Needless to say, these ideas were not commonly known by the students. In fact, these ideas were completely unknown to all but one student in the class.

Sticky Note Reading

To assist the students with the First Dare reading, that is, comprehending new, difficult, and perhaps unsettling information, we provided them with a set of colored *sticky notes*. Sometimes called by the brand name Post-it Notes, sticky notes are a wonderful reading-tracking device.

We instructed the students to use color-coded sticky notes as they read the article.

- On the yellow sticky notes write down any *feeling* you have as you read the author's ideas.

- On the lime-colored stickies write your *opinion* of his ideas (agreement, disagreement, interesting, confusing, ridiculous, . . .whatever).

- And on the pink stickies, write down any *questions* you have for the author that need answering to help your comprehension.

The students used two of each color and stuck them right on the article. Student Divneet wrote two questions on her pink stickies, both about vocabulary words: "What does *enmity* mean?" and later, "What is an *idealogue*?"

The "processing paragraph" and the Pacific News article with stickies attached were filed inside the KWT blue folder for safekeeping of important work.

Stop Signs for Guided Reading

I returned to Dorothy's class the following day to continue co-teaching with her. This time she had an article from *Teen Newsweek* ("Why Do They Hate Us?" 2001) for them to read. The article suggested four possible theories for anti-American sentiment abroad.

To facilitate their reading comprehension of this challenging informative text, we employed an activity called Stop Signs. Stop Signs are cues to the reader to stop reading and do some responding. They can be drawn onto the text (if the assignment is a photocopied worksheet), or they can be posted on the text as a sticky Stop Sign if the assignment is in the textbook. Dorothy opted for the first technique.

When the students arrived at a Stop Sign in the article, they stopped reading to respond to a guided question: "Write a theory (a possible answer or explanation) to the question 'Why do they hate us?' from the section." This prompt for each of the four stop-signed sections of the article caused the students to pause, to think about, to review, to summarize, and to record what they had just comprehended from the article about possible reasons for anti-U.S. attitudes. Molly, one of the students, gave the answers to the stop-sign questions shown in Figure 2.3.

The *Teen Newsweek* article and answers were stored inside the KWT folder. Later, they were accessed for a culminating activity: a letter-writing assignment. I will describe this reading-writing activity in more detail in Chapter Six.

Evaluate the Text

Struggling readers may not realize that part of their comprehension problem may be caused by the author. As suggested earlier, some writers are considerate of their readers; that is, they structure their writing in a clear manner, they use text features that cue the reader, they select vocabulary that is appropriate, and they use engaging sentence fluency so the ideas flow along. This is true of writers of both non-fiction and fiction.

I call the relationship between writer and reader, author and audience, the "meeting of the minds." I tell students that it takes two to tango in the comprehension dance. This comes as both a surprise and a relief to struggling readers, for they have come to believe that their reading limitations are caused by themselves—

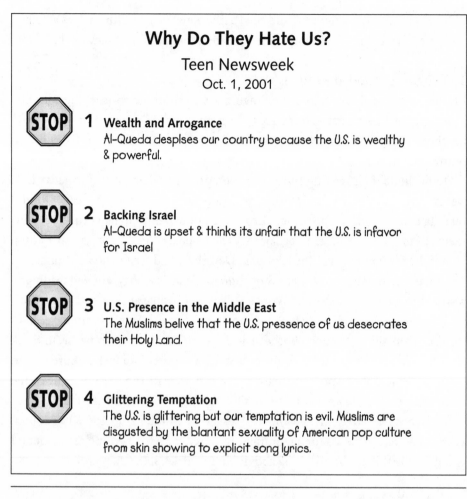

Why Do They Hate Us?

Teen Newsweek

Oct. 1, 2001

STOP 1 **Wealth and Arrogance**
Al-Queda desplses our country because the U.S. is wealthy & powerful.

STOP 2 **Backing Israel**
Al-Queda is upset & thinks its unfair that the U.S. is infavor for Israel

STOP 3 **U.S. Presence in the Middle East**
The Muslims belive that the U.S. pressence of us desecrates their Holy Land.

STOP 4 **Glittering Temptation**
The U.S. is glittering but our temptation is evil. Muslims are disgusted by the blantant sexuality of American pop culture from skin showing to explicit song lyrics.

Figure 2.3 Reflective Answers to Stop Sign Questions.

Source: Dorothy Syfert, teacher, Monroe Middle School, Oregon.

that because of whatever deficiencies they possess, reading failure is their fault. "Meeting of the minds" takes some of the pressure off their backs because now they view reading comprehension as a partnership with the writer instead of a lonely, futile solo. It helps to build their reading confidence.

To help students perceive this new, two-way relationship with the authors of the assigned materials, I use the questionnaire shown in Exhibit 2.5, which asks the students to rate the writer's degree of assistance.

Evaluate the Author
Considerate versus Inconsiderate

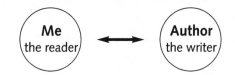

1. Does the **author** use a title that helps me get an accurate idea of what's coming?

2. Is the **layout** obvious and well organized?
   - Any boldface headers?
   - Any italic words?
   - Any font or size changes?
   - Any pictures, diagrams, or charts?

3. Is there a clear **intro**?

4. Any **key vocabulary** identified to check out?

5. Do the paragraphs have useful **topic sentences**?

6. Any **questions** for me to answer?
   - Any interesting ones?
   - Any go beyond simple recall?
   - Any I could add?

7. Is there a clear **conclusion** or summary at the end?

8. Anything **else** that helps or hurts my chances for strong comprehension?

Exhibit 2.5 Survey Form: Evaluate the Author.

Now they get to judge the person who is their partner in comprehension; strugglers love the opportunity to evaluate an author. It is a polite form of talking back to authority. The purpose of the author critique is to remind struggling readers that reading comprehension is actually a two-way street and not exclusively the responsibility of the reader.

I got the idea for this survey from the University of Kansas Center for Research on Learning's "Survey Routine," a work-in-progress the center dates 1997–2002. It listed twenty-five prompted questions designed for college students, which seemed too much for middle and high school students, so I shortened it to eight questions. It could be further adapted by an English teacher to prompt students to evaluate the degree of helpfulness of an author of fiction.

The results of the students' survey analyses of how considerate and helpful or inconsiderate and not helpful their author was can be later employed as a prewriting activity; that is, their answers to the eight evaluation questions can help them Prepare for a writing assignment in which they share their feedback with the author in the form of a memo. I return to this exercise in Chapter Five.

CONCLUSION: IT TAKES A VILLAGE

Because struggling readers in a middle school, junior high, or high school need assistance in their struggle, all their teachers must find ways to help them.

This chapter covered the first two steps of the structured four-step process approach, the Prepare and First Dare, to see how they work in any classroom to give readers a game plan for attacking reading assignments. The third and fourth steps, Repair and Share, form the topics of the next chapter.

To apply the framework, the chapter provided a set of easily implemented reading activities for social studies, math, or science classrooms, most of which could be adapted smoothly to English/language arts: the famous KWL and its offspring the FFF (Folded File Folder), FTL (Folded Time Line), and the KWT (Know-Work-Teach) folder. Additional activities presented were the OM (Open Mind), Stop Signs, and sticky notes.

This chapter also addressed the issue of authors and their responsibility to their readers. Struggling readers should be informed that reading comprehension is actually a two-way street: you, the reader, plus the author, the person who wrote to you. It described the "Meeting of the Minds" activity where students evaluate how considerate or inconsiderate the writer was to them.

Questioning and critiquing an author not only reassures struggling readers that their struggles are not entirely on their own shoulders, it also very nicely leads from reading to writing, a marriage made in heaven.

Why bother with all this? Because in our hearts we know all too well that we really have no choice. Our struggling readers need us. It takes a village to help them succeed.

Now we move on to helping students dig deeper into richer understandings with the Repair and Share stages of reading and writing.

Moving to Richer Comprehension

Repair and Share

Y ou mean, I have to read it *again!??*"

Students typically are not happy about reviewing, revisiting, returning to, or rereading an assigned text. And teachers are not happy to hear students complain about this important and often necessary task. It is difficult enough to get them to Prepare and First Dare an assignment. But even though it will be a great benefit for them to go forward in the process, they firmly believe that once is enough—more than enough. We must show them the way. We must teach them how, why, and when to Repair their initial understandings.

In the preceding chapter I laid out the Prepare and First Dare stages of the reading process. In this chapter I turn to the third and fourth stages, Repair followed by Share in the context of assigned informational text readings. If you teach English/language arts, please stay with me here—the concepts are valuable, and most of the exercises can be retooled for literary sources with little effort.

REPAIRING INITIAL UNDERSTANDINGS

This section clearly will be the most difficult for our challenged readers. Students who struggle to comprehend your lessons are not thrilled to be instructed to "Go back and reread the chapter" (or whatever you assigned). So it's useful to teach them how to Repair.

Repair Strategies

Why do students need the Repair stage of the reading process? It is unlikely that any reader will construct 100 percent perfect comprehension with just the First Dare reading, and struggling students are apt to be far short of the mark.

While this may seem obvious to teachers and other skilled readers, it comes as a surprise to struggling students to hear that once is not usually enough. And worse: not only may it surprise them that they are not expected to gain perfect understanding with just one reading, it may irritate them to hear the claim that returning to the assignment for a Repair is beneficial.

Why the irritation (or outright anger, in some cases)? Because these strugglers have been in school long enough to quickly recognize what is coming next: *rereading*. Let's be frank: The last thing a poor reader wants to be told is to go back and reread something. ("As if it wasn't boring enough to have to read the stupid thing once, now I have to do it *again*.") Repair is rereading, so it needs packaging in a different way to keep the students' reaction from being the opposite of what we intend.

Rather than directing students to "go back and reread" the assignment, I recommend a different approach: "If you need further information from the assignment, it is legal to look back at a key part to find out." This approach comes at rereading from 180 degrees around: instead of mandating a full second reading, it offers the option of a partial reread.

Most teachers are probably thinking, "Sure, when my kids hear this option, they'll likely say, 'No thanks. I'm fine with my comprehension as is. No need for me to go back.' They'll opt out from even a partial reread because they won't see a benefit to more reading."

True. So the next consideration must be how do we convince them that returning to a piece for *fine-tuning* comprehension is worthwhile, helpful, and relatively painless rather than a punishment created by cruel teachers?

Putting it another way: How do we sway suspicious reluctant readers that it is well worth their while *to return to the reading* and apply some of the following Repair strategies (from Shoemaker and Lewin, forthcoming) to *rebuild* the meaning:

- *Fixing-up strategy:* Return to the text to resolve any confusions.

- *Evaluating strategy:* Go back to assess the value, quality, or significance of an element, that is, to evaluate or to examine the author's choices in writing.

- *Analyzing strategy:* Return to examine the key features as they relate to the whole piece.

- *Perspective-taking strategy:* Reread to consider and judge another point of view.

Now, these four Repair strategies are powerful aids to constructing better understanding and appreciation of written material, but they are in the dreaded language of "teacherese." So, I have rewritten the list in student-friendly language with a higher degree of specificity, as shown in Exhibit 3.1.

Notice that all of the strategies in Exhibit 3.1 require only a *selected* rereading rather than a complete second read. Notice also that all the strategies require students to return to the text because it is very unlikely they could recall the information from only their First Dare reading. Notice that the list is far from complete;

Menu of Content Reading Repair Strategies

- Reread an important part slowly to really get it.
- Read a passage aloud softly to hear the words spoken.
- Find out for sure which event happened before (or after) another event.
- Reread a key passage to see if you agree or disagree with it.
- What do you think of the author's decision to [fill in something specific to the text in question]?
- Hunt for a key vocabulary word in its context to determine its meaning.
- Skim for evidence to prove [or disprove] that [fill in something specific to the text in question].
- Reread the title and change it to something better.
- Return to the part where [fill in something specific to the text in question] and look for [some important insight].

Exhibit 3.1 Menu of Content Reading Repair Strategies.

any teacher can easily add some to create a class Repair strategy menu. And notice that all the strategies cause the readers to reconsider, rebuild, refine, revise, revamp, remodel, reformulate, and review their initially constructed understanding. The key is *re-*, which of course means *again*. Good readers know that *re*turning to a text to read again can only boost understanding.

Poor readers don't know this, or they don't care about it. So how do we, their reading coaches, persuade them to give it a try? It is one thing to merely tell them to use these strategies, or any others. It is quite another to convince them to actually do it.

It is up to us to conjure up a context that will provide a motivating purpose. So instead of our strugglers' perceiving all this as more of the usual teacher blah-blah-blah, we must *pave the way* for them to try the strategies out.

Understanding Repair

"If it ain't broke, don't fix it" is probably one of the best-known and most widely followed maxims in American English. Useful as it is, however, it often conceals a huge problem: If you can't tell it's broke, you can't fix it, and it won't even occur to you to try. So before the students can do anything useful by way of improving their understanding, they must understand what they're looking for—the targets of the exercise.

In general, the *targets* are the key areas of concern, the objectives to be met, the characteristics of a quality response, or in the language of assessment, the traits of excellence. Students must know what these are *in advance* of the assignment. We know this. We understand that to withhold this list of targets is to put the students at a serious disadvantage. Just as a gymnastics coach teaches athletes on the point system the judges will be using, we teachers who coach literacy must be forthcoming, clear, and direct about our scoring system.

We have some scoring device options to use, including the rubric, the checklist, and a hybrid I call the "ChecBric."

Rubrics are, by now, well known to teachers. Sometimes called an analytical trait scoring rubric or a scoring guide, a rubric is an itemized list of the key traits required in an assignment. Accompanying each trait is a scoring point scale that shows a student the degree of proficiency achieved. Some state departments of education use a four-point scoring scale, some use a five-point, and many a six-point. I recommend using whichever point scale your state (or district) is using, so that students get practice with it in the classroom prior to any state or district assessment.

A checklist is like a rubric in that it lists the targets, but instead of a scoring point scale, it merely offers students a blank line to check off when a particular target is accomplished. Students like checklists because they are simple—a binary *yes* or *no* as indicated by the presence or absence of a check mark.

Some teachers use rubrics, others prefer checklists, but I like to combine them into a *ChecBric* (Checklist + Rubric = ChecBric). Designed for an in-class performance assessment, the ChecBric is a two-column scoring device: left column a checklist for students to check their work on all the targets, and right column a rubric for teachers to record the score earned for each targeted trait (Lewin and Shoemaker, 1998). Exhibit 3.2 shows a sample ChecBric form. This one is set up for the following Translation exercise; you can plug in the student and teacher requirements suitable for any given lesson.

EASILY IMPLEMENTED CLASSROOM ACTIVITIES

To sway our challenged students, to guide them into better reading behavior, we must create engaging tasks that inspire, motivate, and encourage them to revisit a selection and improve upon their initial understanding. That is, we must come up with new activities that do not irritate, annoy, turn off, or frustrate these kids, but rather make Repairing a First Dare appear easy enough, rewarding enough, and important enough that they will be willing to try out review strategies. We can do this. We have to.

Translation

When you empower readers to improve upon the author's work, they find it natural to go back and read it over to decide what to do. Many struggling readers do not think about the role of the author in facilitating comprehension. As suggested in Chapter Two, there are *considerate* and *inconsiderate* authors who write for students. (See Exhibit 2.5.) Start by telling the students that the assignment they just read could be rewritten in a more considerate way by using "student-friendly language"—wording more familiar to students—to remove some obstacles that get in the way of understanding.

ChecBric: Translation

Target 1: I understand the reading.

___ I identified the author's main ideas:
- accurate translation—no confusions
- complete translation—no biggies missing

___ I commented on the author's key supporting details:
- included important details
- skipped less important details

___ I've shown that I "read between the lines" to make inferences:
- included ideas that the book implies

___ I offered support by referring back to the book:
- quotes
- paraphrases

Target 2: I have improved the writing to make it more understandable.

___ I used words that students can understand.

___ I used examples that students can relate to.

___ I have organized the translation into a simple structure that makes it easy to follow.

___ I can add some humor or a story to make it more enjoyable to read.

Student reflections on this assignment

Trait 1: Demonstrates comprehension of the reading.

6 = **exceptional** comprehending; thorough and accurate rendition of the concepts presented in the text, including inferred ideas

5 = **excellent** comprehending; strong understanding of concepts presented in the text

4 = **proficient** comprehending; competent, good enough understanding of the concepts

3 = **inadequate** comprehending; close, but some inaccurate or incomplete understanding of the concepts

2 = **limited** comprehending; confused or inaccurate understanding of the concepts

1 = **missing** comprehending; NO attempt to meet expectations, OR virtually NO understanding

Trait 2: Rewriting

6 = **exceptional** rewriting: new version is vastly superior to original; far more engaging, interesting, informative, or entertaining

5 = **excellent** rewriting: new version is much improved over original; interesting and helpful

4 = **proficient** rewriting: new version is better than original; helpful

3 = **inadequate** rewriting: new version may be somewhat better than original, but also worse in some ways

2 = **limited** rewriting: new version is inferior to original

1 = **missing** rewriting: NO attempt to meet expectations, OR new version shows nothing even resembling the original's information

Teacher comments to student

Exhibit 3.2 ChecBric: Translation Exercise.

Model for them how to edit a paragraph from the assignment by translating it into informal language that would be easier and more engaging for a teenager to read. This can be accomplished by making an overhead transparency of a paragraph from the text and editing it with an overhead pen as you talk your way through the process. (This teaching technique is called the "Think Aloud" because you think out loud to the class, revealing your decision-making process as you edit.)

I tried this translation activity with a community college student named Jonah, who was taking a course in astronomy that used a tough textbook (Bennett, Donahue, Schneider, and Voit, 2003; despite the date, it was actually published early in 2002). He and I practiced translating a chapter on constellations. We wrote the intro together for practice.

Then, on his own, Jonah rewrote the next section, translating it into his own words as follows:

Patterns in the Sky

Have you ever stared up into the clear night sky at all the shining stars? Of course, you have. We all do. And did you know that on a moonless, clear, super-dark night, your eye could see 2000–3000 stars?

As you look up at all these stars, your mind might try to form groups or patterns of them. Like, "Oooo, Shelly, check out the turtle playing a guitar!!" Other people from different cultures do, too.

- The Chinese looked up at the pattern we call Orion and called it Shen, the supreme warrior.
- Hindus in ancient India also saw a warrior but they named it Skanda.
- In Northern Australia, native Aborigines saw the three stars (those on Orion's belt which are the easiest to see) and visualized three fishermen in a canoe.
- In Southern California the same three stars seem to climb straight up in the sky, so the Chemehuevi Indians saw a line of three sure-footed sheep.

As you can see, these people from different cultures visualize star patterns that reflect figures or events from their daily lives.

These imposed patterns are called *constellations*.

He said to me, "It's like rereading, but you're comprehending it better." Right on target, Jonah.

With a whole-class exercise, you could walk everyone through another paragraph, calling on students to assist in the editing process. Then deputize each student to independently rewrite a different passage—one or more paragraphs—by translating it into student-friendly language.

Students will certainly return to the text to carefully reread their assigned passage with a critical eye toward improving it. They are, after all, playing the role of an expert, and looking smart in the eyes of other students is a big motivator, especially for strugglers who rarely feel smart.

Allow them to read their version to a partner, a cooperative team, or the entire class, depending on time availability. It would be considerate to present them with a copy of a scoring ChecBric at this point. See Exhibit 3.2.

Congratulate them for carefully rereading and rewriting. You can award points for this activity, scoring their translations with the ChecBric. You can collect the individual rewrites and compile them into a new account of the text, whatever it is. This integrates reading comprehension and written expression.

Extended Challenges

The Translation activity could be modified to bump up student thinking. Instead of assigning them to translate a paragraph (or section) into more student-friendly language, try requiring that students:

- Add additional useful information gleaned from one or more other sources.

- Generate examples to the text that would be helpful to other readers.

- Add commentary that transcends what the original author provided.

Of course, if you take this approach, the ChecBric should add the extended targets so the students know what you're looking for.

In all these suggested scenarios, we are providing the more able students in our classes with an opportunity to go beyond the basics and reach higher levels of thinking and information processing. Likewise, these extensions could also be assigned to train the less able, more reluctant, resistant, and possibly even repelled readers to do what the smart, skilled, and successful readers do: go back when necessary to Repair their comprehension by rereading portions, parts, or passages of the text.

Further, how about offering bonus points to anyone who will take the rewrites and type them into a word processor, format them nicely, and print up the student-friendly version for distribution to class authors?

You could even honor them by saying, "Your version is so much easier to understand that I am going to save it and use it with my new class next term." Or you can say, "Your version is so much easier to understand that I am going to send a copy to the publisher, so the original author can benefit from your editing."

By saving their work for next term or next year, you are proving to them that you value their work. This will likely be the first time in their entire career of being students that they have experienced this honor. And even if they don't say to you, "Wow, thank you so much for valuing us as productive human beings," you will know it, and they will know it.

Place the translations into a folder and keep it where you will remember it next term. Tell your new class that you have some resources available to assist them in reading and understanding the upcoming chapter in their textbook. Distribute the translations and find out from the students what they think of their predecessors' work. Obviously, this may present the opportunity for the new class to write their own translations—even better than the first batch.

If you choose to send the student translations to the publisher of the textbook, be sure to add a cover letter explaining the context of this assignment, so that the recipient clearly understands the importance of it. Also, you may want to send a query to the publisher, in advance of the students' work, inquiring about the proper person to send them to. And you can certainly request a reply from the publisher or authors; tell them how meaningful a reply will be to your students. (Or how about giving the students the assignment to write a memo to the publisher announcing the translations? I will talk more about student memos in Chapter Five.)

Of course, if you don't have the time or energy to mail the translations to the publisher, that is OK. Sometimes we get swamped and cannot pull off a big-time sharing of student work. No guilt allowed.

These last two suggestions move from the Repair stage into Share because now the students have an audience for what they learned. And these activities are new, different, engaging, empowering, and maybe even *fun*. We are paving the way for student success.

Prove It or Lose It

A second reading Repair activity for informational text is to hand the students a set of statements related to their reading assignment—some true, some untrue, and some partially true. For example, a science teacher who just assigned a textbook chapter on the human respiratory system could generate the following statements and distribute them to the class:

- Respiration is the process of oxygen combining with food to produce energy.
- The epiglottis is a flap that "directs traffic"—allowing food and water down the trachea into the digestive system.
- The nose is a better way to breathe in air than the mouth.
- Trapped particles in the nose are rerouted into the digestive system.

Challenge the students to identify which statements are accurate from the reading and deserve to be kept, and which statements are not accurate and should therefore be rejected; that is, to "prove it or lose it." Each student independently marks the statements:

- A = Accurate (the reading told me so)
- B = Between accurate and inaccurate (could be, not sure, or can't remember)
- C = Completely wrong (the reading definitely did not state this)

The next step is obvious. Thrill the students by telling them, "Before I collect your ABCs, I will let you check your answers by *looking back* in the chapter. If you can prove a statement is accurate by finding it in the chapter, circle the marked 'A' for 'accurate.' If you can find some evidence in the chapter that the statement is partially true, circle the marked 'B' for 'betweener.' If you cannot find any reference to the statement in the chapter, circle the marked 'C' for 'completely wrong.' Of course, you are *free to change any of your answers* based on looking back by crossing out the original letter and replacing it with a new one."

If time allows, do the partner, group, or whole-class debriefing activity to allow students to Share what they discover from this rereading activity. As always, reinforce the importance of reading Repair by rewarding, congratulating, and generally making a big deal out of it.

This activity serves to replace the pop quiz that our strugglers fear and hate. It actually is a pop quiz, but with the *right to return* to the text.

Extended Challenges
As with the Translation activity, a teacher could build in upper-level thinking skills by presenting some of the statements in a Prove It or Lose It activity that cannot

be cited directly in the text. This would challenge the readers to dig more deeply in their repair work by making inferences, hypothesizing, and speculating.

A possible structure for this could be

- In the lines
- Between the lines
- Beyond the lines

That is, students can be trained to look back in the reading to determine if a teacher-posed statement can be verified explicitly in the text, or inferred by "reading between the lines," or supported by a different source. In each case, students are expected to rethink their initial reading (the First Dare) by revisiting the assignment for further scrutiny. And by triggering deeper analysis with some statements that require inferring (between the lines) and extending (beyond the lines), we are building stronger reading comprehension skills—skills that are not only critical for success in school but are also critical for success in life after school. Plus, this helps them meet the required state standards.

The Repair Quiz

Another way to encourage your students to return to the text is to assign the "Repair Quiz." It is quite simple: Before they read an assignment, announce that afterwards they will be quizzed on their comprehension. Nothing new here; kids have routinely been assigned this activity throughout the grades.

But here is the difference. After the quiz is over, do not collect the papers as usual. Rather, tell the class that before they turn in their quizzes, you will allow them the opportunity to "check their answers." This always gets their attention.

"What do you mean?" they will ask. "Can we go back to the reading and look?"

The key here, of course, is to "go back and look," otherwise known as rereading. To the kids this is a form of legalized cheating. Of course, it is not cheating at all to Repair your initial comprehension; it is exactly what smart readers do.

Here is the procedure. Tell them to draw a line beneath their last quiz question answer and to write in big letters the word *Repairs*. Then allow them three to four minutes to return to the reading and check their quiz question answers. If anyone wants to change any answers, that is legal. On one condition: the new answers must be written beneath the line below the original answers, so that they (and you) can see the difference between the First Dare and the Repair stages. Exhibit 3.3 shows how one student did with this exercise.

Why only three to four minutes? To separate out those students who actually First Dare read the assignment from those who did not. A student who has read the material once will know where to look during the Repair Quiz; a few minutes will be sufficient. If a student has not read the assigned material, then the Repair Quiz won't be a Repair, it actually will be the First Dare, and a few minutes will not be enough time to find the answers to the quiz questions. We certainly would not want to encourage the skipping of the assigned First Dare, would we?

Another option: Tell the students that any repaired answer on the Repair Quiz must be written in a different colored pencil, so that they (and you) can see the growth from the First Dare to the Repair.

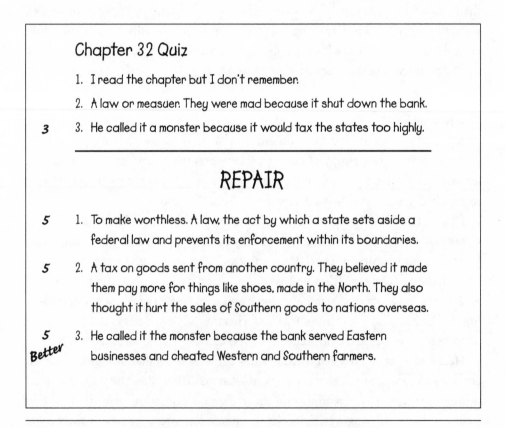

Chapter 32 Quiz

1. I read the chapter but I don't remember.

2. A law or measuer. They were mad because it shut down the bank.

3 3. He called it a monster because it would tax the states too highly.

***

REPAIR

5 1. To make worthless. A law, the act by which a state sets aside a federal law and prevents its enforcement within its boundaries.

5 2. A tax on goods sent from another country. They believed it made them pay more for things like shoes, made in the North. They also thought it hurt the sales of Southern goods to nations overseas.

5
Better 3. He called it the monster because the bank served Eastern businesses and cheated Western and Southern farmers.

Exhibit 3.3 Stephanie's Repair Quiz.

SHARING AND VISUALIZING UNDERSTANDINGS

Share is the label I suggest using for the final step in the general reading comprehension process. *Sharing* means confirming your understanding, revealing your comprehension, and communicating it to an audience. Some shares are relatively quick, while some require more time.

Repair into Share

I have already described a few Share activities in this chapter. For example, the Translation activity has a Share component. Students are prompted to write their new, improved, considerate, student-friendly versions for other students: to a partner, a cooperative team, or the entire class. This audience for their reading-writing serves to inspire them to do good work—they want to look good in the eyes of other students, especially if their teacher wants to use their version with another class. Because it is written and its audience is broader, this Share takes longer.

Interpretive Cards

Interpretative Cards are 3" x 5" index cards with an interpretative question about the topic of the reading assignment on each one. They cover the same sort of ground as the statements in the extended Prove It or Lose It activity, but in question form. The cards support cooperative learning activity among pairs of students, teams, or the class as a whole. Here is one way to use interpretive cards with groups of students:

1. Setup. Divide the class into groups of four. One team member is the *cardholder,* who receives the interp card from the teacher, reads it to the group, and places it face up for any member who wants to reread it. The cardholder is also responsible for not allowing any writing on the precious card and for returning it in perfect shape to the teacher at the end of the activity. (It is ideal if each team gets a different card with a different interpretative question.)

2. Individual activity. Within a certain time allocation ("You have two minutes and nineteen seconds. . .") students independently record their answers to the card question on pieces of scratch paper. Looking back at the text to help answer the question is legal. One team member's role is *timekeeper* and *enforcer* of no talking, independent work.

3. Group work. The team members each get a set amount of time to read their own answers aloud to the team, and other members can comment, agree, disagree, elaborate, question, discuss. Referring back to the text to prove a point is legal. One team member serves as a *moderator* to keep the team at-task on the discussion of every team member's answer to the question.

4. Sharing with other groups. The team prepares a group answer to the question. That is, they compose an all-star, very best possible answer collectively. They can do this by being wowed by one team member's answer and adopt it as their collective answer; by synthesizing pieces of team members' answers into a composite collective answer; by generating a completely new answer based on comments during the discussion in step 3. And if any team members disagree with the collectively composed all-star answer, they have the right to file "minority reports" individually or as a group. One team member's job is to serve as the *scribe* to record the collective answer.

Lots of sharing in this cooperative learning activity. And while the teams work, the teacher can float from group to group pausing to listen in, to monitor progress if necessary, to compliment good work, or to prompt a team that is struggling by asking a leading question.

Further, each team could be given time to read their question and their collective answer to the entire class. Even though the members of other teams didn't prepare equivalent answers because they had different questions, they are welcome to comment on the interpretative answer by agreeing, disagreeing, asking for clarification, complimenting, and so on. Of course, anyone in the class has the right to return to the text to quote a reference that helps prove an interpretative point. If this option of whole-class sharing is used, then one member of each team would take on the additional role of *group reader.*

This Share activity incorporates reading, writing, discussion, and debate. It is time-consuming but powerful. I have had teams demand the right to Share their collective answer even after the bell rang to end the period. I had to promise them time to Share the next day.

Three final notes about interpretive cards. First, looking back to the text is always labeled "legal." I never explicitly require rereading, but rather I try to encourage it by making it available to students for a motivating purpose.

Second, it is useful to collect the card, the collective answer, and each individual answer from each team at the end. I recommend reading them to see what the individual students wrote as compared to the team's collective answer.

Third, a big-time Share could be to assign students to rewrite a section of the reading incorporating their interpretive answers. This makes them editors of their textbook. Besides the benefit of empowerment, of repairing an author's work, it neatly links reading and writing, or as Hillocks describes, "my reading self" with "my writing self."

The Comic Strip

Because some of our struggling readers also struggle with writing, we need to resist the tendency to always use writing to Share reading comprehension. While writing is an excellent mode for sharing, we must be sensitive to how depressing a struggle it is to be in school for years and years with limited literacy skills. And we must remember that some of our strugglers do not qualify for special education assistance. Many of them are the in-betweeners who don't test low enough for special funding but surely are behind their classmates. We can connect to these forgotten students by occasionally assigning visual, graphic, and pictorial tasks to reveal their comprehension of the informational texts they read.

My favorite alternative to writing is the comic strip, which actually is a combination of illustrations with minimal writing. I first learned of using it in conjunction with reading comprehension from former colleague Dorothy Syfert.

Dorothy assigned a historical comic strip in a 1492 U.S. history unit. Her students had read a short account of the December 25th grounding of the *Santa Maria* off the coast of the Caribbean island Hispañola, now Haiti and the Dominican Republic.

Her class was enthusiastic—far more enthusiastic than my class, where I'd assigned a five-question reading comprehension quiz. After she shared with me some of her students' comic strips, naturally I "borrowed" the idea. (Staff development.) And I have shared this activity with hundreds of other teachers, including Amy Gallagher.

Amy's students also read the account of the grounding of the *Santa Maria,* and they created their own versions of this historical event in comic strip form. Check out a panel from Dave's work in Figure 3.1. The exercise assisted his comprehension by inducing visualization, it engaged him by providing a new and enjoyable activity, and it allowed him to reveal his understanding of the historical content information. This made his teacher Amy very happy.

The first time Dorothy and I used the comic strip, for assessing eighth-grade history students' reading comprehension of their textbook's account of a 1492 event, we distributed 11" x 17" sheets of white paper and instructed them to record the key events in five or six panels. But when we scored the resulting comics, we quickly realized that five or six panels was an unfair limitation to some students; that is, some kids could not adequately reveal their understanding of the history event in only five or six pictures.

December 6 1492 Columbus lands on Mole St Nicholes northern haiti

Figure 3.1 Comic Strip Panel: Columbus Reaches the New World.

Source: Amy Gallagher, Marple Newton High School, Newton Square, Pennsylvania.

So we refined this task. Instead of restricting the number of panels on a large paper, the next time we used this reading task, we distributed a stack of smaller panels, made up from letter-size white paper cut into quarters, to each student with these instructions: "Use as many panels as you need to fully explain what happened in your reading assignment." We also gave each kid a printed set of directions called a "Task Sheet" that provided the task's purpose, audience, directions, and assessment targets in the form of a ChecBric.

Because the class could not possibly accomplish all this at a high level of success in just one class period, we extended the time allocation to three periods (actually parts of three periods) and structured it like this:

Day 1   Read the Task Sheet and ChecBric to get clear parameters; read the passage (First Dare), making quick sketches on as many comic panels as you need.

Day 2   Using the Checklist column of the ChecBric, self-assess your comic strip to see if it meets all the task's requirements. If not, revise it by fixing up any panels, adding new panels, removing panels, or reconsidering the sequence of your panels. You can go back and reread the textbook passage at any time to help you double-check your work.

Day 3   Arrange your panels in the order you want; check the mechanics of your writing (spelling, punctuation, grammar, caps); double-check your ChecBric to be sure all targets were hit; use a fine-point black-tipped pen to trace over the words for improved visibility; use colored pencils or pens to decorate your drawings; use a glue stick to affix the panels onto a large piece of colored construction paper; glue the ChecBric onto the back side; sign and date your comic strip.

Readers in science classes also can create comic strips. Mari Radostitz and Joel Bradford, Cascade Middle School, offered their students the opportunity to reveal their understanding of their science textbook's account of the human digestive system. See Figure 3.2 for the opening of Emily's gorgeous digestive comic strip starring Strawberry as the narrator.

Of course, comic strips are not only for informational text assignments in content area classes, they also work very well in high school English and middle school language arts classes. I have assigned literary comic strips to both middle and high

Figure 3.2 Comic Strip Panel: Human Digestion.

Source: Mari Radostitz and Joel Bradford, Cascade Middle School, Bethel School District, Oregon.

school literature students with very good results. Comics help students visualize the characters, the settings, and the events in their minds' eyes as they decipher the words from the author. Plus, it's fun.

SnapShots in Science

Another way to help students visualize what an author is saying is to use a technique I call "SnapShots." This works most naturally with literature assignments so

I describe it in more detail in Chapter Four, but here's a sketch of how it works. Jud Landis, a ninth-grade physical science teacher, invited me to co-teach with him during a unit on Newton's First Law of Motion. Jud had purchased new textbooks, and while they were superior to the ones he used to use in terms of user-friendliness, they still didn't make reading scientific content easy for all his students.

So we employed a variation of SnapShots. We handed each of the students a set of three small sticky pink notes, and told them to make a visual representation—a sketch, illustration, or drawing—of any key concepts presented in the section of the chapter they were working on. We added that if they were not comfortable with their illustration skills, they could trace or copy any figures that supported their understanding of the concepts. Figure 3.3 shows what Brittany came up with for this exercise.

Additionally, we gave each student three blue and three green stickies: blue to write key concept summaries and green to record any questions that emerged during reading. These color-coded sticky notes turned out to help science students apply key reading strategies as they worked, and the general success level of the class improved.

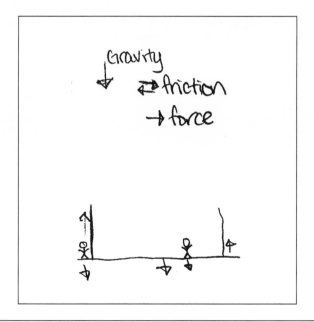

Figure 3.3 SnapShots in Science: Newton's First Law of Motion.

CONCLUSION: THE RIGHT OF RETURN

Struggling readers cannot be expected to get 100 percent perfect comprehension by reading an assignment once. No one should be expected to accomplish this feat. All readers deserve the chance to go back and reconsider their comprehension. This returning to the text to boost understanding is labeled the Repair stage of the reading process.

We addressed a set of strategy families that can be taught to students under the umbrella of the Repair stage: fixing-up strategies, evaluating strategies, analyzing strategies, and perspective-taking strategies. All these strategies reflect what skilled readers do to improve their comprehension.

To encourage students to exercise this right of return, we as their teachers must develop activities that guide them back to the text without making it punishing or painful. The Translation, Prove It or Lose It, and Repair Quiz activities are designed to do just that, and to link nicely to the Share stage. The comic strips and snapshots turn to visual exercises to stimulate comprehension and provide a break from writing.

In the next chapter, I take a look at the four-step process from a different angle, exploring the exercises in the context of literature assignments. Many of the concepts provide useful insights for content area classes as well, so stay tuned. . . .

chapter FOUR

Working with Literary Texts

Comprehension of literature differs from the comprehension of informational text. Although there surely is some overlap in readers' ability to understand fiction and nonfiction, the structure of literary text is typically more engaging than that of informational text. More simply put, most readers like reading stories better than they like reading articles, essays, or technical directions. It is the narrative organizational pattern that engages readers, with characters in settings trying to solve problems. Witness student preference for reading historical fiction novels over the drier version in a history textbook.

Still, the reading of narratives, as in novels, short stories, or plays, requires the active participation of the reader. Just as when reading informational text, the reader of fiction needs to apply reading-attack strategies to navigate successfully through the story, alertly translating the author's cues into a meaningful experience.

PREPARE AND FIRST DARE EXERCISES

The FFF, K-W-L, FTL, and KWT folders, introduced in Chapter Two were originally designed for nonfiction, informational text reading. However, they adapt smoothly for use with fiction assignments. For example, the topic written on the top tab of a Folded File Folder could be the setting of a novel. Or, the "K" column of the K-W-L could be for "what I already know about sibling rivalry" if a short story, novel, or poem deals with this theme.

English/language arts teachers have used several other reading-tracking devices to help coach their literature students toward better comprehension and fuller appreciation of fiction. Some of these devices focus on elements unique to fiction, but others can be adapted for use in content area classes.

The Story Web

The story web, or story map, has a long and glorious history in English/language arts classrooms. I have no idea who originally developed it, but I first learned of it in the middle 1980s from the Oregon Department of Education.

This Prepare tool is a graphic organizer (GO) that prepares a reader of a short story (or a novel chapter) by previewing six critical components of any work of fiction:

- Title
- Characters
- Settings
- Main events
- Problems and conflicts
- Solution or resolution

During the Prepare stage the story web cues the reader to remember that the story will have the six components, so be on the lookout for them. But the story web doesn't stop helping readers at that point, it assists them at the later stages of the reading process. In the First Dare stage it offers a simple means to take notes by filling in the six boxes of the web while reading. In the Repair stage it suggests returning to the story for further investigation of any weak or missing information from any of the six boxes. And in the Share stage it provides a written record of what the reader constructed from the story.

The story web comes in many different formats and layouts. See my favorite in Exhibit 4.1. Or perhaps you would like to modify my version of the story web by adding a seventh box for theme, or author's writing craft, or "what this story reminds me of."

Alternative Device: The E.G.O.

Here's another tool for tracking fiction, be it a novel or short story: the electronic graphic organizer, or E.G.O. It works like a story web, but it offers the real benefits of the electronic medium: built-in spelling checker, ability to cut and paste, palette of fifty colors, easy change-making features, and a library of twelve hundred ready-made shapes, symbols, and icons.

Students can record the same key elements of fiction as with the paper story web, but now at the computer. Figure 4.1 presents a book report on the historical novel *Sarah Bishop* (Odell, 1988) created by a happy middle school student. Why happy? Because she is using a different format, and she is working at a computer. My students always appreciated variety. . . . Anyone else's students, too?

The "Open Mind" Returns

Although I introduced it earlier as a comprehension helper for reading nonfiction, the Open Mind was originally designed for the reading of fiction.

The OM is a tracking device, a classroom reading activity, that accomplishes two critical things. It gets the student to think about the story before actually reading it, and it allows the teacher to take a peek into the student's mind.

Reading is a private event, is it not? Reading comprehension occurs inside the mind of the reader. The only way we, the teachers, can see this would be to drill a hole into the students' heads—not recommended. So we invent other (less invasive) ways, or we borrow them from other teachers.

I used the OM with sixth-grade literature students who were assigned the novel *Lupita Mañana* (Beatty, 1981). They were told to "think like the main character, Lupita" by jotting down her thoughts in the day's reading. Check out Figure 4.2 to see how Evyn used both words and graphics to reveal what the novel's main character was thinking.

Of course, a student may prefer to draw a picture to visualize what is occurring inside the mind, instead of using words. And some students like to use a combination of words and drawings.

Character Emotional Scenes

Instead of assigning writing as a means for supporting reading comprehension, as with the story web, how about another illustrative device? Middle school teacher and long-time colleague Dorothy Syfert invented a device she calls "Character

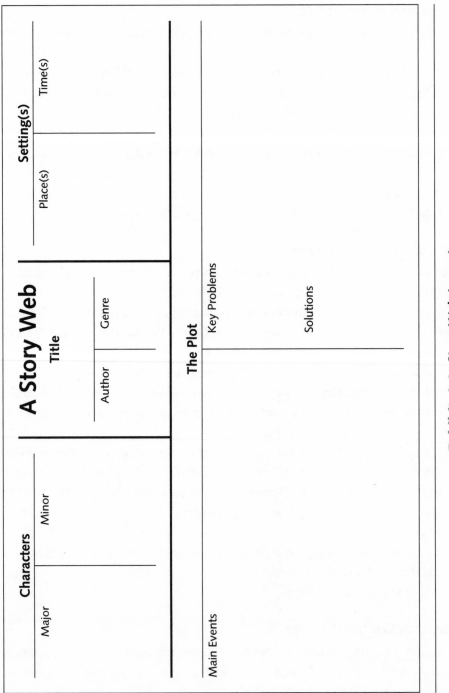

Exhibit 4.1 Story Web Layout.

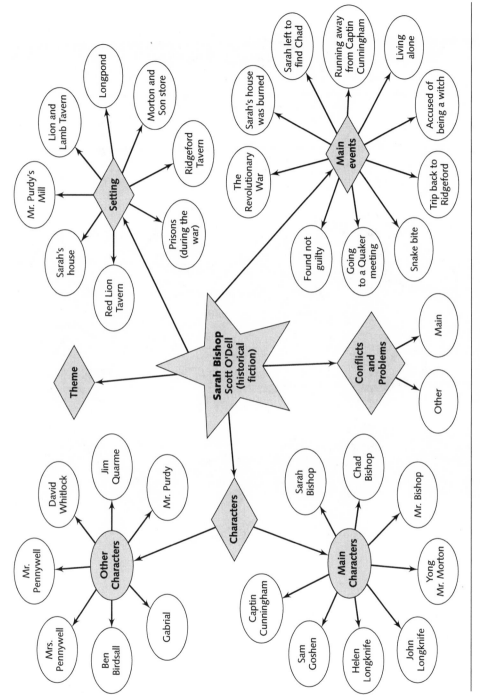

Figure 4.1 Electronic Book Report.

Note: Produced using Inspiration Software.

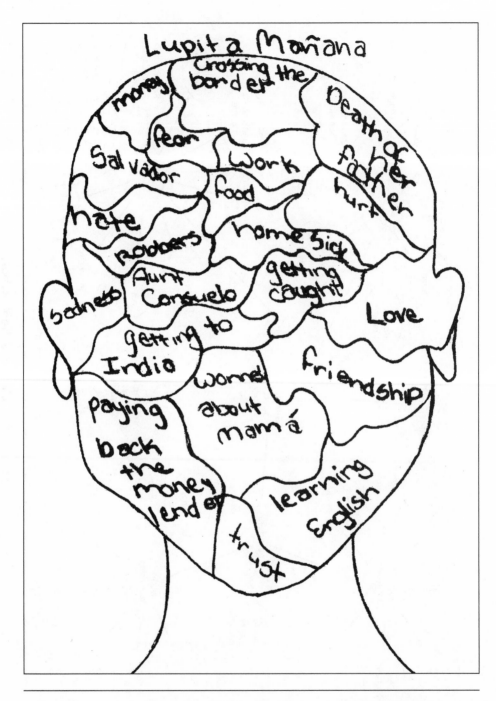

Figure 4.2 The Open Mind of a Character (and a Student).

Emotional Scenes" for supporting the reading of literature. She had her students select a major character and visually portray that character's emotions from a key scene from a book. Figure 4.3 shows Jamie's rendition of Lawrence Yep's feelings in his biographical novel *The Great Rat Hunt* (1996).

Jamie possesses outstanding drawing ability, as you can see, and her written descriptions are also excellent. Clearly not a struggler. But for her classmates with less ability in reading and writing, this "Character Emotional Scenes" activity paved the way for success, too.

To assist the class earlier in the term, Dorothy had them practice a simpler version of this activity: They drew quick facial expressions for the main characters in a Gary Soto short story titled "Born Worker" (2001). Many students like to draw faces even when they don't do much other drawing, and this visualization activity can help solidify their comprehension of fiction. Figure 4.4 shows samples from Mike and Daniel, a couple of struggling students who did well with the exercise.

Advanced Visualizations

Imagine a classroom of tenth-grade literature students having a good time reading an assigned short story. Imagine that some of these students typically experience reading difficulties and usually have a less-than-enthusiastic attitude about reading fiction in a class. But imagine them actually smiling as they read the story, track the story, analyze the story, and evaluate the author's effectiveness in writing the story.

Too good to be true? No, of course not. It can happen. It does happen. It can happen if the story engages the students, and they discover they can clearly *visualize* the story as they read it. Even challenged readers stay alert while constructing a story's meaning once they learn how to see what is going on, to create mental images cued by the author's words. Introduced in earlier exercises as "visualizing what's going on by picturing it," this strategy is the ability to see in the mind's eye the characters, settings, and actions, and it is what makes the story come alive to the reader.

And readers must often visualize by "reading between the lines." Authors of fiction cannot tell every single thing about a story. Instead, they provide what they can and then let the reader fill in the blanks. This ability of nonliteral comprehension is critical to reading success. I call it interpreting, inferring, hypothesizing, speculating.

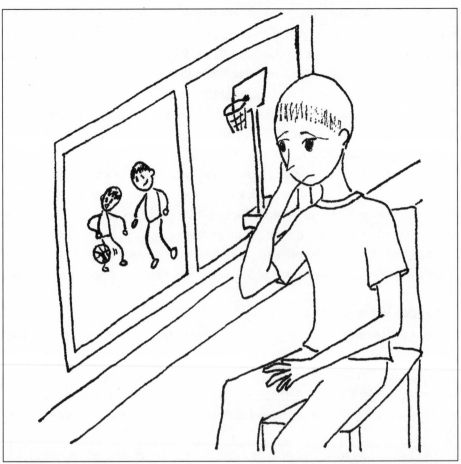

Lawrence has asthma, so he can't play sports. His dad is very good at sports and his dad can only play with his older brother. Lawrence thinks that he can't make his dad proud of him, and sometimes he thinks that his dad thinks his brother is the only true son.

Figure 4.3 An Emotional Scene.

Source: Dorothy Syfert, language arts and social studies teacher, James Monroe Middle School, Eugene, Oregon.

Arnie whined he is surprised and afraid

Dad → Mad

"Work" yelled Jose' Dad "I see years of work

Dad was yelling at Jose'

Figure 4.4 Quick Emotional Sketches.

Source: Dorothy Syfert, language arts and social studies teacher, James Monroe Middle School, Eugene, Oregon.

SnapShots to Improve Visualization Skills

If successful readers are able to visualize scenes in fiction so easily, why do less skilled readers find it difficult? I really don't know. I don't know why some brains can take the words off a printed page and paint a mental picture. I don't know why some brains have trouble doing this. Is television the primary culprit? Video games?

I do know that struggling readers can be helped in learning to visualize as they read. It requires coaching them, training them, helping them practice this skill; you know, paving the way.

My favorite device for visualization improvement is an activity I dubbed Snap-Shots. I co-invented it with twelfth-grade literature teacher Chet Skibinski. We tell students the following:

"Good readers take pictures while they read. That is, they can picture in their mind's eye what is happening. You can do it, too. You *visualize* what is going on in the story because your brain is the camera that snaps away as you read the author's words. You take mental SnapShots. And to help your brain do this, here is a Photo Album to place your mental photographs of the story as you read it."

This reading-tracking device assisted Aaron, a student in Marsha Ruhl's class at Glide Middle School, as he read the assigned story "The Proud Princess." (See Figure 4.5.) He pauses periodically from his reading to make a quick sketch of an important scene. Beneath each SnapShot he quickly jots a caption to support his drawing.

I believe that pausing to think about reading comprehension is a useful "First Dare" reading strategy. It aids metacognition—thinking about what you are thinking about. Plus, the pause occurs in the pictorial mode, which aids the key reading comprehension strategy of visualization. And, perhaps most important, students really enjoy it once they understand that their illustration ability is not relevant here. To help them believe this, I provide assistance to those students who feel uncertain how to draw. (Later in this chapter I'll describe the "cheat sheet" I give them.)

Not only does the SnapShots activity trigger the use of the self-regulating reading strategy of visualization, it actually causes readers to use multiple strategies. Come to think of it, SnapShots engage readers in all of the First Dare strategy families introduced in Chapter Two:

- *Focus strategies:* Selectively attend to significant information.

- *Information-gathering strategies:* Acquire needed new information.

The Baby was Born, a princess.

"On this day when you become of age I will trow you a feast. The Biggest Feast." Said the King.

Her Father ordered 30 head of oxen, she was not happy.

He ordered 40 more head of oxen. But she wass not happy. he did that 5 times.

You have to live here for 1 year and 1 day with a plow, a sleeping mat, water, and Bread.

Figure 4.5 Photo Album: "The Proud Princess."

Source: Marsha Ruhl, teacher, Glide Middle School, Glide, Oregon.

- *Self-regulating strategies:* Monitor one's own construction of meaning (metacognition).

- *Generating strategies:* Produce new information, meanings, ideas, summaries.

- *Organizing strategies:* Track new information, construct meaning, and enhance retention.

Perhaps this is why the SnapShots exercise is so successful.

SnapShots with Sticky Notes

To increase the appeal of this SnapShots activity even more to secondary school students, it can be modified. This modification is introduced to the students in terms similar to the basic SnapShots, but with an important addition:

"Good readers take pictures while they read. Your brain is the camera that snaps away as you read the author's words. And to help your brain do this, here is a 'roll of film' to take your mental photographs of the story as you read it."

The "roll of film" is a set of yellow 3"x3" sticky notes. Each student gets a piece of paper with six sticky notes on it, which I set up before class to make it easier to get everyone started quickly.

I continue with the directions: "As you read the story, periodically pause from your reading to 'take a picture' of a key scene, a key character's action, a key setting, whatever you think is important by drawing a quick sketch on one of your sticky notes. Which SnapShots you take, and when you decide to take them, is up to you. Just be sure that you take enough to show that you are tracking the story well. And if you need more than the six I handed out, just let me know."

This SnapShot activity is helpful to struggling readers because it trains them to apply the important reading comprehension strategy of visualization. It helps them to "develop" images that support comprehension. Beyond helpful, it is an *engaging way* to have them practice visualizing, because everyone enjoys using sticky notes. I've used them at all grade levels—elementary, middle, and high school. All students like them. The only difference is that elementary students readily admit how much they like stickies; middle and high school students may play it cool and pretend to be indifferent or bored when receiving them. (But we know the truth.)

Plus, SnapShots allow kids the chance to draw instead of writing—a nice change of pace to constant use of writing, writing, writing. However, some students are not thrilled about being expected to draw because they think they can't do it well.

So I assure everyone in the class that "drawing ability is not the target here—it is reading comprehension ability. So how well you can or cannot draw is not important. Just make quick sketches as you read. If you need to draw stick figures, fine. That's what I'd have to do, with my drawing ability. Just be sure to add a short written caption beneath the SnapShot to explain it." Figure 4.6 shows a pair of SnapShots a student named Elisabeth drew for "Kelfala's Secret Something," an assigned African folk tale from a seventh-grade literature anthology titled *The Language of Literature.*

REPAIRING LITERARY UNDERSTANDING

Just as with nonfiction reading, students reading literature cannot guarantee perfect comprehension during a First Dare. This is not only true for our students, it also happens to be true for us. Therefore, it is very likely that some repairing of the initial understandings will be needed when reading fiction.

Now some readers know this and take measures to boost their comprehension during the initial reading. That is, they apply a quick fix-up strategy: they stop the flow, put on the brakes, and back up to reread a section of a story that didn't quite

Nothing or no one could resist Kelfa's charm. Except the beautiful Wambuna, she wouldn't even look at him! But Kelfala loved Wambuna!

Wambuna had taken an oath that said, "The first man she talked to outside of her family she had to marry." That was tradition.

Figure 4.6. SnapShot: "Kelfala's Secret Something."

make sense. This strategy is sometimes accompanied by another Repair strategy, slowing down the reading rate.

Of course, as noted earlier, many of our challenged readers do not use any strategy because it would lengthen the reading time, and they just want to get it over with ASAP. We need to expand our repertoire of strategy-training activities for literature. Exhibit 4.2 recaps the strategy list in a form that applies to reading fiction.

One more word on the Repair stage in reading fiction: Not every student must return to every reading assignment to make repairs. Sometimes stopping at the

Menu of Literature Reading Repair Strategies

- Check back to find out for sure which event happened before (or after) another event. For instance, [list a couple of key events in the action for the students to check].
- Read a dialogue again, but this time softly to yourself to hear the words each character says.
- Go back to see where the setting changed and why the author moved the scene.
- Count up how many times the character made the same mistake in judgment.
- Locate two times the author used a simile to describe something.
- What do you think of the author's decision to [fill in something specific to the text in question]?
- Hunt for a key vocabulary word in its context in the story to determine its meaning.
- Skim for evidence to prove [or disprove] that [fill in something specific to the text in question].
- Search for foreshadows that could have told me that [fill in something specific to the text in question].
- Add another foreshadow the author could have used.
- Reread the title and change it to something better.
- Return to the part where [fill in something specific to the text in question] and look for [some important insight].

Exhibit 4.2 Menu of Literature Reading Repair Strategies.

end of the First Dare is adequate. That is, we shouldn't feel required to assign detailed exercises for every literature selection. First, for some material once is enough; not all fiction warrants rereading. Second, sometimes we can't afford the time investment that Repair requires; we get busy, and the curriculum wheel forces us onward. Third, we don't want to over-use Repair and make our students bored with us or angry at us. Assign Repair activities as needed to help kids, not automatically every time.

The Story Web

Remember the story web from the Prepare section earlier in the chapter? (See Exhibit 4.1.) It not only benefits readers at the Prepare and First Dare stages, it is also helpful at the Repair stage as well.

Students can assess their story webs after finishing a story to see if they are satisfied. They may need some help here—they typically have difficulty recognizing areas in need of improvement. (This resembles the rewriting stage of the writing process: students usually cannot see *anything* in their first draft that warrants revision.) So it's useful to help them examine the results of their First Dare more objectively.

One method is to place an overhead transparency of the story web template on the projector and then lead the students in a whole-class sharing of what they wrote in each of the six boxes. Students are permitted (encouraged) to elaborate on a classmate's response, to modify what another student has shared, or to disagree with anyone. Any of these responses can trigger the need to *go back to the story* and find the key passage and *reread* it to offer support for a comment, opinion, or explanation. Students do not find this approach to Repair punishing. In fact, they usually don't even recognize it as "rereading" because the teacher has not mandated slogging through the text again, but rather allowed fixer-uppers. Big difference.

Likewise, students can be allowed to Repair their story webs in a partner activity. Two students are paired with directions to compare each other's responses in each box of the story webs. Any differences, both major and minor, can be addressed by discussing the reasons for each response. Then, off they go back to the story to look for evidence to support their response. They *legally* can Repair their story webs based on their repaired reading. (As I've said, some students perceive this as "legalized cheating," which adds spice to the lesson. Just make sure they don't lose track of the difference between legalized cheating and the other sort.)

I recommend, though, requiring students to use a different color pencil for their repairs. Why? Two reasons: It draws attention to the act of repairing—a different color makes the changes, modifications, improvements *stand out* to the student. And it allows the teacher to see the changes, too—I like to know what the kid was able to do alone on the independent First Dare compared to the partner activity on the Repair.

As with any cooperative learning activity, this one requires careful planning: how partners are chosen, the procedural rules for the activity, time limits, expectations for behavior, and preannounced grading criteria. I like to select the pairings rather than letting the students choose their own, and I typically try to pair students with differing reading abilities. This increases the chances for different story web responses, which leads to the need to reconcile them "back in the story." Cooperative pairings can be made according to other criteria, of course, and the teacher always has the right to try them differently to see which works best for any class.

Character Analysis Sheet

Another activity that encourages repairing of an initial understanding of a story is to fill out a "Character Analysis Sheet." This is a worksheet designed by the teacher to lead students back to the text (the story, novel, poem, play) for reexamination of a key character's action, appearance, personality trait, thought patterns, or reflection in other characters' perceptions. Typically, most secondary literature students do not fully grasp what an author is doing to develop a character, so it's useful to take them back for a closer look.

Instead of directing the class to "go back to the story and reread it to find out more about the character," we can more fluidly guide them back with a "Character Analysis Sheet."

Exhibit 4.3 shows a sheet set up for the students to work with Jessie, the main character of a short story titled "Bandennammen" (LeWine, 2002).

First, the teacher working with the whole class, pairs of students, or individuals identifies a set of words that describe the character in question. For example, "I found Jessie to be 'self-confident.'" These characteristics go into column 1.

The next step is obvious: cite examples from the story that support this view of the character. In other words, cite examples that prove Jessie is "self-confident." Say a reader can refer to two examples; they are posted in column 2.

Character Analysis Sheet

Jessie in "Bandennammen"

Character Characteristic	Support Examples from Story
1. self-confident	**1a.** she tells her step-mother Erika to back off with the band naming ideas (page ____) **1b.** she jokes around with the corporate big shots in her interview (page ____) **1c.** _____ _____
2.	
3.	
4.	

Exhibit 4.3 Sample Character Analysis Sheet.

Now a student who couldn't remember anything clearly enough to cite could surely go back to the story and hunt for a few instances. This is the purpose of this activity—to revisit the story for improved understanding and analysis. Likewise, a student who remembers just one or two examples can return to the story to pick up a few more to strengthen the view that Jessie is "self-confident." Same for any member of the class. Anyone can write an example on a copy of the "Character Analysis Sheet," and anyone can (should) look for more back in the story. The teacher leads the class through this process for as many character traits as time and interest allow.

Same procedure when students are working with partners. They agree on a set of descriptors (say, three or four, which seems reasonable) and record them in column 1, and they remember or search the text for examples to back up the character trait and record these in column 2.

But what if someone, the teacher or a student, asserts a character trait, and the rest of the class (or most of the class) disagrees? The person suggesting the descriptor has the right (the responsibility) to identify examples from the story that prove the accuracy of the assertion. Obviously, a discussion will ensue arguing the pros and cons as to whether or not this is an apt description of the character's personality.

And this is exactly what a teacher of literature wants: an animated discussion and analysis of the material. As long as everyone feels secure in the classroom, differences of opinion can and should be expressed.

It is up to the teacher to ensure this proper classroom environment by instructing (and modeling for) students throughout the entire course how to handle differing opinions politely and sensitively. Some groups catch on right away how to maturely discuss topics that have more than one perspective, while others need more time and practice.

If I had a class that just could not learn how to deal with this, then I as their teacher would limit the character analysis activity to individuals working alone. I wouldn't risk making anyone feel put down, and I would tell the class this. If they pledged to me that they could handle it properly, then I would tell them I was willing to give them a try.

Here's an idea to reinforce the importance of repairing analysis of a character. Tell the students, "Use a black lead pencil to record in column 2 the examples you can remember from the story, but then switch to a different colored pencil for recording additional examples that you pick up while rereading the story." This will tell both you and the student how understanding grows with review of the material, which may well be the most important insight the students gain from the exercise.

And, depending on the class, a teacher could begin this activity in class and assign its completion for homework.

I like this activity because it causes the students to deal with all the important Repair strategies identified earlier in this chapter: fixing up, evaluating, assessing and analyzing, and perspective-taking. Not a bad day's work. You will see this "Character Analysis Sheet" in more detail in the sample lesson that concludes this chapter.

Interpretative Cards

Literature is rewarding to read because the authors of fiction possess both the craft of writing and the art of telling a story through engaging characters. They reveal universal emotions, and they move us to see the world in new ways.

I love how literature so beautifully orchestrates the writer-reader dance: authors use words to paint a picture of someone, somewhere, doing something of interest to the rest of us, and we, the readers, take those well-crafted words and assemble the story in our minds (and hearts, if it's really good).

This assembly is based not only on the author's words (cues) to us, but also on what the readers bring to those words from their own lives. This is schema theory, which I introduced in Chapter Two. I call it the "meeting of the minds," and it is most prevalent while reading literature. It "takes two to tango" in the reading of fiction.

And we all know that different readers can assemble different versions of a story. We each take the writer's words, and we construct meaning for them based on what we already know, or think we know, about the situation.

That's why, for example, some readers of the same story see the main character as "self-confident," while others may view her as "insecure." As long as either perception can be defended by examples of her behavior or thoughts, we have different but equally valid comprehension of the story. Only the author knows for sure. But sometimes the author doesn't either—because the character is complex and possesses many different (and contradictory) characteristics, or the author has intentionally made the character ambiguous.

All of this is to say that readers of fiction *interpret* stories in different ways. That's why we love to discuss the books we are reading, or talk about a movie we just saw or a favorite TV show episode. And that's why we can use "Interpretative Cards" as reading-repair activity.

As I noted in Chapter Three, Interpretative Cards are 3" x 5" index cards with an interpretative question on each one. Here are several for the story "Banden-nammen" (which is featured in the sample lesson at the end of the chapter):

Why is Jessie worried about boys' interest in her?

Why does the author change the narration from first to third person?

Why would a writer come up with a story idea about this odd topic of band naming?

What is the theme of this story? What does the author want you to come away with?

These are interpretative questions because they are not explicitly answered in the story. Rather, the reader must speculate about the answers. Of course, the reader gets some help speculating, in that the author has provided information in the story that can be helpful in answering (interpreting).

Interpretative, inferential questions cause the reader to dig deeper into a story rather than hanging around the surface. There is nothing wrong with dealing with the surface issues of a story, like getting the basics of the title, characters, settings, problems, main events, and solution or resolution. In fact, the story web is designed to assist with just that.

But deeper reading leads to deeper understanding, and we can agree that any student in our schools deserves this training. Nod your head if you want your students to improve their interpretation skills. Interpretative Cards are a delivery system.

Interpretative Cards can be used with any literature selection that you are already assigning your students. Or they can be generated for a new story added to your curriculum. If you are looking for new selections to consider using, may I suggest visiting Web sites that offer free fiction. (See "Online Content-Area and Literature Selections" in the Appendix.) Where do you get interpretative questions to post on the cards?

- Create them yourself.

- Luck out and get some from your teacher's guide.

- Assign students to create them while they are First Dare reading the story.

A reminder to content area teachers: Interpretative Cards can be used in your classes, too, when you assign informational text readings. Rather than ask students about characters, plot, and theme, you ask them to dig deeper to interpret the main idea, the author's supportive details, an application of a principle to their own life, or any others you dream up.

SHARING UNDERSTANDING AND INTERPRETATION

The various reading-repair activities can all launch writing assignments. For example, students could take the data they recorded on the "Character Analysis Sheet" and use it to write an essay on the selected character's personality. This is the Share stage of the reading process: sharing what you gained from reading. And of course essays are not the only possible way to Share reading experience. The SnapShots drawings can be worked up into critical reviews or comic strips, and the factual information in the stories can be worked up into articles. In addition, memos, postcards, and letters (see Chapter Five) can be especially useful for literature assignments.

SnapShots in a High School Literature Class

The SnapShots tool turns out to work very well in high school. Tenth-grade English teacher Eliza Sher and I discussed the sticky note "film" technique for helping readers monitor their understanding of literature and decided to give it a try. I suggested one of my favorite short stories, Gary Soto's "The Challenge" (1993).

Eliza had not read this story, so she wanted a quick synopsis. I told her the story is a sweet and sad vignette about a middle school boy named José who falls in love with the new girl at school. Her name is Estela, and he longs for her, but he is too shy to introduce himself. So he fantasizes about techniques for getting her to notice him, finally settling on challenging her to a game of racquetball—because he noticed a racquet in her backpack. Bad idea: José has never played the game, but Estela turns out to be a champion player. The theme of learning a life lesson is poignantly told.

Eliza immediately liked the story as well as the SnapShots tool as a visualization inducer, but she wanted to expand the activity into a reading-writing performance assessment task: writing a "critical review" letter of the story.

Why would a seemingly normal teacher want to do more work than is required for a task instead of a simpler activity?

The answer is twofold. First, Eliza teaches in Oregon, a standards-based state whose Department of Education not only administers standardized statewide assessments but also requires a collection of in-class teacher-designed assessments specific to the class content. I agree with Eliza that these classroom-based "performance" assessments are more meaningful to students and their teachers than the state "bubble" tests. *Target practice* in class. Second, Eliza is a teacher who likes to stretch her students' thinking, and a structured performance assessment on reading fiction and writing a critical review will do that.

So the SnapShots activity idea transformed into writing a critical review of the short story. Each student was to select an audience for the review from a list of possibilities, including a friend, the school's newspaper, next semester's class, or to Eliza herself. They were to recommend either continued assignment of the story to future classes or dropping it from the curriculum.

This activity nicely bridges this chapter on reading and visualizing literature to the next chapter, on writing to share learning. (Of course, this is not the first reference to writing about reading. For me it is impossible to teach reading without writing or to teach writing without reading. As many of us know, they go together. They are the twin pillars of literacy.)

Eliza's persuasive writing task not only requires students to compose a convincing argument in the letter, it also first obligates students to *read* the story with excellent comprehension—so that the critique in the letter is both informed and informative. Reading plus writing.

This is where the SnapShots help. While reading the story for the first time, the First Dare, students self-monitor their understanding by taking mental SnapShots, that is, drawing quick sketches. But since this class is tenth grade, the state has raised the bar on expected performance; that is, Oregon's tenth graders have *four targets* to hit while reading:

- Comprehends both literal and inferential meaning.

- Extends understanding beyond the text to other sources.

- Reads critically by analyzing the author's writing ability and ideas.

- Critically analyzes the context in which the writer lived and wrote and how that social, historical, cultural context affected the writer and writing. (For a printer-friendly downloadable rubric for these four reading traits, check out the "Reading and Writing Standards" section of the Appendix.)

To reinforce the four separate targets, Eliza and I handed out four different colors of sticky notes for their picture panels:

- Yellow for retelling the story = target 1, comprehension
- Blue for relating the story to something else = target 2, extension
- Pink for giving feedback to the author = target 3, critical content analysis
- Green for commenting on the author's background as it affected the story = target 4, critical context analysis

Once again, the SnapShots teaching technique worked. It not only facilitates creating mental images while reading (visualization), it then serves as a prewriting tool for the critical review writing task. For example, see Jessi's "Photo Album," complete with captions, in Figure 4.7.

Now read an excerpt from the same student's critical review, which was intended for a student in next semester's class:

Final Draft

"The Challenge"

The book "The Challenge" is a great book for all ages to read because, it's very realistic, evocative, because for many people it brings back old memories of when they were young, and it's stereotypical because it shows how people act when they like someone and how it effects them.

I wanted to write this to the next semesters class, because I know that this story will bring back a lot of good, and very precious memories of when they were going thorugh the same thing.

I said that I thought this story was realistic, well it is. Some examples are how Jose tries to get Estela to pity him for purpossley hurting himself. he goes through a lot of physical and emotional pain. Jose felt like less of a "man" when Estela was beating him at everything they did together. And it hurts Jose emotionally because he really likes her. But she is not showing any feelings towards him!

A classmate had a different opinion of the story. In this student's critical review, framed as a letter to her best friend, she doesn't recommend it because ". . . the characters aren't very complex, and the main character is not very likable." Read on:

Jose is not very strong, he is spanish, american. He speaks both languages.

He is from both, Mexico and America. there is a part of both in him.

I noticed how the author is really making Jose work really hard for estela to like him. But as Jose is getting to know her better he sees that she wasn't as great as he thought.

I can connect to this story because when I was in middle school, I had a huge crush on someone, and I did everything I could to talk to him!

Figure 4.7 Simple Photo Album: "The Challenge."

Dear Kalie,

In my english class they gave us a book to read called "Local News." The one particular story they had us read was called "The Challenge." It's basically about this mexican-american kid who develops a crush on a girl in his eigth-grade class, and when he finds out she likes to play raquitball, he decides to challenge her to a game (even though he has no idea how to play). He challenges and she accepts, and when they play, she beats him.

I don't know about other middle schools, but I remember things were different in our middle school. When a guy liked a girl, he would try to be friends with her first. It was nothing like what this guy did.

I wouldn't recommend this book to you, the characters aren't very complex, and the main character is not very likable.

Your best friend,
Kelli

Although this analysis is a legitimate critique, it falls short of the assignment's targets in that it misses the mark on Trait 2 (connections) and Trait 3 (critiquing the author's literary devices) and Trait 4 (analyzing the social and cultural context that influenced the author).

However, and fortunately for the writer, her SnapShots are outstanding in their ability to reveal her understanding and analysis of the story, namely the missing parts of her written review. In fact, her visualization and illustration skills are so strong, that the SnapShots actually became a comic book version of the short story. I was so impressed with both Kelli's comprehension and her illustrations that I sent the author, Gary Soto, a copy of it. Gary wrote back complimenting the idea. Take a look at part of her version in Figure 4.8.

Kelli's success on this assignment would be reflected in the scores she earned for each of the targeted elements. I recommend providing students with a scoring device in advance of the assignment, so that they are clear about the assignment's parameters and how they will be scored. I like to use a ChecBric for this so the students can see just what their teacher will be looking for. Exhibit 4.4 shows the ChecBric Eliza and I designed for her students' SnapShots.

Many students in Eliza's class benefited from the visualization assistance of the activity. Heather wrote in her review: "When you read this story, you actually get a *mental picture* of this teenage boy who does really stupid things to impress girls."

Jose is in love with Estella, but she doesn't know he exists.

He notices a racquetball racquet in her back pack and thinks that he should challenge her to a game.

He brags

She accepts

Figure 4.8 Complex Photo Album: "The Challenge."

Major Foreshadowing

Figure 4.8 Continued.

(Italics mine.)   Although this is meant as a compliment to writing talents of the author Gary Soto, I will also take it as a testimonial to the benefits of SnapShots.

Of course, not all of our students arrive in class possessing visualization and illustration skills. Even though I always introduce this SnapShots assignment with, "Your drawing ability is not important here. You are to take mental pictures as you read by making quick sketches . . . ," some high school students (and middle school, too) worry about embarrassment. So I always provide them with the "cheat sheet" of cartoon facial expressions that I found on a free graphics clip art Web site. Students are free to trace expressions onto their SnapShots from the sheet shown in Figure 4.9.

Some students like to speed up drawing their SnapShots by using much-simplified figures rather than trying for a cartoon look. Jimmy, a fourteen-year-old student in Vicky Hoag's class, used simple drawings in his SnapShots of the short story "Fear" (Soto, 1992). They work well to reveal his understanding and analysis. Notice the role of captions beneath the quick sketches in Figure 4.10.

And some students prefer to use text, reducing the images to symbols or skipping them entirely. Ryan, a tenth grader in Eliza's class, used a whole 3" x 3" sticky note to draw a pair of glasses labeled "José's view of things" and then wrote an

"SnapShots" Book Review
ChecBric

Target 1: I Understand the Reading

____ I identified the author's main ideas
  • characters
  • setting
  • problem
  • ending

____ I commented on the author's key supporting details

____ I've shown that I "read between the lines" to make inferences
  • the theme

____ I offered support by referring back to the story

Trait 1: Demonstrates Comprehension of the Reading

6 = **exceptional** comprehending; thorough and convincing

5 = **excellent** comprehending; strong and understanding

4 = **proficient** comprehending; competent, good enough

3 = **inadequate** comprehending; close, but inconsistent, incomplete

2 = **limited** comprehending; confused or inaccurate

1 = **missing** comprehending; NO attempt to meet expectations, OR virtually NO understanding

Target 2: I Connect the Reading to Another Source

____ I've connected the reading to something that *happened to me*

____ I've connected the reading to something that *happened to someone* I know

____ I've connected the reading to something that I *read*

____ I've connected the reading to something that I watched on *TV*

____ I've connected the reading to a *movie or videotape*

____ I've connected the reading to some *issue or event* in my community or the world at large

Note: You do *not* need to do all of these, but you must *explain why* you are making the connection.

Trait 2: Extends Understanding Beyond the Reading

6 = **exceptional** connecting; thorough and complex

5 = **excellent** connecting; outstanding and strong

4 = **proficient** connecting; competent, good enough

3 = **inadequate** connecting; scant or inconsistent; fails to explain why and how the source connects to the story

2 = **limited** connecting; superficial or flawed; no explanation

1 = **missing** connecting; NO attempt to meet expectations, OR does NOT show a connection to anything

---

Exhibit 4.4 ChecBric: "The Challenge."

Source: "SnapShots" from Chet Skibinski, Beaverton, Oregon. Traits are taken from Oregon Department of Education "Reading Informative and Literary Texts Scoring Guide," 1998. Office of Assessment and Evaluation, O.D.E., 255 Capitol Street NE, Salem, Oregon 97310.

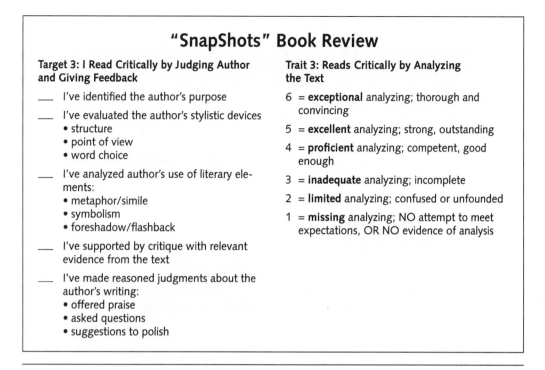

"SnapShots" Book Review

Target 3: I Read Critically by Judging Author and Giving Feedback

____ I've identified the author's purpose

____ I've evaluated the author's stylistic devices
 • structure
 • point of view
 • word choice

____ I've analyzed author's use of literary elements:
 • metaphor/simile
 • symbolism
 • foreshadow/flashback

____ I've supported by critique with relevant evidence from the text

____ I've made reasoned judgments about the author's writing:
 • offered praise
 • asked questions
 • suggestions to polish

Trait 3: Reads Critically by Analyzing the Text

6 = **exceptional** analyzing; thorough and convincing

5 = **excellent** analyzing; strong, outstanding

4 = **proficient** analyzing; competent, good enough

3 = **inadequate** analyzing; incomplete

2 = **limited** analyzing; confused or unfounded

1 = **missing** analyzing; NO attempt to meet expectations, OR NO evidence of analysis

Exhibit 4.4 Continued

extensive caption: "This story would never work unless it was told from the point of view of José. The actions of José wouldn't be all that important unless you knew what he was thinking and his feelings and reasoning. Ideas seem to be very brilliant to the one who thought them up, no matter how stupid they really are." There's a key literary concept—point of view—captured by a student who won't forget it.

Meanwhile, also writing on a pink sticky note, Sara shared her insight into the static nature of the character Estela, who "stays the same not expressing anything to José *or the readers*" (emphasis mine). This character analysis reveals an awesome awareness on Sara's part; not only did she read the story, she was thinking deeply as she read. Her teacher and I know this because of her SnapShots. And Tom sketched a simple frowny face labeled "José" and wrote, "I know how he feels after he lost to Estela in the game, I have my fair share of embarasing moments in front of girls too." Under the sticky note, he added, "Yeah. I know exactly how he feels. I have had that happen lots of times."

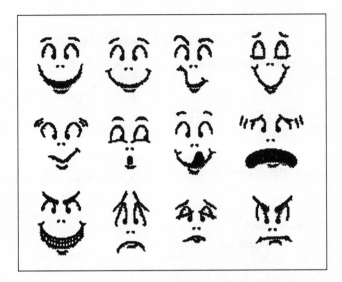

Figure 4.9 Clip Art for SnapShots.

The use of text instead of drawing is an acceptable option. And if a student needed some help with deciding what words to write on a sticky note, the teacher could certainly help things along by asking:

- Who do you see in this scene? (character identification)
- What is the person doing? (character action)
- Where is this happening? (setting)

These and any other prompts not only stimulate student thinking, they also assist in meeting a key challenge of this tool: selection. Students must determine which parts in the story warrant a SnapShot. Obviously, a student cannot make a sketch for every single scene in a story, but rather must discriminate the most important from the less important elements.

SnapShots also help capture relevant experience the students can bring to bear on the lesson. For example, while reading this story, Ahra, a tenth-grader from

This is Frankie picking on me behind a backstop at school

Here he is telling me about his thanksgiving dinner and christmas on the monkey bars.

He told me about all of his thanksgiving food and christmas stuff. When I knew he wouldn't get any of it.

This is were he looked at me like he was gonna hit me I was scared, but he just warned me and walked away

Figure 4.10 Photo Album: "Fear."

Source: Vicky Hoag, teacher, Sierra High School, Tollhouse, California.

Korea, connected it to a Korean story, "The Rainfall," that she remembered. Good news: here's a kid who is thinking as she reads and relating it to another literary piece. (See Figure 4.11.)

SnapShots with sticky notes very well may be my favorite reading-attack method. I use it frequently in the many schools I visit to model reading support activities to teachers. The rewards are constant, as when Tom wrote (about another character in the story), "I could really *see an image in my head* of Freddie working out." (Italics mine.)

In fact, at the beginning of fourth period at Glide High School, Cori, a girl I hadn't met yet, acknowledged me as "Mr. Post-it Man." I asked her why she named me that. She replied, "My friends in first, second, and third periods told me about you. . . . When do I get *my* Post-its?"

Story Boards as an Alternative

SnapShots are a true crowd-pleaser in the secondary grades. Students like this activity not because they necessarily are delighted to be practicing the key reading comprehension strategy of visualization, but more likely because they love sticky notes with their kinesthetic and tactile attraction and the novelty of doing something new, something different. Our challenged readers deserve new activities to engage them and to give them a new chance at succeeding. (And our more skilled, less challenged readers also enjoy them—nice for the multi-ability classes we teach.)

However, I have found that high school students are sometimes less than thrilled with SnapShots. It may be that some older students misperceive this activity as being for younger kids, that is, *babyish*. Now, the very last thing I want to have happen is for students to be turned off by an activity that I am counting on to engage and entice them into practicing an important reading strategy.

So, if you try SnapShots with juniors or seniors who complain that it is beneath them, or if they reject the activity before even trying it, switch to Story Boards.

Here's how to introduce Story Boards:

"Class, I have good news for you. Today we are going to Hollywood." This should trigger some initial interest.

Continue on: "Who knows how movie directors and producers decide how to map out a movie?"

There is a Korean story called "Rain Fall". It is also about boy and girl's love story. In that story, the boy likes the girl, very much, but doesn't have any courage to talk to her.

Figure 4.11 SnapShot: "The Rainfall."

The answer you're looking for is: "They create a story board—a set of still frames quickly drawn on paper and posted in sequence on a large bulletin board." Provide this info if no one in the class can do so, but you'll probably find someone who already knows.

Story Boards are essentially the same as SnapShots in that they both are a vehicle for practicing visualization skills, for selecting which story elements are the major ones deserving attention, and for sequencing the order of these key elements. The difference is minor: they use letter-size paper instead of sticky notes. But the packaging of the activity is very different: it assures older students that they are mature learners (not babies) who can handle Hollywood.

Beth Kolbush uses Story Boards in her literature classes. She distributes a piece of blank white paper to her tenth graders and directs them to fold it into eight panels to track the scenes. Here are a few optional teaching tips to consider for assigning Story Boards:

- Distribute large paper, such as 17"x24" or even larger, like sheets torn off from a roll of butcher paper.

- Instruct students to pause while reading to sketch a scene onto the paper.

- To help them remember to pause periodically, use a kitchen timer set for five minutes.

- Discuss which scenes, or characters, or events warranted inclusion in the Story Board and why some did not.

- Postpone the large paper, and provide students with small squares of paper to make quick sketches as a First Dare Story Board. Later, provide large paper and colored marking pens to students to create a repaired story board worthy of sharing with others.

- Provide students with a set of instructions to assist them in successful completion of this assignment.

SnapShots and Story Boards are both excellent activities to inspire students to visualize what is going on as they read. The examples I've given show how easily they engage readers, even readers who struggle. And even though they relate to the visualization of literature, both SnapShots and Story Boards can be used in content area classrooms—that is, they work just as well for comprehending informational text in a science, social studies, health, business, or math class. Your students have seen hundreds of educational films and videos on the subjects they study, after all, so the lesson can be packaged as a Story Board for a new offering on the topic.

Articles Based on Historical Literature

Teachers can easily connect expository writing with literature. Instead of always relying on the tired old book report, we can assign news articles about the fiction. Ruth King, teacher at Brookside School in Cranford, New Jersey, assigned her sixth graders the Newbery Award–winning historical novel *Number the Stars* (Lowery, 1989). She applied many reading comprehension and appreciation strategies to assist her students through the Prepare, First Dare, and Repair reading stages.

To get them to Share what they learned, Ruth asked them to write news articles about the content learned from the novel. Students coauthored articles with a partner at the computer. The final word-processed articles were published in a class magazine called *De Frie Danske* (A Free Denmark). For example, one student wrote:

156 Jews Escaped From Camp

Yesterday around 4:00 am. 156 Jews escaped from Sobibor. The guard fell asleep on duty and the Jews escaped.

People in a nearby town saw the Jews fleeing for their lives. They took refuge in people's lower floors of their houses.

Many of the Jews that were fleeing were killed in the process.

For more information on the 'Net, http://haven.ios.com/~kimel19/resist6.html

What's the incentive for writing articles about literature? What is the students' purpose? To look good, to look smart, to look knowledgeable about an important historical event. And to be published in a magazine underscores their importance as students and writers.

A SAMPLE LESSON

I love fiction that stars teenagers as main characters. Obviously, middle school or high school protagonists connect to secondary readers. In a new short story, oddly titled "Bandennammen," an interesting high school girl named Jessie creates for herself an unusual and high-paying job.

I used this story to co-design another mini-unit with high school literature teacher Eliza Sher.

Prepare for Reading

Eliza's tenth graders started out with time to Prepare, to get ready to read the story.

First, we provided them with an E.G.O., an electronic graphic organizer (see Figure 4.12), to engage them with four Prepare strategies: read the title and make a prediction or ask a question; sample a few intro paragraphs to see what you can quickly learn or predict about the story; skim the entire story to pick up proper names, places, dialogue, or illustrations; check out the author.

Additionally, Eliza prepared her students for character analysis by reviewing with them what they had already learned earlier in the term. They generated the following list of author techniques for characterization:

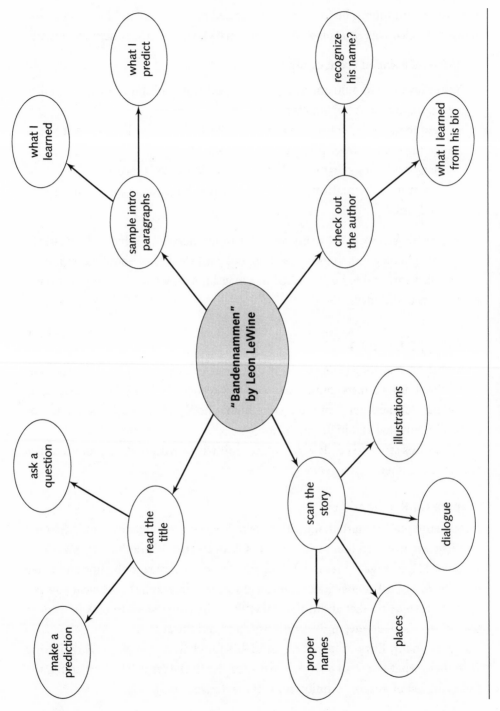

Figure 4.12 E.G.O.: "Bandennammen."

- Character's words or actions
- Character's physical traits
- Narrator's words describing character's actions, thoughts
- Other characters' reactions

How much time was invested in these two Prepare activities? Just 12.7 minutes. Well worth it.

Finally, and most important, we helped the class set a motivating purpose for reading this short story: "Assist the author in improving his characterization of Jessie. His short story has promise, but at this point, it needs work because the character is still too undefined. The author has expressed interest in converting the story into a screenplay to sell as a movie script to a film studio. By 'fleshing out' Jessie, you can help the author improve the plot, which improves his chances of getting a film contract."

Not the usual literature assignment.

The First Dare

None of Eliza's students had ever read the story "Bandennammen," so it was a First Dare read for them.

Sticky Stories

- Blue stickies were for congratulating the author on successful characterizations of the main character Jessie; parts of the story that generated understanding of her.

- Green stickies were to indicate a missed chance where the author could have provided important information to the reader about Jessie and thereby improve the story.

But there are lots more colors available. A class could use different colors for as many different First Dare techniques as were useful for a given lesson. For example, students could receive a set of yellow 3" x 3" stickies to jot down questions that arise during the reading that need clarification for understanding. Or students could be instructed to use pink stickies to record predictions at key plot events.

Sticky note reading always works for me when I teach. Students love the novelty, the hands-on approach, and the brevity of using them to track their reading purpose. To cue them to record a comment on a sticky, I set a timer for five-minute intervals. Of course, a teacher could orally prompt the class by periodically saying, "Sorry to interrupt, but if you haven't used a sticky lately, now would be a good time."

If you'd like to use sticky notes with the story "Bandennammen," a printable copy is available at my Web site. (See first section of the Appendix.)

Embedded Strategy Prompts

Instead of supplying students with sticky notes for their First Dare reading, we could have provided them with First Dare reading strategies embedded in the story, like the ones shown in Exhibit 4.5. As they read, a periodic strategy prompt interjects into the story, requiring them to think about a key aspect of the story.

As the sophomores read this new story, they could practice trying out the strategies their teachers embedded in the text for them and labeled *First Dare*. To see the entire story with seventeen embedded reading strategies, go to my Web site and print a copy.

Embedded First Dare Reading Strategies

Jessie is available to help. She's a rock band namer, and a very good one.

She never intended on getting into the band-naming biz. How could anyone, really? It just sort of happened. And it sort of happened in a funny way, when you think about it.

> **1st Dare Strategy**—Ask a question to myself: Do I really understand what her job is and what this story will be about? Or do I kind of understand? Or am I pretty much lost?

* * * * *

The rave was held in a warehouse I'd never been to, somewhere off Buffalo St., down in the industrial section. It wasn't billed as a rave, but rather the posters had advertised it as an "anti-rave" . . . you know, to fool the parents.

> **1st Dare Strategy**—Tap prior knowledge: What, if anything, do I already know about "raves"?

Exhibit 4.5 Strategy Prompts: "Bandennammen."

Do you predict that the inserted First Dare reading strategies would assist your students in their comprehension and appreciation of the story? Will the prompts pave the way for them to achieve maximum understanding in their first reading? It is a good way to remind the reader to be an active participant in the construction of meaning—it takes two to tango in the reading comprehension dance.

Some teachers, as well as some students, might appreciate the cued responses but still dislike the frequent interruptions from the strategy prompts. Maybe seventeen is too many; perhaps five or six would be sufficiently helpful to you or your students. We want to pave the way to enjoyable reading, not bulldoze the reader off the road.

And some students may also object to being forced to stop the flow of the fiction to respond. I understand these objections, but without the cued strategy prompts, how can a teacher be sure that a reader will be practicing the selected strategies instead of blowing right through the story with limited understanding or analysis? That's why I like using sticky notes—they make the reader's growing understanding leave tracks.

Repair Reading

Despite the obvious benefits of the First Dare activities, we know they cannot guarantee perfect comprehension. This is not only true for our students, it is also true for us. Therefore, it is very likely that some repairing of the initial understandings will be needed.

As I noted in Chapter Three, the Repair stage of the reading process does not mean that the reader must go back and reread the entire selection. Rather, it means revisiting only certain key parts to boost comprehension.

And this comprehension boosting may have already occurred to some readers. During the First Dare reading, many readers apply a quick fix-up strategy: they stop the flow, put on the brakes, and back up to reread a section that didn't quite make sense. This strategy is sometimes accompanied by another Repair strategy, slowing down the reading rate.

Of course, many of our challenged readers avoid using these strategies with fiction, just as they do with content-area materials. Going back or going slowly would lengthen the reading time, and their only goal is to get to the end.

So we must teach them the benefits of returning to the text by alerting them to the key Repair strategies: fixing up, evaluating, analyzing, and perspective taking.

Character Analysis Sheets in Action

Typically, most secondary students do not fully grasp what an author is doing to develop a character, so it's useful to take them back for a closer look. Instead of directing the class to "go back to the story and reread it to find out more about the character," Eliza and I handed out Character Analysis Sheets to provide a reason to return.

Recall that the first step is for the teacher, or the whole class, or pairs of students, or individuals to identify a set of words that describe the character. These words go into column 1.

For example, I have selected "self-confident" as the first descriptor of Jessie in "Bandennammen" because that is, to me, a key trait of this spunky lead character. Most readers would agree with that. (The story is available on my Web site, if you'd like to check for yourself—see the Appendix.) So if we are working through this activity as a whole class, we could agree to write "self-confident" in column 1 of our copy of the Character Analysis Sheet.

The next step is obvious: cite examples from the story that support this view of her. In other words, cite examples that prove she is self-confident. I can refer to two: she tells her stepmom Erica to back off band-naming and she jokes around with the corporate big shots in her interview. These incidents are posted in column 2 next to "self-confident."

Now, I was able to remember these two examples—I have read this story several times, and I know it quite well. However, if I couldn't remember, I surely could go back to the story and hunt for a few. This is the purpose of this activity—to revisit the story for improved understanding through *analysis*.

Likewise, if I remember one or two examples, I still can return to the story to pick up a few more to strengthen my position. For example, in the scene where she meets Donald "Devious" Decoutte at the coffeehouse for a band-naming meeting, she doesn't even offer him a second or third choice of names. She is very comfortable with her friend Bernie at school, with bluesman Karl Altoona, and in English class she jokes about band names related to literature.

Same for any member of the class. I asked the students if anyone agreed that Jessie is "self-confident." Some did. I asked them to write examples on their copies of the Character Analysis Sheet, pointing out that if necessary, anyone could (should) look for more back in the story. The teacher leads the class through this process for as many character traits as time or interest allows.

The class generated a wide range of characteristics for Jessie: stuck-up, popular, insecure, easily bothered, humorous, un-funny, uncomfortable around boys, rude, poor student, and bright student. How is it that different students reading the exact same story generated such differing character traits? I told them, "Yes, the words you read on your copy of the story are exactly the same as your classmates' copies, but your brain is different. You take the author's words and mix them into your own memories, experiences, assumptions. That's what readers do." I resisted the temptation to tell them about schema theory.

Finally, I told them, "Any characteristic is accurate as long as you can defend it with examples from the story." And they made good use of this freedom. Matt filled in the other three blanks (besides *self-confident*) on his Character Analysis Sheet with *Stuck-Up* ("I allready knew on the bus over that their name would be shattered [page 80] I have to listen to his rambling epic account of the band's History [page 80] These amateurs lacked that rare combination of humor and word play, and the sublime balance between the irreverent, and the melcilous, the insolent, and flippant [pg. 81]"), *Popular* ("At school, kids would now holler out a cleever band name as they passed her in the hall [page 81] Her family and friends got into naming names for bands [page 81] Word spread about her giving out names for bands [page 80]"), and *easily bothered* ("I have to listen to his rambling epic account of the band's History [page 80] Her Mom would not stop new names for bands, which made her mad [page 81] A boy at school liked her, yet she was never interested, and would shoot him down [page 82]"). Based on the same reading, Eric used *conceited* ("Says that nobody else is any good at naming bands but her [pg. 81, 82]"), *insecure* ("Doesn't like to talk to guys about dates [pg. 79, 80, 82]"), and *popular* ("People know her all around school and her town [pg. 80, 81, 82, 84]"). Two different readers; two different responses. But notice that both cited their examples with the page numbers from the story.

Practical Interpretative Cards

As I've noted, reading and comprehending fiction requires interpreting what the author is portraying. Authors use words to paint a picture, to tell a story, and readers assemble those words in their minds to recreate the story. Different minds recreate slightly different versions. That's why some readers of "Bandennammen" see Jessie as self-confident while others may view her as insecure. As long as either perception can be defended by examples of her behavior or thoughts, we have different but equally valid comprehension of the story. And that's why Eliza and I could have used Interpretative Cards as a reading-repair activity.

Here's one of the questions we could have used:

Why is Jessie worried about boys' interest in her?

This question requires interpretation because the author of the story does not come right out and tell the reader why Jessie acts concerned about boys. Here's all a kid is likely to know from reading the story (or rereading it):

- She feels that Donald "Devious" Doucette, band member of Shattered, kind of hit on her a little bit at the coffeehouse meeting.

- Her semi-friend from freshman year who invited her to the Backstreet Boys concert caused her discomfort, though she doesn't talk about it.

- The author says, "Not that guys' interest in her happened so often, but it did happen—enough to make her feel uncomfortable. . ."

When we discussed this with the class, we pointed out that there might be other pieces of evidence in the story that Jessie is worried about boys' being interested in her. We asked, "Can you remember any? Could you return to the story and hunt for more?"

After retrieving the story examples, the students now have to generate an answer. Some get the feeling that Jessie lacks self-confidence with boys. She acts confidently in a group, like at a rave or in a class, but one-on-one makes her feel inadequate and fearful of rejection. The author doesn't say this about her, but "reading between the lines," it's easy to get this impression.

This is a legitimate inference. However, others point out the scene where she and Karl "the Tuna" joke around and talk about bands and band names. We asked, "Does she seem insecure with him, acting self-consciously due to fear of his rejection? Do you remember, or might you want to go back to that part of the story and review it?"

A third interpretation is she is too busy to be interested in a relationship right now. School, art, band-naming all take up her time, and she is completely happy with her life as it is. We asked, "What evidence from the story supports this hypothesis?"

A last interpretation is a rejection of the question "Why is she worried about boys' interest in her?" Some students may not agree at all that this is how she feels. That's fine—as long as they can point to evidence from the story that refutes it.

It's a good idea to have other Interpretative Card questions, so that different students can address different questions. A set of four to eight cards would be sufficient. Here's another of the ones we used:

Why does the author change the narration from first to third person?

We asked, "Did you notice during your First Dare reading that sometimes a narrator is telling the story about Jessie, and at other times she takes over and tells it in first person? If so, why do you think the author alternates the narration? If not, go back to the story, and check it out." (Is it OK for a reader to return to the text for further consideration?)

A teacher attending one of my workshops answered this question with, "Because the author, like my students, got careless with verb tense." Another teacher posited a different answer: "To make certain scenes more immediate, more inviting, more 'in the now.'" And several complained, "The shift in person was confusing and disruptive."

Then we asked,

Why would a writer come up with a story idea about this odd topic of band-naming?

This question prompts the reader to remember that fiction is created by authors; that is, human beings write stories, and these humans have lots of choices to make in the composition of fiction. Most struggling readers do not think about authors, the choices they make, and the effects of those choices on the story's appeal or lack of appeal to a reader. So now students must "think like a writer" and ponder the reason, or the inspiration, or the mistake of generating a story on this particular topic.

We also asked

What is the theme of this story?
What does the author want you to come away with?

These interpretative questions are universal ones that could be used with any piece of fiction.

Once you read the story, you'll find you can come up with many additional interpretative questions for "Bandennammen" if you want to use it with your own students.

Sharing Reading

The results of the Character Analysis Sheet reading-repair activity feed smoothly into the next stage of the process. Eliza returned to the movie-script idea and invented a brand new writing assignment, "a character in search of a conflict," whereby her students would make suggestions to the author for improving the main character Jessie, to "flesh her out" with more information about her in an effort to generate more conflict, which in turn would drive the story's plot into a new direction. Eliza explained that as of now, the studio executives are not convinced "Bandennammen" is a go for production.

This puts the students into the role of film studio script writers and editors whose job is to critique the story in order to help the author improve it. As the exercise developed, Eliza wisely prevented some students from adding conflicts that would take the plot way off in other directions by advising them not to "overly Hollywoodize" the story with violence, sex, or fantasy.

My contribution was to suggest formatting this advice and critique into a "studio memo" to the author. The idea caught on with the kids, as shown in the following cogent memo from Janet—not the usual output of kid who doesn't always feel plugged into assignments.

To: Leon Lewine
Fr: Janet
Date: Oct. 4, 2002
RE: Characterization
c/c: Sher & Lewin

You can read many stories in your life time, but when you read a short storie or even a novel, something happens that you never thought was going to happen, and you have comments and ideas you wish you could have told the author what you thought could have been a little different, and what they could have added. Well now I have the chance to tell you ideas you could add or change. I also have questions about the storie "Bandennamen."

While reading "Bandennamen" I started to think of some questions and ideas for your short story.

You bring up Germany in your story in the very begining, but you never say anything else about Germany. Why didn't you end up bring up Germany again?

When Jessie is at the "anti-rave" she says it was "to fool the parents." Then she says that this "anti-rave" had no drugs and no smoking. How do we know she is telling the truth, because she lied about the rave and said it was the "anti-rave." So maybe you could add some more things so we know if she is telling the truth or not.

Jessie thinks of the cool name "Altoids" and two guys where standing beside her and one says "The 'Altoids' Yuh totally. Really. Much better name" but Jessie never looks at the guys to say thank you. Why doesn't she look over at them? You could have said she was shy of guys, or maybe added that she had seen these guys before, and they weren't attractive.

On page 81 you start to tell us about Jessie and her background, you could have added what she looked like and tell us how she was when she was growing up. was Jessie short, tall, brown hair, blonde hair, blue eyes?

On page 82 she goes to the Backstreet boys concert. Why did you pick them and not a hip-hop artist or maybe punk?

Again Jessie tells her mom that she will finish high school and pass and everything. You could have added again what year was she in high school.

On the very last page you say something about her still wanting to go to Art School. Why would she want to go to Art School when she can do band naming.

Jessie has some conflicts in this storie. You can tell she is trying to find who she really is, and trying to understand the outside world. What I don't understand is that it doesn't sound like Jessie is like very sure about the band naming thing because she keeps bringing up how she likes to do art so you could have made her an artist for CD covers and maybe not band naming. Maybe she could make up titles for the CD and then create the covers for the CD.

Some good comments on the story is on page 81. When you tell us how she started band naming. On page 80 Jessie says what a metal band name should involve such as "always sounded stark, cold, and hard." Also another good thing is Jessie is going to finish High School. Most stories have the kids drop out or they try everything not to be in school. So saying Jessie is going to finish High School is good.

Well that's all I have to comment on the storie. I hope you understand the comments I have made about the story.

Hitting the Targets

Of course, the students' success depended not only on their reading, the Character Analysis Sheet answers, discussion with classmates, and their prior knowledge of characterization techniques, they also needed to know what the expectations for their memo critiques were.

Eliza and I came up with the ChecBric shown in Exhibit 4.6 to pave the way for her young editors.

Celebration

The students' engagement in composing their plot treatments was quite high. They were motivated to work hard on them because they were given a satisfying role: expert reader (looking smart) providing feedback to a pro writer (speaking up) by writing in a new, engaging form (plot treatment memo).

Eliza decided to send them to the author through his publisher. This wonderful human being took the time to write back:

> Dear Honest Readers,
>
> Thanks very much for taking the time to write me. It is unusual for me to receive feedback from an entire class of Lit students.
>
> Your analysis of Jessie has been interesting to me. I never perceived her as undeveloped or underdeveloped, nor did I view the plot as needing more conflict. I liked it the way I wrote it (and rewrote and rewrote it) because I really like Jessie.
>
> It was my decision to make the bandnamer character a female instead of male. When I originally conceived the story, I just assumed that she would be a "he." As a male, this just naturally happens. So it was a stretch for me to write it from a girl's perspective, and I am proud at how she turned out: a cool kid with a great future.
>
> But. . . . I think you are correct that she has it too easy. It is true that fiction, a story, relies on conflict to drive the plot development. No conflict, no plot.
>
> I am considering rewriting it with some of your suggested plot treatments: that another young bandnamer "steals her thunder," that her relationship with her family gets more attention, and that she bogs down on inventing a band name and eventually ends up using her art to design CD covers.
>
> As for the (many) suggestions that she gets involved with a boy (and expe-

"Bandennammen" Critique Memo
ChecBric

Target 1: I have interesting, convincing ideas about characterization and plot

____ My writing is clear, focused, and in control.

____ My writing keeps the readers' attention.

____ My main idea(s) stand out clearly.

____ I have a thorough, balanced, in-depth explanation/exploration of the topic.

____ My supporting details Share examples from the story that give strong, accurate, credible support to my position.

____ My supporting details Share examples from the story that give credit to the author when successful characterization appears.

____ Main ideas & details fit my audience & purpose which is to convince the author to make the changes that I suggest.

____ My writing makes connections and shares insights.

Trait 1: Communicates Knowledge on the Topic

6 = **exceptionally** clear, focused, interesting writing that keeps reader's attention throughout

5 = **excellent** clear, focused, interesting writing that keeps reader's attention throughout

4 = **proficient** writing with enough focus and clarity to help reader understand the main ideas

3 = **inadequate**ly focused writing that is overly broad or simplistic

2 = **limited** focus and clarity causing unclear or undeveloped ideas

1 = **missing** clarity and focus, lacking central idea or purpose

Target 2: I have organized my ideas clearly

____ My introduction grabs the reader's attention and helps him know what I will be writing about.

____ My ideas are presented in an order that makes sense.

____ I use transitions between paragraphs that help the reader see how my ideas connect to each other.

____ I use transitions within paragraphs to show how my ideas are related to each other.

____ My conclusion ties together my main points and leaves the reader persuaded, or at least thinking about my points.

Trait 2: Organizes Ideas

6 = **exceptional** use of organization that enhances the ideas and compels the reader through the text easily

5 = **excellent** use of organization that strongly moves the reader through the text

4 = **proficient** use of organization that is clear and coherent, but may be formulaic

3 = **inadequate** use of organization; an attempt was made, but is inconsistent or skeletal

2 = **limited** use of organization; lacks clear organizational structure making reading difficult to follow; or writing is too short to demonstrate organizational skill

1 = **missing** use of organization; lacks coherence, is disjointed, haphazard. Reader gets confused

Exhibit 4.6 ChecBric: "Bandennammen" Critique Memo.

"Bandennammen" Critique Memo

Target 3: I have followed the rules of writing

___ I have correct spelling, even of more difficult words.

___ I have paragraph breaks that help organize my ideas.

___ I have correct grammar and usage that help communicate my ideas.

___ I use punctuation to guide the reader through my writing.

___ I am skilled in using these conventions; there is little or no need for editing.

Trait 3: Controls the conventions of writing

6 = **exceptional** use of conventions that support the reader's understanding

5 = **excellent** use of conventions that support the reader's understanding; maybe a few minor errors

4 = **proficient** use of conventions; errors do not interrupt reader's understanding

3 = **inadequate** control of conventions; errors interrupt flow of ideas and cause some confusion

2 = **limited** control of conventions; errors substantially interrupt flow of ideas and cause breakdown of meaning

1 = **missing** control of conventions; numerous errors ruin message and throw reader off into frustration

OVER for Student Self-Reflections

OVER for Teacher Comments

Exhibit 4.6 Continued

riences the pluses and minuses of a relationship), I think not. I intentionally left her relationship with boys ambiguous—just to stimulate your own interpretations. I love to force readers to speculate. Plus, even though a relationship may seem like a necessity at your age, it is not crucial to every teenager.

Again, thanks mucho for your energy and your ideas, and thanks to your teacher for teaching you. You are fortunate to be in her class.

Big payoff for the students.

CONCLUSION: SETTING STUDENTS UP FOR SUCCESS

Reading quality literature in school can be an engaging and rewarding experience for all students—if their teacher sets them up for success. In this chapter I have presented a set of classroom activities that are designed to pave the way to comprehension, appreciation, and analysis of literary texts.

Some of the activities, such as the Story Web, Open Mind, and Character Analysis Sheet, have been available to literature teachers. Others are brand new ones to consider: the E.G.O., Interpretative Cards, and the visualization activities (Snap-Shots, Character Emotional Scenes, Story Boards).

All of them plug into the general process approach of "Prepare, First Dare, Repair, and Share," and they all serve to facilitate understanding of fiction reading. The next chapter moves on to the ultimate Share activity: writing to share learning. I will show how the process approach works with writing, and how to develop new, different, and engaging writing assignments to turn on our resistant writers.

Writing for Content Learning

Allright, class. Take out paper and a pencil, and begin writing a description of setting of the play."

Guess whose spirits and posture sag visibly upon receiving these directions for a writing assignment?

Why do we assign our students to write?

Why does anyone write?

To communicate, right? Why else would anyone bother with all the blood, sweat, and tears associated with composing thoughts onto paper? But our struggling students misunderstand writing. They have come to believe writing is only to fulfill a school assignment. No big motivation here.

I suggest that writers write because they are motivated to communicate their ideas to an audience. Their purpose is to share their thoughts, feelings, opinions, joy, anger, criticism, or thanks with someone else.

The problem in school is that some kids don't want to do this, they don't know how to do this, and they don't know why their teachers want them to do this.

This chapter addresses the use of writing in the service of learning. Writing to learn accomplishes two critical tasks in a classroom. First, writing enables students to think about, to process, to grow ideas about the topics we are teaching them in science, math, social studies, personal finance, English, the arts, health. Writing about course content boosts their understanding in middle school, junior high, or high school. Second, writing enables them to gain proficiency in a critically important skill: writing itself—which is obviously a key communication tool. All schools want their students to write better, so it's worthwhile to practice writing in every classroom.

INSTRUCTIONAL FRAMEWORK

Throughout this book, I have addressed the tight connection between reading and writing, between constructing meaning *from* text (reading) and constructing meaning *through* text (writing). Periodically, I presented writing activities in the context of reading instruction. Now I turn direct attention to writing by bringing it into the foreground.

Informational Versus Creative Writing

First, a clarification. This type of writing that I am addressing here is different from creative writing, which is often assigned in English/language arts classes and generally comes from personal experiences or personal observations. The role of the personal in writing is well-founded and well-deserved. Many of our most revered authors write creatively about their own lives, other people's lives, or adaptations from real life into fictionalized accounts. It is the act of creative invention known as fiction.

I am in awe of fiction writers. I have tried writing several short stories myself, with so-so results. I know how difficult it is to tell a story in an engaging and meaningful way. Creative writing deserves a place in our curriculum. Both in the middle school grades and at high school, students should be exposed to writing creatively. It is a skill and an art worthy of our instructional time.

It also has a place in the study of content material, especially history. But the special techniques that develop it as a skill will not be addressed in this book because my focus here, my purpose, is to show ways to use reading and writing as vehicles for learning, not for the creative invention of new realities. Therefore, the examples in this section will illustrate how teachers can assign writing as a means for processing class work to a deeper and more astute level and for inspiring students to then share their understandings with others—mostly by reporting facts, occasionally by making a mental leap into the scene and writing what amounts to fiction, but always with the goal of promoting their learning rather than launching their literary careers.

Traditional Expository Assignments

Writing to share learning often seems to begin and end with expository writing, and expository writing, as we surely know, has served education well. For centuries students have written in this mode to "explain and inform" about the material they are learning. The classic expository assignments are the research paper, the five-paragraph essay, and the book report. These three are being employed in classrooms today, and I have used them as well. But the sad truth is that they are not particularly inspirational to struggling students. In fact, I surmise that although the classic book report is famous in the annals of education, it is *infamous* in the eyes of many students.

The problem with the traditional expository assignments like the book report is that they tend to be a turn-off rather than a turn-on to students who have seen them before, again and again, over and over, and who may have experienced less than successful results. And for what purpose is a book report assigned? To regurgitate the plot, setting, characters to a teacher who no doubt has read the book and already knows the plot, setting, and characters. In other words, no real purpose, just an artificial school purpose. We can do better than the "same ole, same ole."

I am not knocking book reports or research papers or five-paragraph essays or chapter summaries. I just think we need to figure out a way to repackage these writing assignments into more engaging, enticing, and *enthusing* writing experiences with real purposes that our disaffected students can adopt as their own.

We can come up with newer, more interesting, and seemingly easier writing tasks that actually grab the students' attention, which stimulates energy and hope instead of inertia and despondency. You know what I mean by inertia and despondency—you have witnessed it, right?

Not a Lockstep Approach

Before addressing my general four-step process as it relates to writing, two important comments about the process approach. First, as noted in Chapter One, it looks linear, sequential, and step-by-step, but in reality it is *recursive*. This means that a writer can actually go backward in the process as well as forward depending on what is needed.

For example, say a writer is at the First Dare (sometimes labeled the first draft or rough draft) stage and stops writing to read a just-composed paragraph. A word or two or a sentence doesn't seem to do its job, so the writer quickly makes an alteration before moving forward. What the writer has done is to jump forward to the Repair stage for a quick fix-up and then backward to the First Dare to continue drafting.

Similarly, a writer who experiences "writer's block" while drafting (First Daring) can reverse direction and go back to the Prepare stage to do more thinking, pondering, researching, discussing to hatch new ideas to stimulate the writing. The process allows writers to loop forward and back as needed.

Second important comment: This writing process needs flexibility built into it. And not just with the recursive directions, but also with the role of each step, how many steps there are to follow, and when a step can shortened or even skipped.

This can be a touchy issue. Professional authors sometimes feel frustrated when asked to describe their personal version of the writing process approach. While understanding its importance as a teaching tool, they can worry about its being used too rigidly to lockstep kids through what is really a more fluid procedure.

I had the opportunity years ago to hear the wonderful young adult author Gary Paulsen speak at a book-signing event. He is one my favorite writers (not just for young adult readers, but for me, too). After his talk, he fielded questions from the audience.

I patiently waited until it was my turn and asked him, "Mr. Paulsen, as a schoolteacher, I'd appreciate your comments on the role of the 'writing process' in your work as an author."

He looked at me blankly and replied, "What's that?"

I said, "Uh, you know, the 'writing process'—what steps writers take to overcome difficulties and compose text. . . ."

He immediately said, "I don't know anything about that. What I do is write. And before I write, I read. I read all the time."

Well, while I appreciated his connecting reading to writing, I think he knew about the writing process, and that, in fact, he had developed his own version of it as a writer, and that whatever it was, it certainly worked for him. But he refused, I believe, to institutionalize it, to formalize it, because he probably worried that would harm it or maybe even kill it.

It is a good reminder not to get so attached to the writing process that it becomes overbearing and chokes off our student writers. We should definitely show the kids a general process, model it for them, and teach them some options for using each stage. And then we should encourage them to create their *own version* of it that works for them. It's essential to be careful and not overdo it to the point of rigid control. Having warned about that, I'll now proceed to an overview of the general process and see what the options are at each step.

Writing Strategies and Skills: The General Process

The writing revolution that began in the early 1970s and continues today altered writing instruction from a grammar-based approach to a problem-solving approach. The traditional "skill and drill" has been and still is being replaced by imitating what professional authors do: They invent a process to enable them to transfer their thoughts from mind onto paper to share with readers while readily admitting that composing text to communicate their ideas is tough sledding. The processes they invent have in common the ability to facilitate overcoming obstacles in that transfer. Traditionally, the sequence has been labeled

- Prewriting
- Rough drafting
- Rewriting
- Publishing

Of course, the number of steps in the process and the particular labels for those steps is debatable and open to many different opinions. What does matter is that a writer, whether a professionally published author or a kid struggling in school, needs a plan of attack to meet and defeat the many obstacles inherent in composing thoughts in a coherent, interesting, and informative way. So why not imitate what the pros do by teaching students this kind of procedure?

I have taken this writing process approach and relabeled the four steps in the rhyming sequence of "Prepare, First Dare, Repair, and Share." As mentioned back in Chapter Two, be my guest and use it if you think it will resonate with your students.

To ensure student success in writing, to pave the way for them, we guide them in learning how to Prepare, how to First Dare, how to go back and Repair, and how to effectively Share (publish) their work. Without the process, the strugglers will struggle painfully. With it, over time, they will find ways to alter this general process into a personal one that allows them to proceed with far less struggle.

Prepare Strategies

Prepare is a critical step in the process of composing text. If preparation is lacking, then the first draft will suffer. This is obvious. How often have we heard students struggling with a writing assignment complain, "I don't know what to write"?

As teachers, as coaches of learning, we must prevent this from happening. We need to help students "front-end load" enough ideas or opinions or feelings about the topic that they have a place to begin.

Preparation strategies for writing that we can teach students include

- How to recognize a reason for writing

- How to tap prior knowledge (from the course content)

- How to brainstorm ideas

- How to tentatively organize those ideas

- How to be aware of a specific audience and to address that audience for a purpose

- How to use a particular form and structure

- How the writing will be assessed

With writing about class material, this front-end loading is a fairly straight-forward process—we are doing it all the time. That is, whenever we are teaching our students the content of a course, they are acquiring ideas worth writing about. In fact, all our instruction in science, math, literature, language arts, history, and the rest is a giant prewriting activity, is it not? I believe that it is, and I use course content for writing assignments. The trick is to help students feel motivated, inspired, energized to write about it—that is, to have a purpose to write rather than an external compulsion to regurgitate what their teachers have "inflicted" on them.

First Dare Strategies

The First Dare truly is a dare because now, at this stage in the writing process, it is *show time*. After the writer has taken the time to Prepare, the curtain rises and it's necessary to put that preparation into play by attempting to write out the information in a meaningful, coherent, and interesting manner. Not easy. It fact, it is extremely difficult to do. As I've said, that's why I named this stage the First Dare—it implies taking a risk, making a venture into new territory.

To assist our students, we can teach them these first Dare strategies (a.k.a. writing a rough draft):

- Go for the flow, not perfection.
- Keep interruptions of that flow to a minimum by postponing attention to precise spelling, capitalization, and other mechanics.
- Make any quick fix-ups that occur to you, but do not get hung up on perfection.
- Skip lines for ease of making any changes later.
- Consider writing only on one side of the paper for ease of making any changes later.
- Keep your audience and purpose in mind; be considerate to them.
- Find your true voice to speak to your audience.
- Use your materials from the Prepare phase to guide you but not to collar you.
- Know what to do if writer's block sets in.

That's quite a bit to handle at one time. Fortunately, the First Dare is not the final say in the matter. The First Dare is just that: a first try, the initial attempt, the opening bid. There is nothing automatically permanent about a First Dare. Writers just do the best they can, knowing that they have the right to return to their draft at any time to rethink it, to improve it, to spruce it up.

Realistically, this "right to return" may not come as very good news to struggling student writers. It may, indeed, come as bad news, as in, "What? I gotta go back and do this stupid thing again??" The next section addresses ways to cope with the reluctance to try Repair work.

Repair Strategies

It hardly will come as news to any teacher, but this stage is really hard to do. We all know how hard it is. Even professional authors admit to the difficulty of revision. (And they have the big advantage of professional editors helping them. As I write, rewrite, rewrite, and rewrite this chapter, I am in constant touch with my editor; I need her help.)

So it's useful to provide students with a menu of Repair strategies (a.k.a. revising a draft to improve it):

- Add new ideas to help the reader understand my message.

- Remove unnecessary ideas that may bore or sidetrack the reader.

- Move information around to improve the organization.

- Tighten up the meaning.

- Smooth out the sentence flow.

- Scrutinize the *sound* of the writing (the voice or tone).

- Adjust the conventions (mechanics) to guide the reader along through the ideas.

- Add visuals to support the text.

But even with a list of strategies, an honest appraisal of the Repair stage reveals, I believe, that it is useless to expect students—especially those who struggle with writing—to achieve perfection in their revision. Rather, after teaching writing for twenty-four years, I believe that *improvement* is the only reasonable goal here.

Now what constitutes improvement in the Repair stage is a matter of disagreement. For the student, it may mean, "Hey, I fixed up some spelling and rewrote it neater. I'm done!" For the teacher, it may mean, "Eradicate all sentence fragments and run-ons, and insert topic sentences for each paragraph—because by now *you should know* these things."

It gets frustrating negotiating the gap between expectation levels for revision. I will attempt to mediate with the following suggestions:

- Teachers should hold on to high but realistic expectations.

- Students should be held accountable, but they should not be expected to fix up every possible area in need of improvement.

- Revision is a developmental rather than stationary bar we set for students, meaning that even though these students are in middle or high school, developmentally (realistically) they can only handle making minor changes to a draft, perhaps dealing with only one or two categories of possible changes at a time.

To assist students at the Repair stage, we must examine several concepts. First, I suggest that we *teach the writer instead of correcting the writing*. That means that marking mistakes in red ink is a fruitless endeavor. That in fact it retards student writing ability. Do you agree? Disagree? Not sure? I'd better deal with this issue, and I will in a moment.

Second, give students *three rounds of Repair work* with a solid structure for accomplishing each. What are these three rounds, and how are they managed in a classroom? I'll lay out this procedure in detail in Chapter Seven, with other useful tips on classroom management.

And third, subdivide Repair work into *editing* versus *proofreading* and differentiate them. In this context, editing means improving the meaning of the communication (ideas, organization, vocabulary, sentences); proofreading means locating and correcting errors that interfere with the meaning (spelling, grammar, capitalization, punctuation). Perhaps the writing process should be relabeled "Prepare, First Dare, Repair, *Ensnare Errors,* and Share." This may help students realize that mechanical fix-ups, while immensely important, do not constitute everything there is about Repair. Or maybe not. Perhaps they more realistically view the process as: "Prepare, First Dare, Repair, *I Really Don't Care,* and Share." More on this later.

Share Strategies

The Share stage basically means making a big deal out of the students' efforts to work hard at writing. Sharing is the culmination, the conclusion, the payoff for preparing, first daring, and repairing.

Here are some strategies for this final stage of the writing process:

- Provide motivation to student writers to go through the hard work of the first three stages.
- Lay out a procedure and support for producing a finished, attractive, proud version.
- Extend the definition of *publishing* from the narrow "publish a booklet of student work" to include many options (sometimes simple and sometimes elaborate).
- Deliver the finished work (a.k.a. the final copy) to the intended audience.
- Turn the completion into a celebration (even if minor) of student achievement.

PLANNING ASSIGNMENTS

When assigning writing in our classes, we have choices, many choices. One early decision that must be made is, Why are my students going to write? Putting this question another way, What is the purpose for their writing?

It would be wonderful if every student could answer this question independently of the teacher. That is, all students would benefit if they could determine a reason for writing in all their classes. But this is not likely to be more than a goal, a worthy objective to achieve. In the meantime, the reality is that we, their teachers, typically need to assist with establishing a purpose for writing. We need to pave the way.

Introducing the Modes

One way to help students achieve a purpose for writing is to determine which *mode* we want our students to write in. A mode is the method of development, the structure of expression.

Many English/language arts teachers know the six common writing modes—narrative, imaginative, descriptive, expositive, persuasive, and reflective—quite well and have been teaching students how to write in each one. Many states are assessing student writing in these modes as well. Mode determination is one way to go because each mode has a built-in purpose. Traditionally, the modes have been defined as follows:

- *Narrative:* Tell a story to your audience, either true, partly true, or invented.

- *Imaginative:* Tell a story to your audience but include elements of fantasy and make-believe.

- *Descriptive:* Describe someone, something, or some place clearly for your audience.

- *Expositive:* Explain a topic and inform your audience on it.

- *Persuasive:* Convince your audience that they should agree with your position on a topic.

- *Reflective:* Think about your learning on a topic; you are your own audience.

To content area specialists, who may have little or no instruction in the teaching of writing, the simple fact that writing *has* modes may come as news. In either case, we must understand the differing modes and their differing purposes before we decide which one to assign a class of students. Or, as some teachers have found, let students select which mode they think will best work to fulfill the writing assignment. Of course, students would first need adequate practice in all the modes so they could make good choices. Otherwise, when given a choice, some kids will always select the narrative mode they customarily used in the elementary grades.

A Problem with the Modes

Unfortunately, the modes often overlap, and this can make them harder to use as a teaching device than they may at first appear. That is, rather than having nice, clear, distinct definitions with different purposes, they typically blend into each other. Consider writing a memorandum, for example. Memo writing, you will soon find, is a great way to inspire students to write about what they are learning in class. I like to use the memo format as a way to encourage students to critique an author they are reading. It works because memos have an attractive appeal to students.

However, which mode are students to write their memos in? When they tell the author what they liked or didn't like about the writing, they are informing that author, explaining to that author, that is, engaging in exposition. But when they make suggestions to the author for possible improvements, they now are trying to persuade the author to change something. So we have a merger of the expository and persuasive modes.

This is not bad news. In fact, it is good news that students are writing for multiple purposes. This merging of modes happens in other assignments, too. Descriptive writing rarely remains a singular purpose, as in "describe your bedroom using the five senses." Rather, descriptive writing shows up in narrative, in imaginative, and hopefully in expository, persuasive, and reflective writing as well. Likewise, narrative writing's purpose is to tell a story, but good fiction authors also explain the background and inform their readers at the same time.

All of this is to say that teaching the modes may appear to be a useful structure for writing instruction, but it seems too blurry to me. And I am not alone. In fact, the leading researcher on effective writing practices, George Hillocks Jr., states: "One of the chief problems with the typography is that its categories are not mutually exclusive. In fact, they overlap to a point that eliminates their usefulness as categories. . . . The categories are hopelessly confused and, therefore, of little use in the analysis of writing tasks" (Hillocks, 1995, pp. 113–114).

Real Purposes for Real Kids

Here's an alternative to using the modes to help teach students a purpose for writing: Think about what really moves your students to write.

Perhaps the answer comes quickly to you: Not much.

Well, the better students probably do have at least one motivation to write, and that would be to get a good grade to keep up their precious grade point average. But what about the less able students? What moves them to write? Not much, you say.

I can relate to this stark answer. Struggling writers are not often inspired to put pencil to paper or fingers to keyboard. In fact, most of them will loudly declare their distaste for writing, meaning they have no reason to write other than when some cruel teacher requires it.

Upon pondering my own response to this question of what really moved my students to write, I finally came up with an answer: *When they have something to say*. When they want to give voice to something, they will find it worthwhile to go to the effort to say it.

And why would they want to "say something to someone" in writing? Three reasons that I can think of:

- To look good in front of that someone

- To talk back to someone

- To appear funny or clever to someone

I do not mean to belittle or ridicule these reasons. I really think that these three are actual purposes likely to be motivating to students who struggle with writing. And I think we can use them to inspire our students to write.

It's worth exploring the trio more carefully. To "look good" really means to look smart, to be knowledgeable, to have something worth saying (writing), to have some expertise to share on a topic, to feel effective, to help someone understand something worth understanding, to be respected. To "talk back" actually means to speak up, to provide feedback to an authority (authors), to evaluate someone's work, to think about it, to critique it, to offer suggestions for improvement, to be honest, to tell someone what they really need to know. To "appear funny" means to have the ability to amuse someone, to entertain, to get their attention, to be clever, maybe to satirize, to parody, to lampoon in order to make a point worth making on a topic in a memorable way.

To be honest, I am motivated by these same three reasons. I admit that I like to look good, look smart, look helpful to other people. I also like to tell someone what I think of their ideas to let them know how I feel. And I doubt that I am the only adult who enjoys appearing funny and clever.

Humans write to communicate ideas. But our strugglers have so many obstacles built up over the years that the urge to communicate ideas *in writing* has been thoroughly suppressed. The thought is just too overwhelming. So what if we tap into their legitimate desires to look good, to talk back, or to appear clever? What if we tap into these real human needs to instill the energy required to write?

Assessment of Student Writing

Beyond teaching a structured way to attack an assignment and making sure the students have a purpose they can relate to, we need to make sure they know what constitutes a successful composition and reveal to them how this writing assignment will be assessed. This is a another good place to use a ChecBric, because it tells the students both what they should look for and what the teacher will be looking for. Exhibit 5.1 shows a ChecBric I have used for memo-writing assignments.

Another useful scoring option is to provide students with an assessment list. Also called a "criterion-based performance list" (McTigue, 2000), it is just like a checklist of key targets, but it also has a point-value associated with each target. Some targets are more important, so they get ten or fifteen or twenty points allotted to them. Other targets get weighted less. Many teachers use assessment lists in their classes, and they structure them so that the total number of points equals a hundred—a nice way to convert a score on the assignment into a percentage for a grade.

For a more detailed look at scoring devices, samples of each, and their pros and cons, see *Great Performances: Creating Classroom-Based Performance Assessments* (Lewin and Shoemaker, 1998).

And don't forget: You can have your students participate in the design of a scoring device by assisting you in the generation of the targets. When they do this, they understand the targets, they buy into the assignment, and the veil of assessment mystery gets lifted. Just be sure to distribute the device early in the Prepare phase, so the students have it in front of them.

BASIC WRITING ACTIVITIES: TALKING BACK WITH MEMOS

It's time to use the writing process for some writing. As I mentioned earlier, I really like the memorandum format—it gives the kids a short, relatively easy writing assignment that effectively elicits their understandings of information while tapping into their desire to communicate their ideas about that information.

MemoChecBric

Student Checklist	Teacher Rubric
Target 1: Expressing My Ideas	**Trait 1: Ideas and Content**

Target 1: Expressing My Ideas

____ My memo comments on the author's successes.

____ My memo comments on the author's missing ideas.

____ My memo offers suggestions for improvement.

____ My memo shows that I "read between the lines" to make inferences, to "speculate" on ideas.

____ My memo offers support by referring back to the text.

____ My memo is brief but to the point.

Trait 1: Ideas and Content

6 = **exceptional,** compelling ideas and content; clear, focused; way above expectations

5 = **excellent,** outstanding ideas and content; easy meeting of expectations

4 = **proficient,** interesting ideas and content; good enough to meet expectations

3 = **inadequate** ideas and content; close, but overly broad or simplistic; not good enough to meet expectations

2 = **limited,** obvious ideas and content; unclear or minimal; tried to meet expectations, but a ways to go to meet expectations

1 = **missing,** absent ideas and content; lacks central idea or purpose; way off on the requirements OR: no attempt to meet expectations

Target 6: I Follow the Rules of Writing

____ My memo follows the standard format: To: From: Date: RE:.

____ My memo has been checked to eliminate spelling errors.

____ My memo has been checked to fix any capitalization errors.

____ My memo has been checked to fix any punctuation errors.

____ My memo has been checked to fix any paragraph identification errors.

Trait 6: Writing Conventions

6 = **exceptionally** strong control of writing conventions; way above expectations

5 = **excellent,** outstanding writing conventions that help deliver content; easy meeting of expectations

4 = **proficient,** adequate writing conventions; some minor errors, but good enough to meet expectations

3 = **inadequate** writing conventions; close, but errors interrupt ideas; not good enough to meet expectations

2 = **limited** writing conventions; frequent significant errors; tried to meet expectations, but errors disrupt ideas, quite a ways to go to meet expectations

1 = **missing,** absent writing conventions; numerous errors cause breakdown of meaning; way off on the requirements OR: no attempt to meet expectations

Student **Reflections** on this assignment

Teacher **Comments** to student

Exhibit 5.1 ChecBric: Memo Writing.

Source: Traits are taken from Oregon Department of Education "Writing Scoring Guide," 2001. Office of Assessment and Evaluation, O.D.E., 255 Capitol Street NE, Salem, Oregon 97310.

The memo idea typically surprises teachers, who rarely think of memo writing as an assignment. This is odd, I believe, given the number of memos we receive from our administrators. (Perhaps that's why we tend to overlook them.)

Memos have never failed me as an engaging writing task. Three reasons they work with secondary students: They are short. (Short is good.) They are unusual; it's rare that a high school or middle school student has ever written a memo. (New is good.) And they have a cool text structure; To: From: Date: RE: is very cool if you've never used it. (Cool is good.)

I like memos for these reasons as well. But additionally, and what is more important, memo writing allows the memo writer to talk back to authority but in a polite and structured way, and to look good in the process. Again, these are legitimate purposes for writing. More than legitimate; they are powerful.

Plus, I very much like how memos can be used to merge two of the important writing modes, exposition and persuasive writing. But they give these modes a new twist.

The Content Area Memo

My former student Britni composed a memo to Dr. Ernest L. May, the senior author of the American history textbook, *Proud Nation*. She wrote:

To: Ernest R. May
From: Britni Jones
Date: September 30, 1997
RE: Proud Nation, p. 35

I thought that the Christmas day, 1492 page was good. I think that you did a pretty good job explaining what happened on Christmas, but you didn't say anything about how the La Navidad burnt down.

I think you did a good job explaining how the Santa Maria ran into the coral reefs, too. The only other thing I would put in the article besides how the La Navidad burnt down is talking more about the Tainos and Indians.

Overall I thought that your article was well written and easy to understand.

Sincerely,

What is an eighth-grade kid doing writing a memo to a senior textbook author? Three things, actually:

- Informing Dr. May that she appreciated some elements in his passage about the sinking of Columbus's ship the *Santa Maria* on Christmas Day, 1492 (exposition)

- Explaining to him the shortcomings of the passage (exposition)

- Suggesting to him that he should add additional information to improve it for his audience (persuasion)

Paving the Way

These three required elements, the three targets, ask quite a bit from an eighth-grade memo writer. To pull off this assignment, Britni needed to read the history textbook, and read it well; she needed to consider the effect (both positive and negative) it was having on her as a student of history; she needed to organize her thinking into the categories of "what I liked, what was missing, and what improvements I wanted," and she needed to write all this down using the memo format.

Naturally, most middle and high school students would have difficulty accomplishing all this on their own. First, they have never before written a memo. Most kids don't really know what a memo is. They may have heard the word *memo*, but few have seen or read one. Second, this memo-writing assignment demands upper-level critical thinking. To complete the three required elements they will have lots of thinking to do. Third, all this critical reading and thinking must be transposed into writing in both the expository and persuasive modes. And fourth, they have only a small space to pull this off: a memo.

So we pave the way. First, to help them Prepare, students must become acquainted with the memo format. I was fortunate. My principal was a memo freak. I constantly received memos in my mailbox (some even were thoughtful thank-yous to me for working hard to help kids . . . really, he sent these to the staff). Some other memos were announcements of upcoming issues, meetings, policy matters, or administrivia.

I took one memo (not confidential), made an overhead transparency, turned on the overhead projector, and asked the class, "Who has ever written a memo?"

Well, no student had ever written one, of course, and they really didn't know what a memo was or what it looked like or what purpose it had. So, we discussed all this.

Now, if you are thinking, "I like this memo idea. It is new, it is different, and it is *short*. My students could get into this, but sadly, my administrator is not a memo freak...," you could write your own memo as a sample for the students. They are very easy to write. Write a memo to them about an upcoming event or assignment.

Text Structure of the Memo

All memos always have the same text structure at the top—the familiar *To: From: Date: RE:* headings. Students love this, they really do. I'm not sure why, but probably because it is different enough to get their attention. And the RE: for "regarding" is very cool—that is, cool if you are a middle or high school student who has never seen it before.

Now, do not expect your students to reveal to you that they love this memo idea or that the RE: is super-cool to them. No doubt they will sit in their desks and stare blankly (or even glumly) at you, as usual. But that doesn't mean you haven't caught their attention. You have, and you're on your way to a great writing assignment.

Once the memo has been introduced, be sure to discuss that the format requires brevity. That is, after the To: From: Date: and RE:, a memo's message must fit onto a half-page of paper—two or three paragraphs maximum. While this is good news to struggling writers who have difficulty writing more than two paragraphs anyway, it does require them to make decisions about what goes into the memo.

Now, for the better writers in a class, the memo may cause anxiety: They may be accustomed to verbosity in their writing, overloading their poor teachers, wearing them down, and thus ensuring the award of another "A." Memos enforce economy of ideas and the words that express them.

More Preparation Possibilities

At this point an opportunity for a practice memo arrives. You could have students write a memo *to you* to get introduced to its format and purpose. Maybe assign a memo to you with the RE: being a review of how to write a memo.... Or a memo to you about what should be on the unit test next week, or a memo with feedback on your teaching of the unit. Practicing with a new structure is essential; novice writers need guided support.

For a student to successfully write a memo to a textbook author, some serious prewriting needs to occur. Before they can do their First Dare draft, writers must first Prepare. As I noted earlier, for a class assignment most of the preparation is automatically built into the unit. My students were studying 1492 by reading about it in their textbook, reading supplementary resources I provided from quality Web sites, listening to my fascinating mini-lectures, reading a few children's picture books, and watching a videotape. All this learning can serve as a launching pad for the memo writing.

Additionally, to help them Prepare for the feedback memo, I could provide them with the "Evaluating the Author" survey, which prompts students to rate the degree of considerateness or inconsiderateness of the author's writing. Presented in Exhibit 2.5, this form trains students to be critical evaluators of the authors they are assigned to read. I remind them, "It takes two to tango in the reading comprehension dance."

Students provide the textbook author with feedback on the writing by incorporating their answers to the eight survey questions. This nicely links reading and writing, the twin pillars of literacy. And it works in any classroom that uses textbooks or other outside reading assignments.

Finally, to facilitate memo writing, the teacher could produce a memo template like the one shown in Exhibit 5.2, photocopy it, and distribute it to students. This speeds up the writing process by removing time spent on formatting.

Early Repairs

Memos are perfect for providing feedback. Do you have any students who like to talk back to authority? Well, the memo is a proper vehicle for this because it offers a short format, a clear purpose, and a polite tone.

Providing feedback. This is what the memo to the textbook author accomplishes. It is the motivating purpose for writing. Compare the following memo from Tana to the one from Britni quoted earlier. Tana wrote the same headings, but her message is different because she had a different reaction to the assigned textbook reading. Also, Tana decided to recursively Repair her memo by inserting the sentence shown here in italics, which she added in a bubble in the margin.

To: Ernest R. May
From: Tana Gardner
Date: September 30, 1997
RE: "Christmas Day, 1492"

I think the story *Christmas Day, 1492* is well written. *I liked the part about it being God's will that the ship sank.* It is short, but you didn't leave out a lot of detail. You could have added what, exactly, happened to Fort La Navidad. I want to know who burned it and killed the men, and I want to know why they did it.

```
To:
From:
Date:
RE:
_____

_____

_____

_____

_____

_____

_____

_____

_____

_____

_____

_____

_____

_____

_____
```

Exhibit 5.2 Sample Memo Template.

Tana added the italicized line because I had told the class that when offering feedback to the author, you need to provide evidence from the text to support your feedback. This tip is even included on the ChecBric. See Exhibit 5.1.

She is making a basic Repair while she is drafting her memo. Recall the recursive nature of the composing process: writers move forward and back as needed to solve problems. Tana identified a problem in her early memo, not enough supporting detail, and she realized this without an external source (teacher, peer partner, editing group) telling her. Good job, Tana. This is what alert writers do; they pay attention to their communication to their audience and work to smooth it out, to make it better, to be a considerate writer.

Tana has repaired her First Dare memo before the official Repair stage has begun by inserting additional needed information. Maybe we should refer to this fixing up while First Daring as "round 0" of Repair.

Regardless of what we call it, all students should be made aware of the usefulness of spontaneous revision because all authors do it. However, we do not want to stress this recursive repair so much that students become overly fixated on editing their work as they are writing, because this may serve to overload their writing systems and interrupt the necessary flow of a draft.

Memos in Literature Classes

High school special education teacher Sherry Stoddard in Livermore, California, had her students write a memo to Leon LeWine, author of the short story *The First Time* (1983). Sherry's students read the story, thought about it, discussed it, critiqued it, and then wrote to the author.

Sherry explains the procedure she followed:

> The first thing my class did is read the story, *The First Time.* I have two English classes in my SDC program [special day class], and the first one read the story after my presenting the idea that a successful writer fills the reader's head with visual images and giving examples. As we read, one boy immediately knew that the vehicle was a motorcycle! I gave him a lot of credit for being so perceptive. I had the students write the author a memo telling him about the image that he had helped the student visualize.
>
> I did much better with the second class, and we built up more slowly and deliberately to reading the story, talking at greater length beforehand about what good authors' responsibilities are to their readers and stopping along the way, identifying passages that prompted a mental image. We used highlighters to identify these passages. Again, I had the students write a memo to the author to say which part helped the reader get that mental picture. The students were very wrapped up in their responses, so of course I was as pleased as punch to put this new technique into play and have it work!!!

Bob (one of Sherry's students) wrote, "I like the way you describe the girl. I can picture her on the motorcycle with me and haveing her hiar flying in the Wind. Please give me a picture of her," and signed the memo, "Always your friend."

Other memo ideas with reading literature include writing a memo to a character revealing something you, the reader, know that the character does not yet know; a memo critiquing a character's action or attitude; a memo to a character from another character discussing a problem.

Finally, your students could write memos about literature to each other. I figure they like to pass notes to each other anyway, so why not legalize and formalize it? The memos could be mini–book reviews recommending (or not) a particular book.

Another audience for the memo could be "To: My Parents" (or whoever stands in that role for the student). The purpose could be "RE: the novel I am reading in Ms. Kim's Lit class." Maybe offer extra credit to those students who get a memo back from the person they address. (Involving parents is a good idea, after all, and it will be interesting to the class to see how many grownups write memos as a matter of routine.)

Other Memo Audiences

I learned of memo writing from my colleague Dorothy Syfert who used it in a content area class, U.S. history, so when I borrowed it, I also used it for critiquing a history textbook author. Clearly, though, memos work in any context.

One way to get students' attention is to invite them to write and send memos to their principal or vice principal about what they are learning. Why? I think the administrators might enjoy learning what is going on in a class. Aren't they usually too swamped with other duties to observe instruction in classrooms? Help them out by using them as the memo's audience.

Two tips if you do like this idea: First, make sure you send a memo to the administrator in advance of the students' offerings to provide a heads-up. Otherwise, this memo assignment may not turn out to be as cool as you planned. And remind students of the purpose of the memo and the proper tone. You would not want a student who has a vendetta against the principal or vice principal to use the memo inappropriately.

Here's a great idea from MaryEtta Taylor, a special education teacher who introduced herself to me at a workshop. She assigned her students to write a memo to another teacher, with the subject "to help me do better." Nicholas addressed his memo to two teachers and a coach, writing,

> I learn best when I see it as you explain it. I also like to practice.
>
> I do well in groups. I take notes. I have good calculator skills.
>
> One thing that gives me trouble is giving answers out loud. I have trouble doing long written assignments.

MaryEtta wrote to me: "I've had really good responses from our teachers. They liked hearing directly from the students."

With any audience for a memo, a teacher could tell the students to add cc: at the top just below the RE: line. This stands for "carbon copy" or, these days, "courtesy copy." After the cc:, students write in your name, so that they know you will read the memo before it goes to the audience. They do not actually need to provide you with another copy; the cc: means that they know you will see it and perhaps assess it.

PREPARING SHORT CRITIQUES: THE POSTCARD

Postcards make another effective writing assignment. They're even shorter than memos, but they still get the kids thinking about communicating. These two postcards, written to the young adult author Gary Soto, are examples of expository and persuasive writing:

> Gary Soto, your stories are boring. After the opening scene the story took a minute to reach its climax. The story also couldn't hold interest. It's just about some kid who liked a big girl. This is an unsatisfying story to read.
>
> Dear Mr. Soto, I wanted to write to tell you, I enjoyed your story "The Challenge." It was also easy to follow. However, I hoped for a different ending. Maybe after the game, she could've invited him over. I liked the Spanish dialect used—like for instance, nada, vatos. Great story.

The Literature Postcard

The tenth- and eleventh-grade students who wrote these two memos had as their purpose to share with their audience, Gary Soto, a critical analysis of his work—that is, to explain, inform, and convince. The modes of exposition and persuasion are more challenging than the first three modes because they require deeper thought, critical analysis, and synthesis—which is exactly what our instruction aims for. Both modes are perfectly suited to middle and high school learners in any subject.

Eliza Sher, literature teacher at Sheldon High School, agreed to let me co-teach her sophomore and junior literature class to try out the short story "The Challenge." As mentioned earlier, I love Gary Soto's work because he so beautifully captures the trials and errors of adolescents trying to grow up.

During the reading Prepare stage, I introduced the story and the author and asked the class to preview the story's layout (text structure). We briefly discussed the game of racquetball. I previewed a few Spanish words and phrases in the story, and I asked students to think back a few years to remember how middle schoolers handle crushes. Finally, I distributed colored sticky notes to them to assist their First Dare reading. (For a review of sticky note reading, return to Chapter Two.) All these reading comprehension strategies were applied to boost student comprehension and appreciation of literature. And they did assist the students' understanding of the short story.

Planting the Seed

As an important bonus, the reading strategies additionally helped the students' writing skills because, as a final Prepare strategy, I helped them set a motivating purpose for reading: writing a postcard to the author.

I told them, "When you are finished with the story, you will tell Gary Soto what you think of his work by writing him a postcard critiquing his story."

At first, they thought I was kidding. A postcard? To an author? They didn't know me; I was just some teacher visiting their classroom for some reason. But I convinced them I was serious about their critiquing Gary Soto in a postcard.

I explained to them, "A critique does not mean just the bad things. Being critical has come to mean stressing only the negative, but actually, criticism includes both the positive and the negative, like what a movie critic does on TV or in the newspaper."

I also told them, "Use your sticky notes to record your likes, dislikes, and suggestions as you read the story, so at the end you'll be ready to write to Gary."

Silence.

Then one kid asked, "Are you gonna send these critiques to him?"

I paused dramatically, and responded, "Sure. But only if you want me to. Your choice. You're the postcard author. See how it goes."

A follow-up question came next. "How do you know where he lives?"

"I don't, but on his Web site he has posted his e-mail address. I'll e-mail him and find out."

All of this surely is not what most students have come to expect when a short story is assigned in a literature class. That is exactly my intent. I want to surprise them, to grab their attention, to cause them to momentarily forget any past negative feelings about reading fiction or writing, and maybe even make them forget they are doing a school assignment. Most critically, they got to talk back to a big-shot author. They felt important even before the writing began.

It worked. All the students gamely read the story, scribbled notes on the sticky notes, and wrote the postcards. Many of them put a little checkmark in the upper corner signaling to me that they wanted their postcard mailed to Gary Soto.

Basic Repairs: Fixing Up Postcards

That's the good news. The bad news is I didn't want to mail their postcards just yet because they were, shall I say, in need of *Repair*.

No surprise here: The postcards were merely a First Dare. So I suggested to the class that in order for Gary to understand, appreciate, and respect their feedback, they needed to "clean up the cards." I figured that would be incentive to engage in revising and editing.

No. Their repairs were just minimal. A few i's were dotted, some t's crossed, easy misspellings corrected, maybe an example from the story inserted. . . . Not bad, considering my honest appraisal of the Repair stage: as I've said, I believe it is useless to expect students, especially those who struggle with writing, to achieve perfection in their first attempts at revision.

Given the shortness of the writing assignment and the limited time frame available, it was good to see that the repairs showed any improvement. The kids had improved their postcards, albeit at a minor to middling degree. However, I admit that I got nervous that we would look bad when the audience, in this case a talented, famous author, saw the errors, read the choppy sentences, or got lost in lack of organization.

Anyone else get nervous about student First Dares leaving the sanctity of the classroom? I do, so I like to consider *three rounds of Repair:*

- Self-editing (independent student)
- Partner editing (peer review)
- Adult editing (one-on-one conference where you, or a surrogate, ask the student questions to clarify any confusions)

In this particular writing assignment, time permitted only round 1; the students were on their own to make modifications in their postcards. I was unhappy about this, and so was their teacher Eliza, but hey, we didn't have the time to pull off rounds 2 and 3. Are we in danger of being charged with *instructional malpractice?* No, we are not because teachers do the best we can under the circumstances. If time allowed, I would have taught the students how to self-edit with a "Sentence Opening Sheet" (from the Stack the Deck Writing Program). I will get to that device later in this chapter, and go into detail on making the three rounds work in Chapter Seven.

However, to maximize round 1, self-repair, I provided the students with a 5"x8" lined index card. Why? Because index cards are cool, they are short, they have lines on one side for handwriting help, and a blank side to draw a picture of a character, event, or symbol from the story to make a *picture postcard.*

I distributed the index cards and said, "Write the best postcard you can to Gary Soto on the card. Copy any parts from your "First Dare" postcard that you like, add any new parts, and double-check your work, so that Gary won't be confused by anything you write."

The results of this Repair round were clearly better. Here are two postcards, the first from a nonstruggler, and the second from one who found the exercise harder.

Dear Mr. Soto,

I have just got done reading your short story "The Challenge." I thought it was a sweet and interesting love story, for a 6th grader. But I am a sophmore in high school, so I wasn't as appealing to me. I really Liked the concept of the story and the ending was unusual. Im tired of reading "happly ever after" storys, and yours wasn't. I have been in a lot of situations, where It wasn't always a happy ending, Im glad someone is finally writting about it. The Spanish that was thrown in the story were nice, but added inappropiantly in unusual sentences. It would have been less annoying if you would have left those words out. I thought other than that it was great! Keep the good work!

Alison C.

Dear Gary Soto,

Your story, "The Challenge," was very interesting. I was enjoying it a lot and was getting into the flow of it. All of a sudden it stoped. It left me dissapointed. I wanted to know what was going to happen between José and Estella. I speculate José wouldn't talk to her anymore and Stinger would always make fun of him. I don't really know though. So why don't you re-write the story and make it longer.

Thank you,
Matt E.

Alison checked the upper corner to tell me she'd decided to have hers mailed. But even though she made important improvements, I was still worried. So I appointed myself editor-in-chief, and stepped in to clean things up. That is, despite my very real doubts of the long-term benefits of marking up student work, I recognize the short-term necessity. In this case, in light pencil I noted any remaining fix-ups, returned the cards, and the students did one more final Repair. Though not all perfect, the postcards were very good, even from the students who reside "on the edge" of school.

I mailed the postcards to the man himself, and, bless his heart, Gary replied by thanking the kids for writing and recommending some books and authors he likes.

Postcards from Other Places

Other teachers have found postcards to be a useful teaching and learning tool. Read this e-mail note I received from Victoria Lamkey, a teacher in Haysville, Kansas, after she attended one of my workshops:

I use the postcards with Walter Dean Myers *Fallen Angels,* a book about the Vietnam Conflict [1991]. As we read the book, each student assumes the role of soldier in the platoon and then writes home in character to a mother, sibling, loved one, or significant other. The purpose is to provide brief glimpses of what goes on in their lives on the front lines. People die, new members join the group, and with a scrapbook culminating activity, you can trace the year the draftees spent in Vietnam. This was one of the most popular books I have ever selected and the assignments were wonderful reflections of how they *interpreted* the characters and the theme. [Italics mine.]

Interpreted. That's the ticket. Upper-level reading comprehension. Taking the author's words and moving past them into deeper territory. And the postcard technique gets the assist.

How about a postcard written by your students in a content area class to their parents informing them about what they are learning? High school teacher Mary Mansell assigned "Aztec" postcards: Pretend you are on a field trip to Mexico to study Teotihuacan and write a postcard home informing the family about your findings. Stephanie's postcard in Figure 5.1 succeeds nicely.

Dear Mom

Hello from the ancient city of Teotihuacan, "Place of the Gods"! Oh Mom, if only you were here to see the magnificent pieces and monuments. Our guide filled us with so much information, like how most of the art was religiously inspired, and how the culture is like that of the Egyptians. Both Cultures built the step pyramids, but the difference between them was that the Egyptian Pyramids were just the burial tombs of the great pharaohs and their worldly possessions, and those of Teotihuacan were much larger and were like temples dedicated to the sun and the moon, in which rituals such as human and animal sacrifices took place, and some of these remains might even be housed below it.

When I bought this postcard, my guide told me that the sculpture of the goddess of water, on the front, used to be in front of the pyramid of the sun. The picture is only of the replica that they have in the museum there, and the real one had been taken to the National Anthropology Museum in 1885. He also said that the statue is not really considered a piece from their culture because it was actually made and put in front of the Pyramid of the Sun by the Aztecs when they came to Teotihuacan because they believed it must have been made by the gods.

Well Mom, I will be coming home soon. I can't wait to tell you about how the rest of my trip went! Until then, I send my love to you and Will!

love, Stephanie

RACHEL GRIFFIN
4415 Griffin Ave.
Los Angeles, CA, U.SA. 90031

Figure 5.1 A Postcard from Teotihuacan.

Source: Mary Mansell, teacher, Ramona Convent Secondary School, Alhambra, California.

Postcards, like memos, are turn-ons to struggling writers. They are short, they have a unique (and cool) format, and they make a connection to the real world. They are different from typical school writing assignments, they seem easy to do, they are written to a real audience for a genuine purpose, and they just might turn out to be fun. Imagine that.

But let's not get cocky. The reality is, some strugglers may not be enthusiastic about a memo or postcard assignment. They should be, of course, but sometimes our best ideas fail to connect with every kid in every class. Some strugglers may not successfully complete a memo or postcard. You know this is true, and so do I. We just need to realize this, not be surprised if it happens, and not feel inadequate as teachers. Struggling writers can also be struggling human beings with lots of problems confronting them in life. These problems can sometimes overwhelm even our best lesson plans. We feel unhappy, but we do not beat ourselves up over it. We don't give up; we will try again and again to connect.

EXPOSITORY EXERCISES: THE NEWS ARTICLES

Another expository writing assignment is a news article, written for publication in a classroom magazine or newspaper. News articles, like memos and postcards, are different. They stand apart from essays and reports. They reflect real-world writing, they are written for an audience other than just the teacher, and they get published. But they are not really so easy. Therefore, students need the writing process to expedite the task.

To Prepare for writing an article, students first need a topic. This is quite doable in that they are always studying some topic in class, say, the Boston Massacre. Instruction on this history topic may include the usual materials: textbook reading, supplementary readings, mini-lectures, videotape viewing, reenactments, and the like.

Writing in the expository mode would be a likely Share vehicle, with the option of writing the news article from either a British or Colonial perspective. By requiring that students adopt a perspective, a point of view on the topic, we bump up the expectation from mere regurgitation of the content to perspective-taking. Eighth-grade historian Ryan revealed his understanding of this important event in these terms:

Volume 3, March 5, 1770

The Boston News

Boston, MA—It all started one night when some kids were throwing snowballs. After that, the people of the great city of Boston started ganging up on the British soldiers. Then someone from Boston had a major stupid attack and started firing at them. We have reports of only five people being killed, but we will keep you posted.

Ryan's content revelations could be (should be) more extensive, but his formatting caught my eye. He knew the text structure of a newspaper article, and he used it to package his ideas. I congratulated him and asked how he knew the standard organizational pattern of articles.

He replied, "My dad's a reporter, you know. He writes articles all the time in the paper. He even had one in *Sports Illustrated*. He showed me how."

From that moment on, whenever I assigned news article writing, at the Prepare stage I showed the young journalists in my classes the article format, including multiple columns, the five journalistic questions (who, what, where, when, and why), and how to set up a by-line. These insights helped Megan the following semester, when she wrote the article shown in Figure 5.2.

Looking back, Megan, now a university student, had a few observations to share. In a note granting me permission to reproduce her article, she wrote, "Thanks for considering my paper for your book. I remember writing it, and six years later, I notice several errors and things I might have done differently. I was actually impressed at how well I wrote in 8th grade. . . ."

One more Prepare strategy to go along with gaining ideas and recognizing text structure: show the writers what their targets are and how their articles will be evaluated. Give the students a news article ChecBric or some other scoring device in advance of their writing.

I've said it before, but it's worth saying again: Students like having a checklist for an assignment because they can use it before writing to check out the targets, during writing to check on their progress, and after writing to double-check if anything is missing. However, teachers realize that when assessing student writing, we

I'm part of the 1/3 of the people who are neutral about the Revolutionary War. The loyalists' side is out of the question because I'm not in favor of supporting the king. I would consider being a patriot, but I don't really want to be involved in the war at all unless I have to. Fortunately, I haven't been forced to take a side yet....

Then, March 5, 1770, was the Boston Massacre. A crowd of people threw snowballs at a British soldier. The soldiers fired back, killing five people and two more died later.

There was also the Boston Tea Party which began December 16, 1773. The colonists didn't want to pay taxes for the tea, so they dumped it into the Boston Harbor.

Some of the patriots have protested by tarring and feathering loyalists. They've also raided their homes, stolen their property, and some of them were even put to death.

The loyalists used New....

Figure 5.2 News Article: "The Revolutionary War."

cannot merely inform them what they did, or did not, do. We must show them *their degree of proficiency*—how their work measures up to a standard. Teachers use rubrics for communicating this to students. That is what the ChecBric's right-hand column is for.

THE INFORMATIVE NARRATIVE

Another motivating writing assignment is the informative narrative, a hybrid of the expository and narrative modes. This is a story written about the content in the first person, which causes the student writer to become *personally involved* in the topic.

History students can write informative narratives. For example, while studying the industrialization of the United States in the 1800s, my students learned about Lowell's Mill, the textile factory boom town in Massachusetts. Besides a history textbook, the historical novel *Lyddie* (Patterson, 1991) was assigned as a supplemental source. To process this content, students were asked to write first-person accounts of what it might have been like to have experienced this historical period. Students needed to combine historical facts with personal reactions, as with this example:

> I started working at Lowell's Mills about a year ago. I made cotton into thread and then I wove the thread into clothes. I can remember the first time getting paid. The feeling was indescribable; it was so wonderful. I got paid $1.01 an hour along with the other girls.
>
> Then one day the owner came and told us that each of our wages would be cut. We were so angry! They took away our independence. We took to the streets! We sang out, "Oh, isn't it a pity such a pretty girl as I should be sent to the factory to pine away and die?"

The personal reaction to the horrid working conditions for these young women was to take to the streets to protest. Although it was made up for the assignment, it reveals the student's strong feelings to injustice.

When the informative narrative is set back in a historical period, the writing becomes *historical fiction*. It is the merger of the expository and narrative modes. Typically, narratives are used in the early grades. Many primary and intermediate grade teachers assign story writing.

But stories have a place in the middle and high school grades, too. For example, an American history teacher could opt for a historical fiction writing assignment during a unit on 1492. The students would be expected to write a story about this historical event, starring Columbus, his Spanish sailors, and the Taino Indians, using the content information gleaned from the unit of study. When a story contains elements dreamed up by the student, the mode becomes historical fiction narrative. Of course, the narrative must be heavy on the historical and light on the fictional; otherwise, the purpose of the assignment would be compromised.

My former student Mac based his 1492 story "Sky Eyes" on solid historical ground while adding some fictitious events and characters, including the narrator, Pablo Espolo, a cabin boy working on board the *Niña*. Here's the opening of his second draft:

> **"Sky Eyes" ~Repaired~**
>
> Lost........the creaking of the hull squeezed his head filling his mind with quiet desperation for of all things: dirt, grass, rocks, trees anything, not this blue hell that stretched forever.... Above blue skies, below the blue ocean. The blue sadness reminded him of the hopeless death that surely awaited him.
>
> "God does not want us here," he thought "God will kill us here, it's too late, turn back we are lost, I know we are lost. He does not say we are but I know we are. We are dead already."
>
> A tear rolled down his cheek "Hail Mary full of grace blessed thou art amongst woman and blessed is the fruit of your womb Jesus hail Mary mother of God bless us now and at the hour of our death." He repeated this over and over each time quieter than before until whisper turned into silence....to sleep.
>
> The boy lay sound onboard the Nina deck as the night slid in. The morning will bring his cold destiny but for Poblo Espolo will sleep.

REPAIR AND EDITING ACTIVITIES: THE SENTENCE OPENING SHEET

Of course, some repairs are always in order on a First Dare. Round 1 of Repair is self-editing. Needless to say, few students are excited about this. Most student writers resist revising due to the difficulties inherent in this third stage of the writing process.

So we help them. One technique for fostering student self-repairing is the great "Sentence Opening Sheet" (SOS). Developed by Herb Hrebic and Bob Cahill, two former high school teachers in Chicago, it is a four-column worksheet that guides students through *independent analysis* of their draft. Really. It is so good that Bob and Herb published it in their writing textbook *Stack the Deck.* (This is not a gambling manual. They gave it this title because they were rigging their writing instruction so that all students would be successful—"stacking the deck" so all would be winners.) In the quarter-century-plus it has been out, the SOS has received rave reviews from teachers who use it with their students.

It also got a rave review from the College Board, administrator of the SAT: "As a revision technique for a student's own writing, completion of an SOS may signal various writing problems (repetitiveness in sentence opening, possible run-ons and fragments, passive voice, poor verb choice, lack of variety of sentence lengths, etc." (Hrebic and Cahill, 2002, p. 2).

Here is how the Sentence Opening Sheet works: When students finish their First Dares, they number each sentence. In column 1 of the SOS they copy the *first four words* from each sentence. Examining the initial four words, students decide if they have good variety of sentence beginnings or redundancy of beginnings. If they decide the piece is redundant, they return to their First Dare and make the needed repairs by combining sentences, rearranging sentences, or substituting words in the sentence beginnings. Also in column 1, they double-check to make sure they capitalized each sentence's first word. Of course, students who struggle with handwriting can copy just the first two or three words.

In column 2 they record the *total number of words* in each sentence. Analyzing this data, the students are on the lookout for variety of sentence length, possible run-ons (long sentences), and possible fragments (shorts). Back to the First Dare to double-check on changing any sentences' length, on whether long sentences are run-ons or OK, and on shorts as fragments or OK.

Exhibit 5.3 shows the first two columns of an SOS prepared by a student named Sequoia. It shows that the third sentence is twenty-five words long and that at least four other sentences are more than twenty words long. This is useful data to consider. And the SOS let her do this alone, without help. Without such a format, seeing potential problems is difficult because they are embedded in the writing. The SOS *reformats* the writing so that the data is visible.

Of course, in order to use a Sentence Opening Sheet effectively, a student must be trained in how to use it. That's why I made an overhead transparency of the SOS and walked the entire class through columns 1 and 2. As I wrote on the overhead analyzing a sample draft paper, the students imitated me on their own copies of the SOS at their desks. Practice. And I stopped after introducing columns 1 and 2. I figured that was enough; columns 3 and 4 could wait until another day. I didn't want to overload anyone.

Later, I taught the students that column 3 is for recording the verbs in each sentence. "Why a column just for verbs?" the students wanted to know.

"Because," I replied, "verbs run the sentences. They are the engines that drive the sentences forward. Verbs are critically important in writing well."

First Four Words	Total Number of Words
I can remember it	9
Being humiliated physically and	17
It all stated 1873	25
Someone wanted in despartly	13
So I ran to	25
From the looks of	16
"Yes, may I help	8
"Look here you N---	22
"No not my baby	9
Please I'm begging you	24

Exhibit 5.3 A Sentence Opening Sheet.

So, in column 3 the students analyze their verbs for tense (past, present, or annoying switching); subject-verb agreement (or annoying disagreement); active versus passive voice. Plus, if some students can't even identify which word is the verb, this important information surfaces with a glance at their SOS.

Column 4 is the "wild card" column: it is for any *pet peeve* you have with your students' writing. Maybe you are sick of telling them to "avoid overusing *said* when writing dialogue." So, in column 4 they must write down each use of *said* to self-examine if it is being overused. Then back to the First Dare to Repair some *saids* by replacing them with synonyms for said. Visit the Stack the Deck Web site (listed under "Other Instructional Support Sites" in the Appendix) to see "100 Synonyms for Said."

Other pet peeves teachers want students to eradicate include dull adjectives, using *a lot* a lot, overusing *then,* and misuse of quotation marks in dialog.

The Stack the Deck Writing Program includes the Sentence Opening Sheet in each of its eleven grade level books. All the books have lots of other writing techniques, assignments, and trouble-shooting procedures. (I know this because I authored or coauthored three of the books in their series.) Check out "Teaching Tips for using the Sentence Opening Sheet" at the Stack the Deck Web site for further help on using this outstanding teaching device.

Of course, teachers are tempted to modify other teachers' ideas, and the SOS is no exception. I modified it by moving the "total number of words" count from column 4, its original position, to column 2. I made this adjustment because word count is an easy analysis for students and works well alongside with column 1—even the ones uncertain of their verbs can count as high as the number of words they're likely to write.

Variations on a Good Idea

Sue Borkon, a sixth-grade teacher from the Shorewood School District, Wisconsin, modified the SOS into seven columns: First 3 Words, Action Verbs, Cap Letters, Pet Peeves 1, Pet Peeves 2, Longest Sentence, and Fragments. She shared this alteration with Stack the Deck Web Site in "Teaching Tip #3."

Marge McCormick, Latin/English teacher in Tamaqua, Pennsylvania, used a modified SOS with column 3 labeled "point made." She writes,

First, thank you so much for your enlightening workshop! Just when I had become jaded and discouraged, it gave me the pick-me-up I needed!

I had my students go to their writing portfolios and take out the first paragraph of the year, the mock robbery. Being the first writing assignment of the year, and written on the spur of the moment, there are lots of repetitive sentences and fragments/run-ons. Since we worked on varying sentences immediately after that first assignment, they have improved greatly in the meantime, but they don't see it.

I drew a chart on the board for them to copy: first four words, # of words, and *point made* (2–3 words). They filled it out, and I asked, "How many of you have two or more sentences that start the same way?" At least half of the students—the honest half—raise their hands. "Can you see anything you could improve here now?" Nods of assent, murmurs, and voilà! the realization that they HAVE actually learned something in the time they have spent with me! (Also, that dazed look in a few pairs of eyes. . . . I can just see them thinking, "Gee, maybe the ole lady ain't so dumb after all!") Thank you!!!

Also, I noticed something. I have them write, in two or three words, what the main idea, or point, of each sentence is. In a good paragraph, one with an introduction, logical order, etc., when you read down the list (sentence #1, #2,—down through #5), it reads almost like a thesis statement—a summary of what the paragraph is about. (Two robbers/big men/dressed in black/stole desk supplies/ran from room.) Of course, the ones that aren't done properly make no sense at all! I have a decent sample, which I will be happy to scan and send when I get my hands on it Thursday.

Again, thanks for all your help, and for inspiring me all over again (just in time)!

Thanks to you, Marge, for the kind words and for sharing your *point made* idea. I bet other teachers will be trying it out with their students.

CONCLUSION: MAKING THE CASE FOR WRITING

Writing about course content accomplishes two goals for middle and high school students. First, when writing about a science, social studies, math, language arts, health, or personal finance topic, the student is compelled to process that content far more deeply than when simply answering questions about it on a test.

Second, writing in all these classes fosters a schoolwide atmosphere of the importance of writing. This has been named "writing across the curriculum," and it has been a goal for many secondary schools on and off for nearly twenty-five years. Writing is important: Its benefits extend beyond the students' classroom lives and reach into the real-world lives awaiting them.

This chapter has expanded the role of writing—writing to explain to and inform a reader about what the student is learning. Additionally, it explored ways to exploit the students' desire to talk back, to speak up, by writing persuasively.

Whether assigning the memo, the postcard, a news article, or an informative narrative, we invite the students to deliver the content in new and more motivated ways. This is especially critical when working with our more learning-challenged students.

When students use writing to help them learn new content information, we must do all we can to support them. Writing, like its "literacy twin" reading, is a very challenging enterprise. And for those students of ours who, for whatever reason, are behind in their writing development, it can seem totally impossible.

The general four-step process approach formed a framework for helping students overcome the many obstacles inherent in writing. In short, we pave the way by smoothing out the writing road.

Next, in Chapter Six, we examine more writing assignments designed to help our students learn and to be motivated to process their learning, to think about it, to come to a position on it, and to confidently share it with others.

Developing Advanced Writing Skills

Anyone in the class familiar with this?" asked as I held up a CliffNotes booklet. Not one tenth grader responded, but based on the smirks and lowered eyes, I was sure they knew exactly.

But I fooled them: They weren't going to read one, or be warned not to; rather, they were going to *write* one.

This chapter is devoted to writing. Like Chapter Five, it presents writing assignments designed to help students learn. However, this chapter is different because the writing assignments are longer, more complex, and more advanced.

It presents the Study Guide, the related Chapter Review Booklet, persuasive letters, both in literature and content classes, the e-mailed version of a book review, and the more common essay and brochure.

SYNTHESIZING CONTENT: STUDY GUIDE ACTIVITIES

If you decide a class needs to move beyond short and simple memos and postcards (or the middling news articles and informative narratives), and explore longer and more complex reading-writing assignments, consider Jim Burke's "Study Guide" idea. Jim, a high school teacher in Burlingame, California, suggests in his book *Reading Reminders* (2000) that students write their own study guide or CliffNotes for an assigned reading.

This assignment requires a reader to process the content well enough to be able to instruct another reader on the important points the author is communicating. Beyond mere comprehension of the content, it requires analysis, synthesis, summarization, and organization skills. I liked the idea very much. The benefits of this reading-writing task immediately struck me:

- Surprise from the students facing this new, never-before-assigned task
- Interest from the students at being considered expert enough to write a Study Guide for someone else
- Challenge for the students to pull off this upper-level critical thinking

These three benefits should translate into energy, enthusiasm, and effort from the students. It is using writing to share content understanding. But what about the strugglers in the class? How would they perceive this assignment? Do they have a chance at pulling it off?

Awhile back, I called up Eliza Sher, English and literature teacher at Sheldon High School in Eugene, Oregon. At that point I had never met Eliza, but her reputation in the district was very good: a new teacher with great ideas and strong student rapport.

I introduced myself and explained that I had taught for twenty-four years and now worked in teacher training by offering workshops and seminars. I added that I loved my new job but worried about disconnection from the classroom, so I often volunteered to guest-teach in middle and high school classrooms, so please, please could I come in and try the "Literature Study Guide" idea with her students?

Eliza agreed, saying she needed something new to keep the students' attention as the school year was ending. She suggested a Friday (Why a Friday, I wonder), and we planned how to present the lesson to her two sophomore and junior literature classes. The results were quite good, especially in light of its being the first time either of us had tried this assignment.

Introducing the Assignment

As I reported earlier, I introduced this "Study Guide" assignment to the class by holding up a copy of a CliffNotes booklet and asking the students if they had ever seen one—receiving only sly semi-smiles in return. I said, "That's OK. CliffNotes provide the reader with the short version of fiction, a *synopsis*. What is the advantage of reading a synopsis?"

We discussed the advantages and disadvantages of using CliffNotes, and then I announced, "Well, Cliff is dead. Someone will need to carry on his work."

Startled into a reaction, they cried, "He's dead?"

"Yes, he died this year. And today you will begin to take his place." (It's true. Founder Cliff Hillegass passed away in May 2001.)

I went on to introduce the assignment: writing a Study Guide for another student on "The Californian's Tale" by Mark Twain, the upcoming story in their literature anthology. The student audience would be someone in Eliza's class next term.

Right away a student challenged, "Wait a minute. You want us to write a CliffNotes on this story for some lucky student next term . . . what about us? Who wrote the CliffNotes for us?"

"Well," I replied, "there aren't any for you because last term's students did not write them. They didn't know about Study Guides because your teacher and I didn't know about them until last week when I read this book *Reading Reminders*, by Jim Burke, who suggested that they are a cool way to read and write about literature. Have any of you ever written a CliffNotes on anything?"

No. None had.

I continued, "Well, they are very interesting, but they are tough to do well. You have to read the story very carefully to completely understand it; you have to make decisions about what gets included in the synopsis; and you must write it clearly and interestingly for the audience. And, to tell you the truth, I'm really not sure tenth and eleventh graders can pull this off. Your teacher, Ms. Sher, seems to think you can, but I have some doubts. . . ."

Preparation: Setting Up for Success

You get the idea about priming the pump—getting their attention, their interest, and their energy. Without these factors, writing is just too much for many students. And the motivation here for writing is to look good to another student, meaning looking smart, being knowledgeable, helping out. These are powerful purposes for students, especially struggling students who feel that they rarely or never look good in class.

Next I distributed the yellow cardstock covers with the "Cliff" removed from the CliffNotes logo, so that students could write in their own names. Even though this might seem a bit juvenile or excessive, they liked it. I couldn't tell at the time because they were deliberately cool about it, but Eliza confirmed this to me a few days later. More energy brewing.

Then I distributed a ChecBric, a scoring sheet I would be using to assess their Study Guides. The front of the ChecBric targeted the elements of a successful assignment, that is, the four reading traits from the Oregon State Reading Assessment. (See Exhibit 6.1.) Naturally, since these students resided in Oregon and would be tested on these traits, it made sense to do some "target practice" on them.

This reading-writing task provided excellent practice. It was new and different, and it engaged and motivated the students to try their hardest. The back of the ChecBric listed two writing targets, ideas and conventions, from the Oregon Six Trait Writing Model that would be scored by Eliza, along with the steps the kids could take to be sure they did well. (See Exhibit 6.2.)

Because a key issue in composing study guides is how to organize the synopsis, we provided the students with excerpted copies of several CliffNotes guides, so that they could see how Cliff decided to structure his. We told the students, "Imitating Cliff's format is fine, or inventing your own text structure is good, too. Just be sure to be considerate of your lucky audience by making the information easy to digest."

Finally, we spent ten to fifteen minutes preparing to read the story. The students answered five questions on a Prepare worksheet: 1. What do you predict the *setting* will be? 2. What do you know about the *author?* 3. What do these *key vocabulary* words mean? 4. What do you notice about the *text structure* of the story? 5. What are the names of the *characters* coming up in the story?

As indicated repeatedly in earlier chapters, the time spent at the Prepare stage of the reading process is money in the bank. Without it, struggling students will flounder with comprehension and appreciation of everything you give them.

Over the next three class periods, the students read the story, made decisions on content, and drafted their Study Guides.

Here are two excerpts from Haley's Study Guide:

> Synopsis:
> The story starts as the narrator meets Henry. the Narrator had been prospecting all day & was glad when Henry invited him in. the cottage has a noticeable woman's touch, & the narrator quickly picks up on Henry's affectionate worship of his wife.

The narrator soon learns that Henry's wife is out of town, and makes plans to stay & meet her when she returns.

Henry's friend, Tom, stops by. Henry reads a letter sent from his wife & believes Tom has feelings for her upon reading it. When the expected time of his wife's arrival had come, Henry began to worry. . . .

Henry suddenly drifted into a deep sleep. The Narrator becomes confused. Tom & Joe tell the narrator that Henry's wife has been dead for 19 years, & Henry has not been sane since. They do this on the anniversary of her death. . .

—Connection—

This story actually reminds me of myself, in a way, when I was a child. When I would get a cut or scrape, I would scream & cry, and then I was given attention to make me calm down & act normal. They would do this by comforting me & giving me a bandaid. Once the bandaid had been on a few days & fell off, though, I would cry all over again. Henry is like me, being emotionally wounded by his wife's death. The calming parents are represented by Henry's friends, Tom & Joe. The bandaid represents the time when Henry is okay. The time that the bandaid comes off represents the time when his wife's anniversary rolls around. . . .

Myke, another student in the class, was successful, too. He took a different approach. (See Exhibit 6.3.) This assignment was challenging to him, but he successfully completed it, I think, for three reasons. First, he was motivated to try. In his Student Self-Reflection, required at the end of the assignment, he wrote: "This task was interesting. I was never asked to do a 'Cliff's Notes' for anything before." He liked it. Myke liked it! I believe he liked writing his "Myke's Notes" because it elevated him to a position of expert. He'd never been asked to be the expert before, and it made him feel good. He had something worth sharing with the world (specifically, Eliza's next year's class).

Second, the assignment's structure gave him a fighting chance at success.

And third, his teacher had prepared him for this earlier in the semester by teaching him the elements of fiction, key literary terms, and how to critique literature. Even though he had never written a Study Guide before, he had important prior experiences.

ChecBric for a Study Guide

"The Californian's Tale"
by Mark Twain

Checklist	Rubric

Checklist

Target 1: I proved my understanding of the story.

___ My "study guide" summarizes the plot

___ My "study guide" introduces the characters

___ My "study guide" explains the setting

___ My "study guide" evaluates the theme

Rubric

Trait 1: Demonstrates comprehension

6 = **thorough** degree of understanding of the content

5 = **strong** degree of understanding of the content

4 = **competent** degree of understanding of the content

3 = **limited, inconsistent, incomplete** understanding

2 = **confused or inaccurate** understanding of the content

1 = **missing** degree of understanding of the content

Target 2: I am able to connect this story to one or more other sources.

___ My "study guide" connects this story to something else:
an event in my life, or
a friend/family member's life, or
another story, or
a TV show, or
a movie, or
the news

Trait 2: Demonstrates ability to extend understanding of the work to other source(s)

6 = **thorough and complex** degree of extension

5 = **strong** degree of extension

4 = **competent** degree of extension

3 = **limited, inconsistent, incomplete** extension

2 = **superficial or flawed** degree of extension

1 = **missing** degree of extension

Target 3: I provided feedback to the author.

___ My "study guide" critiques the author's writing ability shown in the story

___ My "study guide" critiques the author's ideas in the story [critique = what I liked, disliked, impressed me, confused me, suggestions for improvement . . .]

Trait 3: Demonstrates a text analysis and evaluation of the author's writing

6 = **thorough and convincing** degree of analysis/evaluation

5 = **strong** degree of analysis and evaluation

4 = **competent** degree of analysis and evaluation

3 = **incomplete** degree of analysis and evaluation

2 = **superficial, confused, unfounded** analysis/evaluation

1 = **missing** degree of analysis and evaluation

Exhibit 6.1 Reading ChecBric: "The Californian's Tale" Study Guide.

Exhibit 6.1 Continued

Next Time

The writing process we employed included the Prepare and First Dare stages. And that's as far as we went. It was June, the school year was ending, and we felt that the students had accomplished enough. Remember, the writing process is a flexible problem-solving tool, not a dictatorial lockstep course.

Of course, if we try this expository writing assignment again, we would want to see how far the students could go with it, including self-editing with a Sentence Opening Sheet (from Chapter Five) and a visit to the Editor's Table, as well as peer partner editors and a mini-conference with the teacher, all of which are coming up in Chapter Seven. Then, maybe sign up for the computers and allow the students to word process their guides, print them, and ready them for the next term's class. This is a good example of using writing to share content learning.

Or, if time concerns limited the assignment, perhaps students could be placed into teams to cooperatively put together a Study Guide.

Chemistry Review Booklets

While the real CliffNotes were written as synopses for literature, this same Study Guide idea works across the curriculum. Pat McDougald, a chemistry teacher in Georgia, employed the student-authored Study Guide assignment with her juniors.

ChecBric for a Study Guide

"The Californian's Tale"
by Mark Twain

Checklist	Rubric

Checklist

Target 2: I organized my "Study Guide," so it is easy to follow.

___ My "study guide" is easy to follow.

___ My "study guide" has clear sections.

___ My "study guide" has a sequence.

___ My "study guide" has an inviting introduction.

___ My "study guide" has a strong conclusion.

___ My "study guide" has smooth transitions.

___ My "study guide" has effectively placed details.

Target 6: I followed all the rules of writing.

___ My "study guide" uses punctuation to guide my reader through my ideas.

___ My "study guide" has correct spelling to help my reader understand my ideas.

___ My "study guide" has correct grammar and usage to contribute to my clarity and style.

___ My "study guide" used paragraph breaks to reinforce my organization structure.

___ My "study guide" needs little or no editing—it is publishable.

Student Self-Reflection on this Task

Rubric

Trait 2: Demonstrates clear organization

6 = **compelling** order and structure

5 = **strong** order and structure

4 = **present** order and structure

3 = **inconsistent, skeletal** order and structure

2 = **lacks a clear** order and structure

1 = **haphazard, disjointed** order and structure

Trait 6: Demonstrates control of standard writing conventions

6 = **exceptionally strong** control of conventions

5 = **strong** control of conventions

4 = **control** of conventions

3 = **limited** control of conventions

2 = **little** control of conventions with frequent or significant errors

1 = **numerous errors show no** control of conventions

Teacher Comments on this Task

Exhibit 6.2 **Writing ChecBric: "The Californian's Tale" Study Guide.**

Title: The Californian's Tale
Author: Mark Twain

Author Information: Mark Twain—Died 1910. Also wrote Huck Fin.
    Moved to S/F.

Setting: Takes place in Cali. about 1870 after gold Rush.

Narroration: 1st person limited.

Characters: Henry (main character)
    Tom
    Joe } minor characters.
    Charlie
    Wife (mentioned)
    Narrorator.

Summary:
    The narrorator a mining town from the past and tells how the town looks now. It used to be a busy and booming town, but now it is a ghost town. The narrorator finds a man about 45 yrs old. He did not have a deserted look. His house was cleand a well kept. The narrorator goes in with the man into the cabin. The narrorator is surprised. The cabin was not like a regular cabin of a miner. The Cabin was well kept and well decorated. "Henry" the miner withe cabin seem to be infatuated with his wife.

Exhibit 6.3 Student Sample Study Guide: "The Californian's Tale."

Source: Eliza Sher, English teacher, Sheldon High School, Eugene, Oregon.

She generated the idea while attending my "Practical Strategies for Struggling Readers and Writers" workshop. She combined two suggestions I made: Study Guides and computer desktop publishing.

Her directions to the class were to create a "review for the final exam." The chemistry textbook chapters were divided into boldface sections, and each student chose a section. They were asked to include word problems when applicable, appropriate images to support the words, and rather than just giving simple definitions, the emphasis was placed on concept development. They were given some class time to begin work on this and two ninety-minute periods in the library using Microsoft Publisher.

For sharing the results, Pat ran copies of all the booklets and distributed them to the students, so they would have them as study guides. And they were useful! Check out the excerpts from two student booklets in Exhibit 6.4 and Exhibit 6.5.

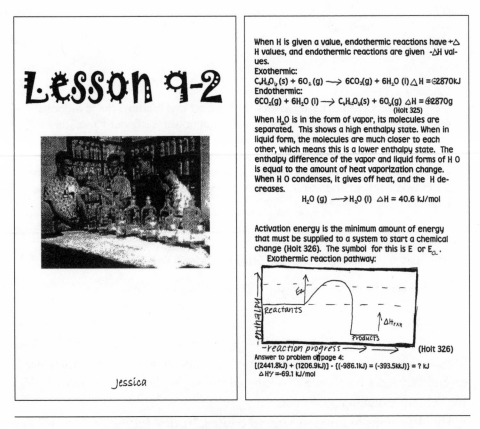

Exhibit 6.4 Chemistry Study Guide: Jessica.

Source: Pat McDougald, chemistry teacher, Harrison High School, Kennesaw, Georgia.

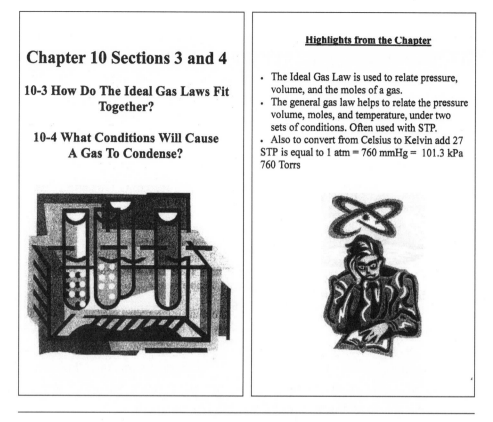

Chapter 10 Sections 3 and 4

10-3 How Do The Ideal Gas Laws Fit Together?

10-4 What Conditions Will Cause A Gas To Condense?

Highlights from the Chapter

- The Ideal Gas Law is used to relate pressure, volume, and the moles of a gas.
- The general gas law helps to relate the pressure volume, moles, and temperature, under two sets of conditions. Often used with STP.
- Also to convert from Celsius to Kelvin add 27 STP is equal to 1 atm = 760 mmHg = 101.3 kPa 760 Torrs

Exhibit 6.5 Chemistry Study Guide: Ryan.

Source: Pat McDougald, chemistry teacher, Harrison High School, Kennesaw, Georgia.

PERSUASIVE WRITING: LETTER ACTIVITIES

Many students appreciate the chance to watch a videotape for learning new content instead of reading a book or listening to a mini-lecture—especially when the video was designed for entertainment rather than instruction. Teacher Amy Gallagher took advantage of this to spice up a class on Colonial American History by assigning Disney's *Pocahontas.*

Of course, Amy is a kindhearted teacher to incorporate a cartoon into the course. But she is more than kindhearted, she is tough. The cartoon viewing was really a prewriting activity because it served to prepare her below-grade-level students for a challenging writing assignment: a persuasive letter about the movie. The students were told before watching it that they would be required to *write* about it; that is, to take a *position* on this controversial film and *defend* the position with reasons.

One of the students wrote this persuasive letter on the computer:

Dear Mr. Roy Disney,

Your movie "Pocahontas" was very successful in teaching kids about her spirit, even though it is not factual. . . . Children have enjoyed this film even though it was not historically accurate.

The movie is accurate in portraying Pocahontas' rebellious spirit. In [real] life, her name was "Matoaka," but her parents gave her the nickname "Pocahontas" which means "hard to control." The movie shows her rebelling against her tribe to save John Smith. The movie also shows Pocahontas rebelling against her father when he says no one should talk to the savages. But she is hard to control, and she goes to talk to John.

The name "Pocahontas" also means playful. In the movie, they show her jump off a cliff to join her friend instead of walking down the side. What is playful is that jumping off the cliff was fun, yet dangerous.

In conclusion, the movie was good even though it wasn't factual. Pocahontas' spirit was expressed nicely, Kids' movies should be for kids to learn that a person was alive, so they will want to learn more about her in school.

Sincerely yours,
Anthony T.

Anthony generated a position on the film ("successful in teaching kids," "accurate in portraying her spirit") and then defended it with evidence from the film. Congratulations. This is upper-level critical thinking that is revealed through the persuasive mode of writing. As I stated in Chapter Five, persuasive writing requires the student not only to understand the content information as well as the expository mode does but to additionally come to a *position* about that content and then to *argue convincingly* to support that position. All students, and especially our struggling students, clearly need work on this.

Daughter of Powhatan, Pocahontas, a indian princess, real name was matoaka. Her Child hood Knickname means "Playful" "hard to control".

Figure 6.1 Student Visualization: Pocahontas.

Amy, Anthony's teacher, picked up this writing assignment idea while attending one of my workshops on and then modified it to better fit her teaching situation. She decided to incorporate drawing into the writing Prepare stage. She recognized that the role of the pictorial is important for readers who struggle with understanding.

Figure 6.1 shows Anthony's visualization of Pocahontas's personality trait "rebellious spirit." By drawing a picture, he solidified his understanding. Then he brought his understanding into his letter writing.

Writing a Historical Persuasive/Informative Letter

Persuasion is the most challenging mode of writing because it goes beyond exposition (explaining, informing) to convincing the reader of the value of a position, belief, or course of action. The letter is a merger of both modes. In Anthony's letter (quoted in the preceding section), the task is easy because surely the recipient will agree with the assertion that the movie is good.

Of course, students were told that they could choose what position to take on the movie. The teacher does not attempt to control students' reactions to any content material. All the teacher does is present that material in meaningful, engaging ways, and then ask the students to react to it.

This reading-writing assignment is based on an inquiry into the content: The students were given a problem with data to analyze. That is, they had to compare and contrast historical sources to construct a position on one of the sources (the movie). Inquiry enlivens the instruction of content because it forces students to process it with a motivating purpose. It allows them to construct their own knowledge. Inquiry helps them develop a "disposition to write" (Hillocks, 1995, p. 34).

Some students reacted negatively to the movie. From another school (mine), a student wrote the following persuasive letter to the Disney Studios:

I' am a eight grade student at James Monroe Middle school in Eugene, Oregon. In my Block class [language arts and U.S. History], we have been learning about Pocahontas. What we did was read a book called *The Double Life of Pocahontas* [Jean Fritz, Viking Press, July 1987]. After that we watched the Disney movie "Pocahontas." The facts are that you made a lot of things up.

For instance, you made Pocahontas look like she was at least 20 years old when she first met John Smith. But when she really met John, she was only 11 or 12 years old. A couple more things about Pocahontas: I find it was weird that she was able to learn English within 3 seconds. I really don't think anyone would be able to do that.

In the movie, she was the only kid [in the family], but she actually had at least 6 brothers or sisters. How about her Grandmother Willo? Come on! A talking tree? I know for a fact that Pocahontas did not go talk to a tree. One more thing about Pocahontas, I really don't think she would sing while she was swimming under water. Now about [Governor] Radcliffe. In the movie you made him out to look like a villain, witch he really wasn't.

One good fact that I saw in the movie was when Chief Powhatan was about to kill John Smith, but just before he did, Pocahontas dove on John, so the Chief would not kill him. That really happened.

Sincerely,

Jr.

His opinion differs, but Jr. is doing the same thing as Anthony: thinking about the content being taught, analyzing a source, comparing it to other sources, arriving at an opinion, writing about it, and then defending it with reasons. That's inquiry.

Congratulations to this student, who was on an Individual Educational Plan for language skills. Despite the punctuation, grammar, and paragraphing errors, Jr.'s message comes through loud and clear.

I will outline a few techniques for guiding him, and his classmates, to the Repair stage shortly. After all, we wouldn't want anyone at the Disney Studios to reject his well-supported opinion due to mechanical errors.

For more student examples of this historical persuasive letter, and a suggested ChecBric for it, see my earlier book *Great Performances* (Lewin and Shoemaker, 1998).

While the memo and postcard described in Chapter Five can offer students an opportunity to go beyond explaining their likes and dislikes to persuading an author to consider an opinion of the author's writing, they are typically too short a format for in-depth argument. The persuasive letter allows space in which to argue convincingly. Plus it simultaneously incorporates the expository mode because the student writers are explaining and informing their reading audience about the topic. And letter writing comes as a welcome break from essay writing.

Various forms of this persuasive letter exist: write to an author expressing likes, dislikes, and persuasive suggestions for improvement (an expanded memo); a letter to a historical figure or to a scientist or researcher; a letter to a fictional character, or a letter to a political figure or a community leader. The audience is important: The person to receive the letters provides the students with incentives for writing. They are sharing their newly acquired content understandings with a real person. Speaking of a real person, how about a letter to an administrator?

Triggering a Change at School

When high school students study difficult and important content, they need help processing the information. That's why teacher Herb Felsenfeld took on the topic of the effects of junk food on the human brain. He began by supplying his special day class at Woodside High School in California with colored paper to make Folded File Folders (FFFs, introduced in Chapter Two).

The students used their FFFs as tracking devices as they read letters to the local newspaper's editor, a Web site titled "Caffeine, Sugar, and Bone Loss," and an editorial titled "Coke Loses Its Fizz."

The result was active learning. So, active, in fact, that the class questioned why their school offered soft drinks to them. Herb and instructional associate Lucy Lopez guided them through a persuasive letter writing project. They shared a copy of the class letter with me (see Exhibit 6.6).

Herb attached a note to the class letter that said: "Repaired: Our final letter—it worked to stop serving sodas from vending machines at Woodside High." Congratulations to the students for successful learning of new content information followed by putting it to excellent use. Right on. (Write on.)

Talking to the Big Shots

How about a persuasive letter to a corporate CEO? Consider a high school example from Alhambra, California. Social studies teacher John Bonar (at the Ramona Convent Secondary School) instructed his eleventh-grade students on the topic of the globalization of the world economy, the movement toward cheaper labor, and the growth of sweatshops. Writing in teams of four, the juniors wrote persuasive

Mrs. Linda Common, Principal
Woodside High School

Dear Mrs. Common,

In our 2nd period Science class we have discovered that sodas have 1/4 cup of sugar per can. We also found that too much soda can lead to weak bones and osteoporosis, because it depletes calcium from the body. It is especially important for young women to have calcium.

We are requesting healthy choices in the vending machines.

These could be:
Apple juice
Cranberry juice
Apple-grape juice
Orange juice
Natural juices, such as Odwalla

The enclosed article gives you more information about this issue. Would you please tell us if these drinks could be added to the vending machines? Thank you for your time, from the classroom in B-13.

Exhibit 6.6 A Truly Persuasive Letter.

Source: Herb Felsenfeld, special day class teacher, and instructional associate Lucy Lopez, Woodside High School, Woodside, California.

letters to the CEOs of U.S. corporations addressing this important social and economic issue. See Exhibit 6.7 for an example.

As readers, we clearly hear the strong voice of the students coming off the page. They write with passion, conviction, and knowledge about this topic. For students to write with a strong voice, they need confidence in their topic and in their writing abilities. Their teacher supported them in both these critical areas. You can be sure that he employed multiple resources in his instruction, that he provided reading support through comprehension strategies, and that he helped his students consider various text structures for organizing their letters. They were clearly motivated to write: they felt they had something to say, they had gained expertise,

Ramona Convent Secondary School
U.S. Department of Education Blue Ribbon School
1701 West Ramona Road, Alhambra CA 91803-3080

March 29, 2000

Michael Eisner, CEO
Disney
500 South Buena Vista Street
Burbank, CA 91521

Dear Mr. Eisner,

It has recently come to our attention that the Disney Corporation has utilized the services of sweatshops for the manufacture of its products. This fact strikes us as largely appalling considering Disney's long-standing commitment to wholesome programming and family values. These sweatshops are the epitome of injustice and oppression, bearing down on the poor and impoverished of this world who are incapable of standing up for themselves. You have, in effect, become a villain more monstrous than any you have created for the screen.

Are your morals so compromised that you are impervious to the injustice of sweatshops, which you are instituting? Does Disney have a code of conduct for all its factories? If so, how does the company enforce these codes? Are there consequences for the factories that violate these codes?

As representatives of one of 15 Catholic High Schools in the Los Angeles area, we cannot in good conscious support a company rooted in the exploitation of the lives of those who are less fortunate, especially if the well-being of these lives are compromised for mere profits.

Disney should stand for children not on them.

Awaiting your response,

Debbie

Brianna

Cynthia

Kristinne

Exhibit 6.7 High School Students Addressing Public Issues.

Source: John Bonar, teacher, Ramona Convent Secondary School, Alhambra, California.

and they needed to speak up. This is why humans write. And judging by the quality of the letter in Exhibit 6.7, their teacher surely set up some solid Repair activities as well.

This is big-time sharing of ideas, perspectives, opinions. The persuasive letter is the vehicle for the students' thinking, learning, reading, and writing.

Literary Persuasive Letters

Naturally, persuasive writing is not only useful for historical events, global economic issues, or school policies. This writing assignment works across the board, including the study of literature.

Book Review Persuasive E-Mail

Check out this e-mail I received from Jerry Blum, a seventh-grade student in Adina Marcus's class in East Brunswick, New Jersey:

> To: larry@larrylewin.com
> Date: Fri, 08 Jun 2001 12:47:34 GMT
>
> Dear Mr. Lewin:
>
> Anything new on your end? Anyway, I'm writing about The Toilet Paper Tigers by Gordon Korman. It's funny and suspenseful, you know, one of those books you can never seem to put down, which is great coming from me because I'm not a big book fan like Ms. Marcus, but Gordon Korman keeps me coming back for more.
>
> He seems to make you laugh on every page while developing a strong plot that doesn't contradict itself. It also includes a large list of characters that all are very different and hilarious, it's amazing to imagine how he thinks of all of this.
>
> Anyway, the book is about a bunch of kids that are lousy at baseball and missed being picked so they all wound up being on a team with a coach that doesn't know anything about baseball and with his niece that takes a picture of them changing and blackmails them with it! Its a load of laughs and you should really read it over the summer. See how the worst team somehow manages to climb the champion's ladder.
>
> Sincerely,
> Jerry

Adina had attended my workshop and suggested a nice replacement for the traditional book report: A letter to a friend urging the reading (or rejection) of a book. I expressed interest in the idea, and the next thing I knew I was volunteering to be a "friend"—an audience for her students.

Adina e-mailed me to say that the combination of a new, authentic audience (me) and the use of technology (e-mail) made this writing assignment a crowd-pleaser for her literature students.

All the students succeeded with it. They all had an opinion of their book, they stated it clearly, and then they supported it. Congratulations. They had a real purpose for writing and e-mailing. They shared their book critiques by merging expository and persuasive writing. Upper-level critical thinking coupled with reading and writing. And congratulations to their teacher, Adina, for paving the way for them. She is very interested in "distance learning" with technology. She was featured in a fine article about her efforts; see the "General Information" section of the Appendix.

Short Story Critical Review Letters

Back in Chapter Four, I discussed use of the SnapShots reading-tracking device to evoke a reader's strong visual images during the reading of Gary Soto's short story "The Challenge." In Chapter Five, I discussed how the exercise formed a base for writing postcards to the author. This reading comprehension activity idea transformed itself again, into a longer writing assignment: a critical review of the short story. The teacher, Eliza Sher, wanted to link reading of literature and writing in the persuasive mode. Each student was to select an audience for the review and write a letter to a friend, the school's newspaper, next semester's class, or to Eliza herself recommending continued assignment of the story to future classes or dropping it from the curriculum. Nice linkage: Reading and writing are the twin pillars of literacy.

So the SnapShots reading activity became a prewriting exercise in that the sticky note drawings were now used to generate ideas for the critical review letters. Additionally, to assist her students at the writing Prepare stage, Eliza reviewed the components of a critical book review: brief overview of the story to help your reader get a sense for it; connections to other stories for comparison purposes; pluses, minuses, suggested areas for improvement—the critique (the major focus of the letter) and some analysis of the author's context—the background, historical era, or culture that may have affected the writing.

You may recognize these four components as the state of Oregon's Four Reading Traits (see Reading and Writing Standards in the Appendix). Eliza is always looking for opportunities for target practice on the state's standards.

She made a modification to this persuasive letter assignment. Instead of requiring her tenth and eleventh graders to include all four targeted traits in a letter, she pulled the fourth trait out and made it into its own mini-writing assignment: a one-paragraph "Opener." This served the students well in that it made the critical review letters a bit easier to write, and the author's context seemed to fit the expository mode better than the persuasive. Lindsey wrote in her "Opener":

> Gary Soto was brought up in and around Fresno, California, and he is Mexican-American. I think that all the characters in the story were modeled after [real] people in Soto's life. I think also that he used past experiences to build the story. All the details were too well-structured to be made up off the top of someone's head.

Jeremy decided that he needed more background information than what was provided in class. So at home he researched the author on the Internet and discovered that Gary Soto's grandparents emigrated from Mexico and found jobs as U.S. farm laborers, and Soto learned their work ethic by doing chores, picking grapes, and painting house address numbers on street curbs. Jeremy also learned that Soto's father died in a factory accident, and his mother raised the three kids with help from the grandparents. Soto didn't have books to read as a child and did not start writing until he was in college. Jeremy presented all this material, and correctly remembered to cite his source: http://www.unomaha.edu/~unochlit/soto.html.

Jeremy concluded with his own analysis: "I think that Gary use some of the setting he use to live in. Gary use some Spanaish in his story to make the story feel more realist. I also think that Gary Soto had the same problem when he was in eigth grade."

Congratulations to Jeremy for going beyond the minimum and showing interest and initiative. Teachers love it when students take an assignment and run with it.

Of course, the paragraph quoted from Jeremy's work is his First Dare. It needs some Repair. Depending on whether or not the students will be sending the

"Opener" paragraphs with their critical review letters, he might benefit from some or all of the three rounds of repair, self-repair, peer partners, and teacher conference, which are discussed in more detail in the next chapter.

EXPRESSING IDEAS AND OPINIONS: A SAMPLE LESSON

September 11, 2001, is a tough topic, but it's one that students felt a real need to consider. I discussed one approach to it Chapter Two, in the context of Dorothy Syfert's eighth-grade language arts and social studies block class. Here's how we continued to use the unit.

Dorothy and I used the KWT (What I Already *Know*—Store my *Work*—What I Would *Teach* Someone) to facilitate student processing of both feelings and thoughts, emotions and ideas, in the days following the terrorist attacks on New York and Washington, D.C. On the cover of the KWT folder the students wrote what they already knew about Osama bin Laden. Inside the folder they stored the work they were doing on this topic, including an emotional reaction paragraph they wrote the day after the attacks, an article from a Web site using sticky notes to help track their comprehension, and an article from a magazine with Stop Signs inserted to prompt understanding.

On the back of the KWT folder they created a graphic organizer representing what they would teach another person about this difficult topic. Looking through their KWT folders to review what they had learned, the students now had to summarize, synthesize, prioritize, and organize the information.

The next day Dorothy and I led her students to transition from reading to writing by taking the newly learned information from their reading and applying it in a meaningful writing assignment: writing a letter about the events of September 11.

First, Dorothy led the class in a discussion on the possible audiences for their letters: to a family member of a deceased or injured victim, to the editor of *Teen Newsweek* magazine, to a celebrity, or to a friend.

Next, Dorothy explained to them how their letters would be assessed: three traits from the Oregon Writing Scoring Guide (her rubric). She selected

• Ideas and content

• Voice

• Conventions

Because she knew that organizing ideas can be a giant obstacle to writers, she led the students in a brainstorm of possible formats (organization patterns) for the letter, so that the students each had a game plan for structuring their ideas.

For example, one possible format she and the class developed worked like this:

Paragraph 1 = review of my first feelings, reactions to the attacks

Paragraph 2 = intellectual response, analysis, and explanation why it happened

Paragraph 3 = my hopes, thoughts, fears for the future

Students were free to use this pattern or create their own.

Now the students opened their blue KWT folders and reexamined the contents—the work they had done during this mini-unit—to review what they had read, felt, and discussed. They also studied their graphic organizers on the back of the folder.

All these activities served to help the students Prepare for writing. They took quite a bit of class time to accomplish, but given the difficulty of the topic, it was a necessary investment.

First Dares

With this preparatory work on their desks, they composed their First Dares (rough drafts). Not surprisingly, student letters reflected a wide range of responses with a variety of points of view. Surprisingly, all the students were able to proceed with minimal stalling, balking, complaining, or teacher assistance. No—not really surprising, given the amount and quality of their preparation. They were quite comfortable putting pencil to paper.

Both David and Cas, two students with differing ability levels, were engaged throughout the period. David wrote the following for *Teen Newsweek:*

September 11, 2001 was a horrible day!

I was at my house at around 7:45 when I heard about the bombing. Where were you?

When I heard the news I was shocked, then I felt sad for the people who died. And I wondered what planes crashed into the trade center Buildings.

How were you feelng? I think that was the wrong thing to do. Osama bin Ladon souldn't of done it but He did any way. I mean if He would do anything for His religon why did He bring war to it.

> I Head that a woman was dateing an arabian and on the morning of September 10, 2001 the woman came Home, And found a note that said ", don't fly any planes on spetember 11, 2001 or go in any malls on Howlloween. A I was planing on going to a thing in the gatnay Mall.
>
> What do you think about that insudent. I heard Osama bin Laden is a terrorist but if He's the Brains behind this one I wouldn't know what to call Him.

Compare this article to the letter Cas wrote to his community expressing an opposing point of view:

> Hello Eugene,
> By now you all are surely well informed about the so-called attack on America and our enemy. But have you ever seen from their point of view? Have you ever thought of us as "the enemy?"
> They hate us, our country, and our government. But not without reason. They hate the fact that we're a wealthy superpower, occupying their holy lands and backing Israel rahter than Iraq. They hate us shoving our culture into their faces, with McDonalds, and MTV.
> We can always blame this whole shenanigan on Osama bin Laden, the prime suspect and alleged perpetrator, but the fact is, he isn't the root of the problem. The root, my friends, is the hatred for America, shared by millions across the Middle East. Half of the problem lies with us, because it is important to realize that we are not a perfect country. But it is also important not to take the terrorists' vengeful stance, for you could become just as terrible as them.
> They claim these are acts of God, that Ala is the One that passes judgement on us. But the religion of Islam isn't one of terror & destruction.
> We do not need to single out Muslims in our community ordiscriminate against. Just do whatever you can to help.

Well done, both of them. They were motivated to write, I believe, because they had something to say (they had a real audience to write to), they wanted to look good (they had studied the topic and had learned new information), and they were confident enough to proceed (teacher-orchestrated preparation). Plus, and this is a big plus, they actually were continuing to learn about the topic and their opinions on that topic as they wrote. The learning didn't stop as with a test or a quiz, it continued as they thought, reviewed, reflected, and wrote.

Repairs

Now, before these letters were ready to be sent, some repairs were in order. Ideally, students should go through three rounds of repair: self-editing, peer partners, and the student-teacher conference. In this mini-unit, however, the students only did round 1. And that's OK, right? Remember that no teacher must feel obligated to run all three rounds of repair. In fact, no teacher even needs to get to the Repair stage on every single assignment. The reality of too many students, a ton of curriculum, and too little time sometimes forces us to cut the process short. That's OK.

So, Dorothy and I instructed the students to self-edit their letters by reading them over to see how well they did on the three targets: ideas and content, voice, and conventions. They were given a student-friendly version of the state's scoring guide with language describing the various degrees of proficiency for the three targeted traits, and they were given time to "make any adjustments in their letters" to move up their proficiency. Providing the students with colored pencils increased interest in self-repair.

The End

Because time limits ended the writing process here, the letters were not mailed to their intended audiences. The only sharing was within the class. We kind of felt badly about this but felt no need to overly chastise ourselves. The reading-writing activities were successful, after all. The students employed a number of key reading comprehension strategies, they discussed and debated ideas, they conducted an inquiry into a difficult event, they thought about reasons and causes to add to their emotions, and they composed all this on paper.

I could have chosen a different lesson plan that ended with publication of student-written work and a response from the intended audience—a bigger deal. But the reality is that we cannot pull this off very often, and there's no need to feel guilty when it doesn't happen. Dorothy and I did a good job designing this unit on the fly, and her students benefited from it.

OTHER TRADITIONAL WRITING ASSIGNMENTS

Thus far I've been describing new possibilities for incorporating writing in both content area and literature classrooms: Study Guides, Chapter Review Booklets, persuasive letters, book reviews, and e-mail messages. These writing assignments offer students a chance to look good by sharing knowledge—their understanding—about their studies. Additionally, they provide students with the opportunity to talk back by speaking up and sharing their supported opinions about that content. Very powerful purposes for writing.

But the more traditional writing assignments are still worth considering. Never forget that some of the tried and true expository assignments still work as well as ever to elicit student sharing.

The Good Ole Essay

While the writing assignments described earlier are novel to students and thus apt to be more motivating, essay writing is still an important mode—not only to process content in a secondary classroom but also to prepare for the work kids will encounter if they attend college.

When assigning an essay, as with any expository prompt, always remember to pave the way for student success. First, you can assist students in preparing for writing an essay. Especially important is not to assume that all students understand the purpose of an essay, the audience, and the text structure. Explain whether the task will be to produce a personal essay, one that offers the reflected thinking of the author and includes a first-person stance. (John McPhee is a great example of a skilled personal essayist. His Web site is worth visiting.) Alternatively, you can assign the more formal essay, in which the author stays in the background and writes in the more neutral third person. Likewise it's useful to address some structural options with your students, so that they understand whether you expect a comparison-contrast organizational pattern, a chronological sequence, or an assertion-support format.

Second, make sure students have adequate information under their belts, so that the dreaded "writer's block" is reduced. Naturally, this acquired content comes from your instruction of the topic. Or perhaps it comes from an assigned independent research project.

Third, explain the parameters of the essay assignment—as I've said repeatedly, students must know and understand what success involves if they're to have much hope of succeeding. So provide them with the scoring sheet (a checklist, a rubric, or a hybrid ChecBric) before they begin the writing process. Additionally, some teachers discuss the time parameters of the assignments with due dates for each component. You could even borrow teacher Dorothy Syfert's technique of distributing blank monthly calendars and instructing the students to fill in target dates for completion of each required step.

Fourth, if research is involved in the essay writing, it's essential to address with students the role of citations, bibliographical entries, and paraphrasing versus plagiarism. (All these topics come up in Chapter Seven.)

Brochures

Students like writing brochures. I believe this is because brochures are different from the usual writing assignments in that they have columns, they include graphics, they get folded, and they are relatively short. Different is good. Short is good.

Brochures can be written on any topic in any subject at any grade level. I have seen student-authored brochures from all over the country on topics such as these:

- A novel in literature
- A state or country in social studies
- Grammar rules in middle school language arts
- Fairy tales and bias in high school English

Of course, these examples are meant not to limit a teacher's creative ideas on other topics for brochure writing but to open doors for creative pondering. For example, many schools wrestled with how to commemorate the one-year anniversary of the September 11 terrorist attacks. Dorothy Syfert, my former teaching colleague, called me to brainstorm some appropriate activities.

As described earlier, she and I had collaborated in October 2001, a month after the attacks. Even though I was nervous about addressing this highly emotional topic with eighth graders, we designed a successful mini-unit. Beginning with the students' emotional reactions to the tragic events, we moved them into an analysis of various theories as to why anyone would plan and carry out such actions against the United States. Now, one year later, we needed to come up with an activity to help students process the anniversary of the events. We opted for a brochure on "Various Explanations of September 11."

Why a brochure? Even though it didn't really fit the topic, it seemed like a useful format for students to share their ideas because of the intrinsic rewards of using it. We had considered opting for an essay, but decided that early in the school year, with a new class and with many other topics to get to, a brochure would be a reasonable choice.

And it was. It caught the students' attention because it empowered them to play the role of a knowledgeable analyst who independently brainstormed possible reasons, who met in cooperative teams to discuss ideas, and who read materials presenting differing points of view.

Read Dara's brochure (in Exhibit 6.8) as an example of the good work Dorothy's students produced.

Whatever topic is assigned, the same kinds of teaching issues mentioned for other expository assignments should be addressed, including content acquisition, audience and purpose, text structure and format (number of columns, role of graphics, font and size limitations), time and grading parameters, editing and proofreading requirements (Repair), and the possible option of word processing.

Deputizing the word processor (or even better, publishing software) is a good way to entice strugglers to become energized while writing. Brochures are different, real-world, and fun to compose. If computers are available, and you have the energy to include them, the students will have access to programs for easing the brochure's formatting, that is, removing the giant headache of trying to get the printer to print three columns *front and back*. See "Software and Equipment" in the Appendix.

FINAL THOUGHTS ON WRITING FOR THE SHARE STAGE

All the writing assignments described here promote student sharing of understanding. The Share stage means making a big deal of the students' efforts to work hard at writing. Sharing is the culmination, the conclusion, the payoff. It helps you build the motivation student writers need to go through the hard work of the first three stages in order to arrive here; that is, continuing the motivating purpose to produce a quality paper. When you can do so, move beyond the classroom and actually send the finished work to the audience the students have chosen to address.

But it isn't necessary to overcommit and create a headache for yourself. Not every single student-written piece must be shared. That is, it is OK to create the big-deal payoff only periodically, not for every assignment. This is based on reality: How much time and energy does a teacher have to pull this off? The more the better, but do not be consumed by guilt if you don't do it all the time.

And you don't have to go it alone—help is available to you at the Share stage. Other people are interested in publishing your students' written work. Here are a few magazines that receive student submissions for publication: *Merlyn's Pen, Stone Soup,* and Karen Kellaher at *Adventures in Writing.* Also, a number of Web sites will publish student work. (See Gail Szeliga's article under "Outlets for Student Work" in the Appendix. The section also lists Web sites for magazine contacts.)

Your own school district will have resources, too. Inquire about newsletters, student anthologies, display cases, and Web sites (both the school's site and the district's site). This will take some work on your part, but you know the students will be thrilled to be published—especially those students who perceive themselves as "not good at writing."

Of course, whenever student-written work is submitted to the public, it makes sense to add a fourth round of Repair: the editor-in-chief. That's you. I recommend going over the students' papers very carefully, searching for any last problems before you present them to the outside world. I know this contradicts my assertion that correcting errors retards student writing growth. And it is super-time-consuming. But the last thing you want to occur is for someone outside your classroom to read your students' writing and misperceive all the hard work they (and you) have put in due to some misspellings, choppy sentences, or messiness.

Now, I haven't done that for the student writing samples in this book because it's important for teachers contemplating a lesson to see real-world results, but that creative spelling and punctuation still makes my fingers twitch. (And I only hope my editors have managed to restrain themselves!) When you're publishing material for parents and others in the community to admire, it's worth the intervention's potential impact on student growth to avert the real impact of general embarrassment caused by errors that get into print.

CONCLUSION: SHARING CONTENT UNDERSTANDING

This chapter presented a set of longer, more elaborate, advanced writing assignments to stimulate student sharing of content understanding. Many of the assignments were recommended for newness to students, ability to promote inquiry and thinking, and connection to the real world.

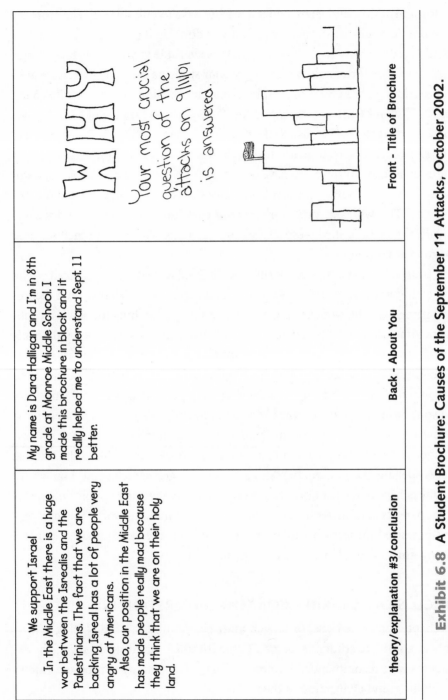

WHY

Your most crucial question of the attacks on 9/11/01 is answered.

Front - Title of Brochure

My name is Dara Halligan and I'm in 8th grade at Monroe Middle School. I made this brochure in block and it really helped me to understand Sept. 11 better.

Back - About You

We support Israel
In the Middle East there is a huge war between the Isrealis and the Palestinians. The fact that we are backing Isreal has a lot of people very angry at Americans.
Also, our position in the Middle East has made people really mad because they think that we are on their holy land.

theory/explanation #3/conclusion

Exhibit 6.8 A Student Brochure: Causes of the September 11 Attacks, October 2002.

Source: Dorothy Syfert, teacher, James Monroe Middle School, Eugene, Oregon.

Introduction

When 2 planes hit the Twin Towers and another hit the Pentagon on the morning of September 11, 2001, no one fully understood what happened. But everyone knew that it was scary, sad, and tragic. The number of deaths went up during the weeks following, along with the number of questions finally being able to be answered.

But one question cannot be answered for sure. Why did this happen, and why do they hate us? Although no one can say for sure, we can make some guesses and theories.

If you find yourself wondering "why?" over and over again, this brochure is perfect for you. In here there is three theories as to why they hate us. Read on to decide for yourself which is the best one.

Our Wealth and Power

Everyone knows that America is one of the most wealthy and powerful countries. Not just rich in possesions, rich in freedoms.

Most countries don't have the luxuries that we have, like freedom to choose, knowing you have enough to eat everyday, etc. This can make people very jealous. In fact, Egyptian playwright Ali Salem says that extremists can become pathologically jealous. Their main goal in life is to destroy America, and there's no compromising with them.

It also doesn't help that people think we are overly-confident. What we call high self esteem, they call arrogance.

Ballot
measure 72
☑ Yes
☐ No

100

theory/explanation #1

Cultures being Erased

Many countries with old and ancient customs and ceremonies hold a grudge against our modern ways erasing their culture. Our music, movies, and ways of life are well known and enjoyed all around the world. And while we don't necessarily mean to erase cultures as one of the most powerful countries, its bound to happen.

theory/explanation #2

Exhibit 6.8 Continued

We considered the Study Guide as a type of CliffNotes synopsis, the related Chapter Review Booklets, persuasive letters both in literature and content classes, the e-mailed version of a book review, and the traditional essay and brochure. In each case the writing process was employed to help remove obstacles.

We are trying our best to make writing less painful and more productive, less "schoolish" and more realistic. We are paving the way to student success with a critically important communication skill: writing.

The next chapter goes into the nitty-gritty of making it all work in a real classroom. It then continues our examination of writing by focusing on a set of special writing skills that must be addressed: spelling, grammar, and researching.

Supporting the Task of Writing

Chapters Five and Six both considered writing as a means for student sharing of their understanding. Both chapters employed the general four-step writing process, both advocated motivating purposes, and both suggested a variety of formats. All key components to "good writing." Yet neither chapter explored some of the details of how you teach this stuff, and neither addressed the critically important issues of spelling and grammar, or what the students could do to collect information beyond what their teacher lays out for them. All these practical elements are an essential part of paving the way for our students—smoothing out the road toward success in school and beyond.

MANAGING WRITING IN THE CLASSROOM

Throughout the book, I've talked about writing assignments and the need to repair them, but aside from a few passing references to First Dare drafting efforts and three rounds of Repair, it may well have seemed as though I came from some pleasant world where writing took care of itself. None of us are that fortunate!

Students need coaching with First Dares and practice with the Repair stage, and—since they start out at such a wide range of ability levels—they're bound to be working on a confusing variety of tasks. After brief discussions of First Dares and of traditional correction efforts and their problems, this section presents the three rounds of the Repair stage in enough detail for you to use them with ease.

Completing a First Dare for Homework

Say you've assigned a news article or some other moderately elaborate piece of writing about the topic you are teaching. And say that your students worked in class on their First Dares during the period, they made some progress, but they did not finish.

An important logistical issue arises here: How much first drafting occurs in class, and how much can be assigned as homework? Tough issue. I really cannot be sure of a formula that truly works in all cases. However, here is my attempt to answer this question.

First, I always conducted the Prepare stage in class, so as to be certain that every student has the same opportunities for getting started on track. Second, the jump from Prepare to First Dare is a big one, so I also allotted class time for this stage, too. I would love to offer ample class time for everyone to finish the First Dare in class. But reality sometimes prevents this, and I tell a class, ". . . Finish up your draft for homework; it is due tomorrow first thing. . . ."

You are clearly aware of the danger of this approach: Some will finish their First Dares as homework, and some will not. Guess which students will not? So the next day you have a split in student readiness: some are ready to move to the next step while others are busy rummaging through notebooks and backpacks looking for the forgotten draft.

Now, a major decision gets made: Allow the nonfinishers to finish their drafts in class? If so, what do the on-timers do while waiting? Really tough call. But is there a choice? How can we proceed to the next stage of the writing process if some students are not yet ready?

Actually, we can move to the Repair stage with the students who have completed their First Dares; they are assigned round 1, *self-repair*. They work independently to revise their work with a "Sentence Opening Sheet" (covered in the "Informative Narrative" section of Chapter Five) or they get to go to the "Editors'

Table" (described with other classroom management tips later in this chapter). The nonfinishers, who probably are the strugglers, use class time to work on their drafts with the benefit of the teacher roving around to offer support because the finishers have been trained to self-repair independently.

Now, this approach can be criticized for rewarding poor homework behavior by letting kids finish in class what was assigned for home. So maybe you can award points to those students who followed through and finished their drafts at home. Or maybe you telephone some students at home when they should be working to ask, "How are you coming along on your First Dare?"

I know, this is not likely. But I will tell you this: I did call students at home to check in on them. Not every student every evening, of course, but I knew which kids in which classes were no doubt struggling to finish writing at home, or were struggling to remember what the assignment was, or were relaxing in front of the TV after assuring family members, "I've got no homework tonight."

So, if I had fifteen or twenty minutes at home after dinner, and if I was not totally wiped out, I would call three, four, maybe five students and spend a couple of minutes checking on their progress.

If a parent or guardian answered the phone, I would introduce myself and offer my assistance to their son or daughter. Typically, the parent would say, "He has homework??!! Robbie, get in here!!!" I then would offer my assistance to the kid. Parents appreciated this overture. And so did the kid. Even though he had to cool down his parents, at least the next day in school he was in better shape on the assignment. And, of course, I'd compliment any kids in class who completed the assignment with my telephoned support. If all my planets were in line the next evening, I would call the students back, congratulate them, and ask to tell mom (or dad, stepmom, grandma) the good news.

My wife objected to my spending nonwork time on the phone to students and parents, and rightly so—like most teachers, I put in more than a reasonable amount of time during the day. But it's paid off very well for me. Now, if this approach is over the top for you, I respect that. No guilt needed here.

Traditional Repairs: Marking Student Errors

When it comes to the Repair stage, one option is for the teacher to collect the First Dares (rough drafts) and mark any errors with a red pen. Anyone familiar with this approach? Sure, we have been using it for centuries. The theory behind this approach is that we model for the students how to write better by identifying the areas in need of improvement. The students use our markings as guideposts for making the necessary corrections.

Good theory. But in twenty-four years of practice I developed concerns about this. First, there is something awkward about defacing a writer's work with bloody red marks. OK, that is a bit strong, but you know what I mean. For a fragile writer, the reaction can be: "I slaved over my hard-earned First Dare and it comes back to me with more red ink than my original blue or black. . . . " This is somewhat of a turn-off. A major turn-off, in fact.

Second, while I was working in my dream job as a part-time teacher and part-time curriculum assistant, I reviewed all the literature I could find on effective practices in teaching writing, and I could not find one study that supported teacher markup of student errors as a way to enhance learning.

In fact, what I found was convincing evidence that this technique has the opposite effect on student writing: it can be detrimental. Why? Because it overly focuses on the mechanics (a.k.a. conventions, rules, errors) and underrates the ideas (a.k.a., content, message, purpose). Both are important to successful writing—errors in the conventions of spelling, capitalization, punctuation, and legibility interfere with the reader's understanding of the precious content. Conventions are a compact between the writer and reader, an agreement to use universal, consistent signposts to facilitate the communication of ideas. So we all spell words the same way, we use commas in certain designated places, and we start new paragraphs at predictable times. Authors do these things to be considerate of their audience and to ensure proper understanding of what they are intending to communicate.

All of which means that lasering in on the students' mistakes can skew their attention away from content delivery. It makes them overly concerned (fearful) of the mechanics of writing—to the detriment of the ideas for writing.

Ask any kid, "What makes for good writing?"

Most will surely say something like, "Spelling, handwriting, length. . . . Did I mention spelling?"

Same for most of the parents of our students. They focus on the surface features of writing, not on the deeper issues of ideas, meaning, structure, coherence. Why? Because they all went to school, and their teachers taught them this.

I don't for a moment suggest that the mechanics of writing are not important.

The opposite is true, as I've already stated: The mechanics reflect critically important agreements that must be fulfilled by all writers for the benefit of all readers. But it's just not useful to overwhelm struggling writers by overdoing it at the wrong time.

Third, marking student mistakes may cause a backlash. Not only the possible anger or resentment factor, but also the ironic outcome of students' actually caring less about making mistakes because they know that "the teacher will pick them up for me later." If a student expects the teacher to spend the weekend marking papers, then maybe the student is getting trained in being careless. Toward the end of my teaching career I began to suspect this more and more.

I was doing the hard work, correcting their writing on an assignment, but amazingly, the *same errors* showed up in the very next writing assignment. Anyone know what I'm talking about?

To correct the errors is short-sighted. It will perhaps improve one particular piece of writing, if the student takes the red prompts and fixes them up. But what is this approach teaching the student? That some teacher will always be there to handle the cleanup? Or that the student will need to make some key decisions about writing? The former, I fear.

So, instead of marking errors, I moved to one-on-one discussions with the students. I changed my approach from "correcting the writing" to "teaching the writer." This occurs in a conference. It is round 3 of Repair, which comes after two other rounds have helped the students learn as much as possible without me.

Round 1 of Repair: Self-Repair

Fixing up a rough draft can be a painful endeavor—as any writer will admit. It is tough enough with word processors on computers, and even more challenging with a handwritten draft facing you on your desk. And if you are a student who is behind in writing skills, it can look like something to avoid at all costs.

Introducing the Editors' Table

To help these kids help themselves, consider setting up an Editors' Table (a table designated for self-repair work) in the back of a classroom—as a place to go when the First Dare is finished. Like the "Sentence Opening Sheet" described in Chapter Five, an Editor's Table trains kids to begin the editing process independently. My former student Leslie is happy at the Editor's Table.

Why a special table for this? Why not? First, students get to move from their desks (where they wrote the First Dare) to the Editors' Table (where they begin to Repair). This physical movement is helpful. Not only does it allow antsy kids to move around, it physically underscores the major role reversal that is occurring.

Changing from an author to an editor is no small distinction. Rather, it is a major transformation. Writers are close to their work; they feel attachment, connection, and ownership. Editors are the opposite. They feel distance from the work; they are critical, suspicious, and strict. Not out of meanness or spite but out of necessity. Editors are the first audience of the writing. It is their job to read critically (in both positive and negative senses) in order to troubleshoot potential problems in the writing that could harm the future audience's understanding and appreciation of the writer's work.

To expect a struggling student writer to make this transition smoothly is naive. So let them leave their desks and move to the Editors' Table to *feel the transition* from writer to editor. They also need access to a new set of tools, and it would be costly to provide enough tools for every desk in the room. Editors' tools are any devices that can be used to fix up a draft—colored pencils and erasers, dictionaries, rulers, and so on. If you follow my practice and limit use of the Editors' Table to four students at a time, it would be a good idea to put sets of tools in four small plastic tubs—one for each self-editor—so there's no contention for supplies.

In addition to hardbound dictionaries, my table included four Franklin Spelling Aces to assist with spelling. These electronic dictionaries are programmed both alphabetically and phonetically, which makes them much easier to use than traditional hardbound dictionaries. Have you heard the joke about the kid who asks the teacher how to spell a word? The teacher says, "Look it up in the dictionary." The kid replies, "I can't. I don't know how to spell it. . . . " Ha-ha. No joke. If you don't know at least the first few letters of a word, you are dead in the water with a paper dictionary. The makers of the Franklin Spelling Ace recognize this and have programmed in 110,000 words and their typical misspellings, so that my students were about 90–95 percent successful finding the proper spelling. Running on four AAA batteries, this device is well worth the $24 it costs. Plus, it has a thesaurus. (For more information on Franklin, visit the company's Web site, which is listed under "Software and Equipment" in the Appendix.)

Procedures for Table Editing

Here are a few rules and procedures I've found it useful to enforce at the Editors' Table:

1. Only four editors at a time may sit at the Table.

2. No talking to any other editor—this is *self*-repair.

3. Pick up a colored pencil—your choice of color.

4. In that color write your name in the top left corner of the First Dare.

5. Read your First Dare softly to yourself.

6. With the colored pencil make any changes you think will benefit your readers.

7. You may use any the other editing tools on the Table—spelling checker, thesaurus, sticky notes, eraser, scissors, Scotch tape, white-out tape. . . .

8. You have seven minutes and thirty-seven seconds to accomplish this.

Here are my reasons for each rule and reg:

1. Too many students at the Editors' Table increases the likelihood that they'll lapse into socializing. This is an important time in the writing process, and it shouldn't be compromised by off-task behavior. (The number four is my subjective preference; you can decide how many of your students to allow at your Editors' Table. The size of the table is a factor, of course.)

2. It's useful for students to talk with each other about their writing—but not at this point in the process. Partner work will occur later, at round 2.

3. The change of pencil is a tangible reminder of the role reversal happening here. It helps the student focus as an editor rather than as the author of the work and remember that an editor has a different purpose. So I tell the students, "If you drafted in black pencil, change to blue or red or whatever color you like for your repairs." This color-coding will continue into rounds 2 and 3 with each additional editor selecting a different color. This allows the teacher to easily see who did what and when.

4. Labeling the editing color choice at the top left corner of a First Dare is for Round 1 of Repair. Round 2 will be with a peer partner who will select a different color pencil and also label that color choice in the corner. This allows all to see who did what. (Thanks to Dorothy Syfert for this technique.)

5. Reading a First Dare aloud allows the writer (now editor) to *actually hear the words* that were written. Teachers know about the gap that usually occurs between what the student was thinking and what actually went onto the paper. Composing

text is a complex act; it requires numerous simultaneous actions. There are bound to be some words or sentences that do not adequately reflect the thought process of the writer. To help students with this, try out this line: "Read your draft to see if your pencil was able to keep up with your brain." Great line. (I picked it up from Leslie Green, a teacher attending one of my workshops. Thank you for this great idea.) This line directly indicates that all writers experience the gap between thinking and writing. As we write, we attempt to move our thoughts out of our brains, down our necks, across the shoulder, down the arm, into the fingers, and out the pencil (or keyboard). Any misstatements, mistakes, or gaps are now blamed on the pencil instead of the brain. Kids like this—it takes some pressure off.

6. It's useful to emphasize that edited changes (the "repairs") are for the benefit of the readers. Amazingly, many students forget this is why we ask them to edit, proofread, rewrite, revise—that is, to Repair. The exercise is not a punishment from the cruel teacher; its purpose is to improve communication between the student as writer and the student's own audience, the readers. This harks back to the "Evaluate the Author" exercise shown in Exhibit 2.5. Having pondered the difference between considerate and inconsiderate authors in the study materials they have to deal with, students find it relatively reasonable when we ask them to be *considerate* authors themselves.

7. Although it's possible to edit with no more than the sort of equipment found in most students' backpacks and desks, having special tools underscores the special nature of the job. Just like Tom Sawyer whitewashing the fence, whatever you can do to make editing a privilege rather than a burden will be effort well spent.

8. The time allocation is purely subjective, but I do want the students not to dally. With limited seating at the Editors' Table, everyone must be thoughtful of classmates who need to get a seat ASAP. Depending on the length of the assignment, I'd say six to ten minutes should be sufficient. To grab their attention and let them know I'm serious about proficiency, I allot "seven minutes and thirty-seven seconds." I always specified an exact time with an activity in class. This precise amount of time is a ploy to get their attention, to impress them with the importance of speed and efficiency. It also scares them because it makes them think I have my teaching down to the second. Sadly, I never did (I usually forgot what day it was), but I was lucky. In every class, I had at least one student with a wristwatch who wasn't afraid to use it: "Mr. Lewin, it's been four minutes and twelve seconds!!" I'd reply, "Thanks, but I know that. . . . I know everything that happens in here." Try it with your students; it will scare them. And you can always extend the time if they need it.

Logistics

Using an Editors' Table involves a few more logistical issues, such as the location. Where you put it depends on the layout of your classroom. And if the room isn't big enough for you to set up a separate table, well, then you may not be able to use this technique. Or maybe you can find a space in the room that could double as the Editors' Table during writing. Or out in the hallway? I don't know about that; it could be problematic, but maybe you want to try it.

Also, what will students do while they are patiently waiting for a place at the Table? It is not likely that you will luck out and have students finish their First Dares in a perfectly staggered sequence of four at a time. More likely, a backlog will develop as the period progresses. So it is mandatory that the class knows exactly what to do while waiting. They need to be trained on the procedure. Some teachers have students work on an illustration while waiting. Others post an early finisher assignment on the board. Or, how about studying spelling list words, reading a library book, writing in the Learning Log (journal)? My students were required to fill out a "Sentence Opening Sheet" before going to the Editors' Table. (Described in Chapter Five.)

Finally, students could be required to bring along their ChecBrics to the Editors' Table, so that they can double-check the targeted elements of the assignment as they engage in round 1 of Repair.

Round 2 of Repair: Peer Partner Editors

When it comes to describing round 2 of Repair, I must begin with an honest assessment: In twenty-four years of teaching writing to middle and high school students, peer partner editing never went as well as I hoped. I tried it in different formats, with different procedures, in different writing modes, at different grade levels, and it never worked as well as I thought it should.

And I know why. Editing is very difficult work. An editor is a *reader,* a very careful reader, whose job is to be on the lookout for potentially troublesome areas, that is, potential bumps in the comprehension highway for other readers who will follow. Editors are highly skilled and trained specialists who help authors become *considerate* to their readers. And they get paid for their services. No professional author would ever (should ever) publish a piece of writing without an editor. (My editor read this chapter well ahead of you, and surely offered suggestions on how to smooth out the road to comprehension for you.)

To expect secondary students, especially those who are challenged by reading and writing, to accomplish this multifaceted task known as editing is asking much. But we do ask it of them, and I believe that we should expect them to step in and do it. However, let's set realistic expectations, and let's structure it for success instead of frustration. Here are seven suggestions for implementing, or modifying, peer editing in your classroom. Some of these I thought of, other ideas come from other teachers.

Shorten Your Sights

You can limit the number of targeted areas to be edited. It is far more doable for a student to edit (read carefully) a classmate's paper for two or three items than for ten or fifteen. Even though quality writing must address numerous (countless?) areas, students get overloaded easily. Keep it simple. And remember: This stage of the writing process can be subdivided into "Repair—editing for content consideration," and "Ensnare—proofreading to find and fix errors." (Professional editors sometimes refer to these as line editing and copyediting.) Both areas are important. Some teachers decide to have separate peer partner sessions for editing and proofreading.

Provide a List of Required Targets

By distributing a list on paper, you reduce the chances for confusion and the ensuing off-task behavior. Be clear and direct. John Collins at the Center for Effective Communication calls these "Peer Evaluation Sheets." For examples, visit the CEC Web site, listed under "Other Instructional Support Sites" in the Appendix. The targets are named "focus correction areas" (FCAs), and the Muskegon, Michigan, School District has been trained in this method. They have posted some samples of student editors working with FCAs on their Web site.

Several alternatives to consider: I have partners use each other's ChecBrics at a peer editing session. Or how about exchanging Sentence Opening Sheets to guide the editing? These provide structured support for the partners. The Stack the Deck Writing Program offers a "Partner Checklist Sheet" for all writing assignments. Visit their Web site, which is also listed under "Other Instructional Support Sites" in the Appendix.

Show the Way

Your list of editing targets should reflect what you have taught (or reviewed) in class. It is overly optimistic to assume that a student will be able to address writing issues in another student's paper if you haven't provided explicit training. I know that by the time they are in middle or high school, students should know how to recognize and eradicate a sentence fragment or when to break a new paragraph. But some of them don't, so *review* it before they are expected to *do* it.

Plan Partner Choice

You should decide whether to allow students to select their own peer editors or to assign the partners yourself. Obvious advantage to the *student choice* option: They will love you for allowing them to pick a partner. Obvious drawback: They will unwisely choose a friend who will not be particularly helpful (but at least they get a chance to gossip about mutual friends. . .). If *you assign* partners, the advantage is that you can use your wisdom to match kids who need each other; the disadvantage is that some kids will hate you for making them work with so-and-so, who is *such a total dork*. When I assign partners, I always forewarn the kids, "You have two choices in reacting to the pairings: You can be satisfied, or you can be neutral. That's it. No put-downs, contorted faces, or hurt feelings allowed in this class." A third option is the *random draw:* kids are paired up by chance. No one can complain that you were unfair, insensitive, or cruel if you do that—but the two weakest writers may well wind up staring at each other's work and seeing nothing for an editor to do. Of course, a teacher may use all the options at different times.

Set Serious Time Limits

Say, "You and your partner have twelve minutes and forty-two seconds to assist each other in repairing your papers. Let's get on with it." If you underestimate the time needed, no problem. Just say, "You are doing well. Need more time? OK, I am extending this activity for another five minutes and ten seconds. Keep up the good work." On the other hand, if you overestimate the time they need, you're in trouble—the kids will take the initiative for filling up the extra minutes. It is far easier to extend time than reduce it.

Offer Fancy Color-Coding Requirements

The students start color-coding their work at the Editors' Table. Now in round 2 the partner picks a different color and labels it beneath the writer's color in the upper left corner, so that everyone knows who did what. Alternatively, some teachers show their students how to use different colors to target different categories of Repair, say, blue for sentence flow suggestions, yellow for punctuation problems, and orange for changing paragraph order. Of course, using fine-point colored marking pens is even more enticing than colored pencils. Highlighter pens are cooler than pencils, but they cost more, and they dry out if you-know-who forgets to put the cap back on. Finally, colored sticky notes can be used in the same way.

Start With the Positive

Require students to identify the successful aspects of a partner's writing. Students in Jennifer Knutson's class in Kenosha, Wisconsin, are directed to use a yellow highlighter pen to indicate strong passages instead of marking the errors they see. Begin with the positive. Or how about the "glows and grows" technique? The "glows" are the strong features of the paper; the "grows" are the areas in need of improvement. I learned this one from a teacher who attended one of my workshops, and I've gotten some good mileage out of it. (I cannot read the name I scribbled. If you read this book, please contact me for proper credit.)

Round 3 of Repair: One-on-One Conference

The word *conference* comes from the root word *confer*. To confer with a student means the give-and-take of a conversation. It does not mean sitting beside a student and marking the errors while the student watches (and grimaces), nor does it mean delivering a monologue pointing out the errors. It is a dialogue.

Here's a sample of this approach in action. Remember "Sky Eyes," the story about Columbus's expedition I introduced in Chapter Five? My former student Mac based his narrative on solid historical ground while adding some fictitious events and characters, including the narrator, Pablo Espolo, a cabin boy working on the *Niña*. You read his repaired version already. Here is the first version he came up with:

"Sky Eyes" ~First Dare~

The creaking of the hull squeezed his head filling his mind with quit dispersion for of all things, dirt, grass, rocks, trees anything not this blue hell that stretched forever about. Above blue skies below the blue ocean. The blue sadness reminded him of the hopeless death that surely awaited him "God does not want us here." he thought "god well kill us here its to late turn back we are lost I know we are lost he dose not say we are but I know we are. we are dead already." A tear rolled down his cheek"hail Mary fall of grace blessed

---

> tho art amongst woman and blessed is the fruit of your womb Jesus hail
> Mary mother of god bless us now and at the hour of are death." he repeated
> this over and over each time quiter than before Intel whisper turned in to si-
> lence . . . . sleep. The boy lay sound on the Nina deck as the night sled in. The
> morning will bring his cold destiny but for poblo Espolo will sleep.
>
> The moon light lite green leafs around a small yellow fire a circle of . . .

As Mac read his draft story with me following along, I avoided the burning
temptation to point out any errors I saw or heard. Instead, I jotted down a few
questions that arose in my mind. These questions were designed to seek clarification on his meaning. In other words, what confused me in his story?

Here are the questions I scribbled on a piece of scratch paper as I followed along:

1. Why is your story titled "Sky Eyes?"

2. Why does he feel "quit dispersion for of all things?"

3. Where did you get the prayer?

4. What are ". . . ." used for?

5. How did you think of the line "as the night slid in?" (Note: I did notice that it
   was "sled" in the original; I'll describe how I dealt with that later in the section.)

Notice that all of these questions to the author are genuine: I really wanted to
know. I was curious, or confused, or intrigued.

For #1 (about his title), Mac replied, "Oh, the Taino Indians in the Caribbean
had never seen Europeans before, and when they saw their blue eyes, they thought
they were looking into the sky." Good answer. Powerful images. Great title.

For question #2 (the peculiar phrase), he replied, "What!!?? I didn't write that."
I said, "Yes, you did. Right here in line 1."

"No," Mac replied, "that's '. . . filling his mind with *quiet desperation* for of all
things. . .'"

"Oh," I said, "Did you run the word processor's spelling checker on the computer?"

"Yeah," he said, "Of course." He realized that the dumb spelling checker had mis-
read his misspellings and inserted the wrong words. Sadly, this happens too often

with struggling spellers. They misspell words so badly that the spelling checker is way off. We should have used the smarter Franklin Spelling Ace. (Described earlier, under "Editors' Table.")

For question #3 (about the prayer), Mac answered proudly, "Yeah, the prayer idea is good. On board the ships, the Spaniards were really scared of dying. I'll bet they prayed like crazy. I wanted a Catholic prayer 'cuz they were all Catholics. I asked my Spanish teacher Senora Jones for one. She helped me translate it into English although in Spanish it might have been more realistic."

Wow.

For question #4 (about the dots), Mac politely informed me, "Oh, those dots show a time delay, a pause for effect. I learned that last year from my language arts teacher."

"Excellent," I said. "Very effective. It's great that you already learned this, and even greater that you remembered to use them."

For question #5 (about the line "as the night slid in"), Mac wasn't sure. "I don't know," he said. "I made it up."

I replied, "I like that line. It captures the gradual coming of night and the character's gradual transition from worried thought to restful sleep."

"Right," said Mac.

You will notice that my questions relate not only to problem areas but also areas of success. And for each answer he gave me, I jotted it down beneath the questions on the scratch paper.

Loaded Teacher Questions

I have a confession to make: Not only did I ask him genuine questions that puzzled me, I also asked a few where I already knew the answers:

- What did you learn about punctuating dialogue—commas, quote marks, and indenting?

- What is the difference between "will" and "well" and "slid" and "sled?"

I asked these loaded, teacher-type questions because they addressed two issues in his writing that were causing problems for me, his audience.

For the dialogue issue, Mac answered, "Well, put quotes around the spoken words."

I said, "Yes, that's right. But a writer also needs to help the reader out by placing the commas properly and to indent whenever the speaker changes or starts talking again even if it's a character thinking to himself."

This serves as a mini-lesson on a key writing skill. Instead of marking his errors, I review the rules. I am teaching the writer for long-term future success, not correcting the writing for a short-term quick fix.

For the question about words such as "slid" and "sled," Mac could see the short vowel differences, but he hadn't *heard* them as he was writing. This learning disability had nagged him for years, so I pointed it out, so that his awareness was heightened.

I am, as his editor, helping him become more considerate of his audience. Remember from Chapter Two the notion that some authors are considerate of their readers by doing whatever is necessary to help them comprehend the ideas? We used this approach with reading; now we turn it around and use it with writing. If students benefit from reading considerate authors, then surely they should return the favor by being considerate writers themselves.

Decision Time

This student-teacher one-on-one conference has truly been a conference in that we *talked* about his writing. I asked the questions. He provided the answers. I explained a few things. The only marking I did was to record his answers.

Why did I write his answers down instead of instructing him to do so? Simple. I can do it much, much faster than he can. If I wait for a student to jot down the answers, the conference could take forty days and forty nights.

After the conference the student-author has a series of decisions to make. Back at his desk, or perhaps at the Editors' Table, for each question he examines the recorded answer and decides whether or not to make a change on the rough draft. In other words, the question and answer trigger a Repair to the First Dare.

Or don't trigger it. It is up to the student. The student is the author, and it is the author's right (and responsibility) to determine what if anything needs fixing, fine-tuning, or refashioning.

As their teacher, who has invested time and energy, I certainly hope they make the improvements to their writing because they will be sharing it with readers. Plus I most certainly will be assessing it. But I cannot mandate the improvements. The writer owns the writing. The writer makes the decisions. And this applies to all writing assignments, long or short, the ones described in this chapter and those from Chapter Five.

Other teachers may disagree. They believe that the student should incorporate at least some of the changes prompted by the writing conference. This is a teacher judgment call. I respect both approaches. Whatever works.

The point is to focus on the student as a writer, not as a producer of errors. I feel confident in this position because the National Council of Teachers of English (NCTE) agrees: "Furthermore, writing teachers who write [themselves] know that effective comments do not focus on pointing out errors, but go on to the more productive task of encouraging revision, which will help student writers to develop their ideas and to achieve greater clarity and honesty" (Online, Accessed November 2, 2002).

Surrogate Teachers

During the one-on-one conference, the teacher jots the answers for the student to save time. And there's not much time. With Mac, I only had five to seven minutes to pull it off because I had about thirty other students in the class needing a conference with me.

Given the increase in class sizes and the increase in students who struggle with writing, the numbers don't add up. Spending a quality five to seven minutes with each student on each writing assignment would mean the conferencing could take five days. No can do. Realistically, a teacher cannot possibly confer with each student in each class period on every writing assignment. It would be ideal if we could, but we teach in the real world, not the ideal.

Until class size is lowered to six students, we probably will have to make compromises with the conferences. I rotated students by assignment. Maybe five to ten kids per assignment. Those I did not get to meet with moved up the priority list for next time. Or maybe the biggest strugglers in the class get more frequent conferences. Tough call here, but what can we do? Too many students, not enough time. Was I subject to arrest for "instructional malpractice" by rotating students? No, of course not. We do the best we can.

One option is to tell the class, "I would love to meet with each and every one of you for a one-on-one conference. You deserve it. But I simply cannot swing that many conferences with this many students. Some of you will be called in for a conference with me. Others of you will get to confer with me on another writing assignment. Meanwhile, since having a teacher-editor to discuss your writing is so helpful, those who don't meet with me will find another adult to take my place for this assignment. The adult is someone over twenty-one years of age who agrees to follow along as you read your paper and ask you questions about it. This helpful human being may be a parent, step-parent, relative, neighbor, coach, clergyperson, or teacher. Be sure to get your adult-editor to use a different color of pencil than you used for round 1 (self-repair) and your partner used for round 2 (peer repair) when jotting down questions and answers. This round 3, adult editor consultation, is due by [date]."

This use of a surrogate teacher is not ideal. Imagine the diversity of skills from the kindhearted adults who agree to edit. And imagine that some of them (most, no doubt) will not understand the genuine questioning approach to editing. They probably will be inclined to mark the errors (choosing a red pencil) and demand to know why the kid can't get this stuff right.

To tighten up this event and make it work as well as it can, I suggest providing students with a cover letter to present to their volunteer adult-editor that expresses gratitude for the help and explains the conference's purpose and procedure. For a sample cover letter to an adult editor, go to my Web site, which is listed in the first section of the Appendix. Feel free to copy it, edit it, and use it.

Or better yet, have the students write a *memo* To: their surrogate teacher-editor RE: "How to help me improve my writing."

Classroom Management

Now, what happens in a classroom when the teacher is meeting with one student? Typically, the other students glance at the teacher to see if the coast is clear for a diversion from the assignment. We need to figure out a way to avoid off-task behavior while a conference is being conducted. We need to do this for two obvious reasons—to avoid wasted learning time in our classes, and to keep from being distracted by time wasters when our undivided attention needs to be on the questions and answers in the conference. I cannot have my antennae toward the class; they must be focused on the student with me in the conference. Nor do I want six or eight kids crowding around my desk.

So classroom rules apply. Students must be trained how to behave during conference time. Here's what I like to use:

- No talking at your desk or at the Editors' Table. I need your total, complete, 100 percent cooperation on this.

- If you have a question for me, write it on one of the blue question slips I have set out for you. Put it in the basket for me, and I'll get to you after the current conference is over. Meanwhile, do something else; be productive. (Provide them with specific directions.)

- When you finish your First Dare while I am in a conference, go ahead and independently begin a Sentence Opening Sheet (SOS). They are located on the shelf over here for you to help yourself. [Exactly: *Help Yourself.*] You may also begin an illustration to accompany your paper. (Or study your spelling list. Or read your book. Or . . . . [anything else that seems relevant to the class].)

- If you want to work with a peer-partner editor, let me know before a conference begins, so that I can find a quiet place for you two.

- If you want a conference with me and you have completed your SOS, sign your name here on the board. I will get to you as soon as I can . . . maybe today or maybe not. Don't get impatient with me; I am working as hard as I can.

- If today is looking like a bad day for you, and you doubt you will be able to follow all these directions, please just say so before we begin, so I can find another location for you to work this period. Otherwise, I will get frustrated with your behavior, and there will be consequences that you'd rather avoid. [The "other location" would be some unappealing place—but not as bad as the promised consequences.]

Of course, you will have your own set of rules for your students during conference time. The key is clear, explicit expectations, accompanied by training students for independent work and seriously following up with consequences for non-compliers. It may take awhile to train some classes, but the effort is essential if you want to use one-on-one instruction.

MAKING USE OF TECHNICAL TOOLS

All the students have pencils and pens and paper, and they mostly know how to use them. But they've been using them since Kindergarten, and it's old hat. Most schools now have the alternative of computer equipment, either in the classroom or in a central lab, that can be used for some assignments. Although I would never advocate using computers for every assignment in every class, I do suggest deputizing them when you can.

Word Processing for Writing

If you have the equipment available, it can be useful to let the students word process their work. What would the advantage of this be? I can think of four advantages to word processing:

- Word processors can check the spelling and advise on corrections. (But they're not foolproof; remember to warn students that the computer can't recognize every error and often suggests the wrong word, so it's still necessary to use a dictionary. Word processors also have grammar checkers, but they are far from intelligent, so be ready to help kids interpret grammar checking.)
- Computers are connected to printers, which have better legibility than most students. (I have never met a printer whose handwriting I couldn't read....)
- Word processors make editing easy with cut, copy, and paste commands. (This is why they were invented: to make Repair less time-consuming and painful.)
- Kids love being on the computer and are apt to be happier and more willing to work than when they're sitting at their desks. (No offense.)

But I'd better be realistic about deputizing computers. I love using them, but they have some definite drawbacks that can reduce or eliminate their effectiveness as a teaching tool:

- Availability. (Some schools don't have computer labs.)
- Availability. (Some schools' labs are booked every period by the technology teacher.)
- Availability. (Some schools have insensitive colleagues who beat us to the lab's sign-up sheet.)
- Dependability. (Some school computers like to crash when our students are using them.)
- Time. (Some students' keyboarding skills lag behind their handwriting skills.)
- Time. (Some students will spend an inordinate amount of time working on the formatting.)

I cannot fix the first five drawbacks, but for that last one, I create a word processed template with all the formatting for a given assignment and save it as a file, so that when the students open the file, they can get started quickly. For a memo, for example, the template provides the To:, From:, Date:, and RE: lines, and the kids fill in the top and then move on to the memo's message. Otherwise, some kids may work forty days and forty nights just selecting a font, size, and style for the headings. And some word processing programs contain ready-made templates for your students to use. For example, my version of Microsoft Word (Word 98) has four memo templates in the File, New dialog box under the "Memos" tab.

Again, deputizing computers can be a big help with teaching struggling writers to struggle less. And even the ones who aren't struggling enjoy the benefits of word processing: ease of editing, legibility of print, cool double-column format, spelling and grammar checkers, and the feeling of empowerment, of being in charge, that a computer can offer.

As helpful as word processing is for composing a first draft (a First Dare), it cannot guarantee perfection. It is still necessary for young writers to go to the third stage of the writing process, Repair. Word processors were invented to facilitate repairing written work. They allow us to process the words in different ways.

A nice technique for round 1 of Repair, if the First Dare was word processed, is using the text color feature. A writer can change some of the text's color from standard black to any other color. For example, the Revolutionary War article in Chapter Five (Figure 5.2) was written at a computer using a word processing program. After typing her First Dare version, the author highlighted all the causes she identified for the war in yellow, read them over, and reconsidered the order she used for presenting them. That allowed her to assess the effectiveness of that order versus reordering them for a better effect on her audience.

This same color-coding technique can be accomplished without computers, of course. Students can use highlighting pens at their desks to color-code key features of their First Dares for self-analysis of their writing. It's just that doing this on a computer is more fun, and no one worries about the caps not being replaced on the pens.

Likewise, the word processor can assist in round 1 by reformatting a First Dare into a Sentence Opening Sheet. The student-writer clicks the mouse at the end of each sentence and presses the Enter key (Return on a Mac) to move the sentences over to the left margin—making a list of sentences. This is Column 1 of the SOS designed to analyze redundancy or variety of sentence beginnings.

School Computers and Home Computers

One last point. If a writing assignment incorporates computer word processing at school, can students finish that assignment at home? This question opens a technological can of worms. First, not all students own computers or have access to them at home. This is an equity issue: we cannot assume all kids can finish at home. If they can, they will need to transport their First Dare home by saving to a floppy disk, by e-mailing it to themselves as an attachment, or printing out a hard copy.

Sending files around either on disk or over the Internet raises the issue of security; school-to-home and back-to-school can bring viruses into the school's network, so discuss this beforehand with your building tech person. The e-mail option requires that students have an e-mail address and that they can access their account from a school computer. Option three, printing out a hard copy at school, requires them to retype their work into their home computer, which defeats—or at least greatly reduces—the benefit of word processing.

Finally, and most important, the student must have the same word processor at home. For example, if your school uses Microsoft Word, then each kid would need Word at home. And if the school has the latest version of the word processing software but the students' home computers do not (or vice versa), they might not be able to open the file with the older system. Again, check with your tech person to explore ways to make this work.

For longer assignments that were to be worked on at home with a computer, I required students to print out and bring to class *each day* a copy of their work in progress. That way, I could see daily where they were in the process and discover who was struggling.

Without a hard copy to look at, I would hear statements from students like, "It's going great. I'm almost done."

Or, "Yeah, I will have it finished on time Friday."

But when Friday arrived, I often would hear, "The computer crashed."

Or, "The printer ran out of ink."

Or, "My dog ate my floppy disk. . . ."

So I am not suggesting that all writing assignments be composed at the computer. I do recognize the powers of word processors, but I also clearly see the problems associated with using them.

BUILDING SPELLING AND GRAMMAR SKILLS

As I said at the beginning of the chapter, if you ask almost any student, "What do good writers do well?" the answer will be, "Spelling."

Ask that student's parent the same question, and guess what the answer will be? "Spelling."

Or maybe "grammar," or "neat handwriting."

Of course, this is not universally true; some kids and adults realize that numerous other factors beyond these "surface features" make for good writing—interesting ideas, helpful organization, sentence variety, cohesion. But many do not. They believe that writing well means correct spelling, grammar, and handwriting.

Spelling

Save the best for last, right? Actually, I have postponed addressing spelling and grammar issues until the end because I have struggled with them as a teacher. These two areas of writing have been, still are, and probably always will be a major challenge to many of our students. But they are very important, so we'd better do something to help them.

Spellings and Misspellings

Why is spelling so important to so many people? I don't really know. It wasn't always true; in Shakespeare's day, well-educated people thought nothing of spelling their own names in different ways, let alone the rest of the language. But I do know that now even the most brilliant piece of writing would be denigrated if it was full of misspellings. People somehow associate spelling with intelligence. We do. We seem to believe that if you can spell well, you are smart. And conversely, if you spell poorly, you must be dumb.

How did we arrive at this assumption? Is it because of all those "spelling bees" held in elementary school? Is it because we confuse possessing a large vocabulary with the ability to spell all the "big words?"

Whatever the reasons for attaching spelling to smartness, they are wrong. Spelling has nothing to do with intelligence. Rather, it has lots to do with good visual memory. Good spellers have the ability to *see* the word in their mind's eye. That's right, they see it. I know that I can see the words. And if I can't clearly visualize a word I need to spell, I write it down in several ways to literally see it on paper, and I can then immediately pick the proper spelling. Anyone else lucky enough to have a good visual memory? For us, spelling comes easily. We would like to be considered highly intelligent for possessing this ability, but it isn't necessarily so. (Although in my case. . . .)

A more likely association is between spelling and reading. The good readers in our classes tend to be better spellers, yes? I suspect this is because reading helps burn words into their visual memories. The more often a reader sees a word in print, the easier it is to see it in the mind's eye.

What about those of us who do not have a flawless visual memory? Spelling surely becomes more of a problem. The same is true for our students because English is not a phonetically regular language like Spanish. In fact, the twenty-six letters of the English alphabet make forty-seven different sounds. The exceptional spellings in English are legendary; just consider the "true" spelling of *fish*. ("G-h-o-t-i," of course: "gh" as in *enough*, "o" as in *women*, and "ti" as in *motion*.)

Spelling Is for Writing

The good news for challenged spellers is that proper spelling is not something that is needed very often. In fact, the *only time* you need to know how to spell a word is when you are using it in your writing. Really, when else do you need spelling? Never, unless, of course, you are interested in becoming a professional spelling bee contestant. Not likely. So, spelling is for writing—it is a subskill of writing.

However, spelling is very important to writing. Although misspelling is not a reflection of intelligence, the reading audience may assume that it is lack of respect to them that allows misspellings. Or perhaps a lack of care on the part of the writer. This is especially important when writing a job application, a college admission essay, or a letter of request. I tell students this: "Do not let your spelling cause your audience to misperceive you. Do not let misspelling ruin your communication, interrupt your message, or deny your purpose."

Spelling Rules

It's useful to begin helping students with their spelling by teaching the spelling rules of English. There are not that many rules, and they are helpful in learning to spell English words. Of course, elementary-level teachers do teach the basic rules of spelling—but the kids often forget them. And some secondary students never truly learned these basics, so they'll profit by having the following list as a reference:

Basic Spelling Rules

- Put *i* before *e* except after *c*, or when the sound is an "a" as in neighbor and weigh. (Write believe, not beleive, but receive, not recieve.)

- A silent *e* at the end of a word makes an earlier vowel long—it sounds like its name. (It turns can into cane.)

- Drop the silent *e* when adding a suffix that begins with a vowel. (Bore turns into boring.)

- Change the final *y* to *i* and add *–es* to make the word plural. (Turn copy into copies.)

- One-syllable words ending in consonant-vowel-consonant (cvc) double the final consonant before adding a suffix beginning with a vowel (–ed, -ing), but multi-syllable words often don't. (Fit turns into fitting, but benefit becomes benefiting.)

- Words ending in *f* become plural by changing to *v* + *-es*. (Turn half into halves.)

For more information on spelling rules, visit the Dyslexia.org Web site or Susan Jones's "Complete List of Spelling Rules for Nouns and Verbs" at Georgia State University. (See "Other Instructional Support Sites" in the Appendix.)

High-Frequency Words

The rules are helpful, but they clearly are not universally applied in English. There are many exceptions to the spelling rules. So the next step would be to teach the exceptions. But of the thousands of words with idiosyncratic spellings, which ones do we teach?

Elementary spelling programs typically decide this by grouping words into *families*. That is, a third grade spelling book might teach a weekly unit on "words that end in –ion (-tion, -sion)." This shows students a pattern that facilitates memorization.

The problem arises when the editors of the spelling program seek twenty words in every family. Sometimes (often) they end up selecting some words that really do not matter. For example, in this list of –ion words, should *induction, objection, abolition,* or *admiration* be included?

No, according to Rebecca Sitton. She is the creator of the "Spelling Sourcebook Series," a spelling program for grades 1–8. Rebecca holds that the only words worth learning to spell are those that are *high-frequency* writing words, meaning the words that are likely to show up in your writing. Since "spelling is for writing," I agree with her and other proponents of this high-frequency approach to spelling instruction.

Rebecca has determined the twelve hundred words most commonly used in student writing and has arranged them into batches for teaching. The words are grouped into lessons by their place in the high-frequency list, not by word families or letter patterns. For example, on her list, words 800 to 810 are *sell, wire, rose, cotton, spoke, rope, fear, shore, throughout,* and *compare. (Spelling Sourcebook 4,* used with permission.)

What do these words have in common? Nothing, really, except that students tend to use them fairly frequently. And amazingly, we have students who, despite being in school for between seven and thirteen years, have not burned these words into their visual memories. Rebecca has many activities for helping students memorize these and other high-frequency words. I used her program when I taught middle school language arts.

A problem arises when students (or their parents or teachers) confuse spelling with vocabulary. Vocabulary includes the words we know how to use when speaking or writing and also words we understand when listening or reading. Spelling all these vocabulary words might be impressive, but it is not really necessary. The only words worth spelling are those that are in your active writing vocabulary, yes? And if you can spell from memory the top twelve hundred words, you are in very good shape.

But what about a science or social studies teacher who cannot afford to spend time teaching these useful spelling words? I suggest creating your own list of high-frequency words—words that are important to the topic you are teaching. For example, when I taught the U.S. Constitution, I knew that my history students would be writing about it, so I made sure they knew how to spell words such as *Constitution, Congress, separation, powers, branches, government.* Even though Rebecca Sitton maintains that research on spelling does not support adding words to the list of twelve hundred, I did it. Why? Because I felt that it would help my students write better in a history class.

Other Spelling Techniques

In addition to teaching the basic spelling rules and the high-frequency word lists, we can provide students with spelling tools. For example, we can borrow an elementary-level technique known as "My Personal Dictionary." This is a small booklet with blank pages for students to record words that are personally difficult for them. They carefully spell the word correctly in their dictionary for future reference. Additionally, they could add the definition, write a sentence with the word, draw a picture of the word, list synonyms or antonyms for the word. Of course, we would rename this activity to make it more appropriate for secondary students. How about "High-Frequency Words Worth Knowing" or "Personal Spelling Checker" or "Biology Dictionary."

A second spelling tool is the computer word processor's spelling checker. I consider it a useful but not totally reliable tool. As demonstrated by Mac in his "Sky Eyes" story (introduced in Chapter Five and revisited earlier in this chapter), the spelling checker is prone to offering false corrections based on very errant student spellings. This is caused by the spelling checker's alphabetical programming, which can put some very strange choices much higher on the list than the word the student really wants—if that word shows up at all.

The third tool is my favorite: the Franklin Spelling Ace (described earlier, in the "Editor's Table" section). Nonetheless, accurate as the Franklin can be with its phonetic as well as alphabetic programming, it is not capable of total perfection in spelling. For example, if a student correctly spells *affect* but really means *effect*, Franklin can't identify this error because it is a usage, not a spelling, error. For a good list of limitations with electronic spellers, visit the Schwab Learning Web site (listed under "Other Instructional Support Sites" in the Appendix).

Some teachers worry that the use of this tool might harm student spelling due to overreliance on it. It can seem all too likely that knowing the Franklin is available for spelling assistance might reduce interest in learning the basic spelling rules and the high-frequency words.

This worry is similar to math teachers' early concern about students' using calculators or language arts teachers' worries about students' using word processors. The new devices are helpful but not omniscient. That is, they are useful to students who know what they are doing. In math a calculator is only as good as the student's inputs. Erroneous inputting results in wildly inaccurate outputs. Same with writing with a word processor. Its features are only useful to a writer who knows how and when to use those features. It cannot make Pulitzer Prize–winning writing by itself.

And, likewise, an electronic spelling checker needs student knowledge to make it effective. That's why I recommend teaching the basic spelling rules and the high-frequency words along with using a Franklin Spelling Ace.

Marking Student Spelling Errors

So what do we do when our students misspell words on their papers? Funny you should ask. Here are the possible reactions a teacher could make to spelling errors.

Mark them. This reaction notifies student writers that the word they selected to help communicate their ideas does not follow the standard American English spelling and needs to be corrected. You can circle the word, underline it, place a check mark above it, or use any other notation you like. Now, once marked, what happens next? Does the student correct the spelling? If so, how? With a hardcopy dictionary, an electronic dictionary, asking a friend, asking you? This must be addressed. Also, what happens if a student fails to follow through on the correction? Point reduction penalty? Returned paper? Teacher-student conference? You need to decide in advance.

Ignore them. This reaction is justified if your focus is on content and content alone, if you are pleased that the student used a good word even if misspelled, or if you lack the time, energy, or interest to enforce spelling.

Value-added spelling. Tell your students that "spelling, while overrated, is an important subskill of writing, and therefore is valued in this class." To prove this to them, say, "You will receive five points on this assignment just for correct spelling. These five points are yours simply for checking the spelling. However, if you'd rather not get them, I will deduct one point for each spelling error." (Later you can bump up the stakes by offering ten points, or by deducting two or even three points for misspellings.)

Reduce spelling errors in the first place. You can do this by teaching high-frequency words likely to be used, employing three rounds of Repair before students submit their writing, or at least saying, "Before you pass in your papers, take forty-two seconds to scan your work for proper spelling. Fix any words that need fixing." Or say, "Before you pass in your papers, take forty-two seconds to scan your work for proper spelling. Circle any words you are unsure of." This is a step in the right direction, and it saves time. Then you decide when to give the class time to fix the errors they marked.

Our Fault?

One final comment on spelling. The problem with student misspelling may be, in part, our own fault. When we teach students to ignore spelling while writing a First Dare, we are encouraging them to use inventive spelling, otherwise known as "guess and go" spelling. Although this facilitates the drafting process by removing a barrier to fluency, it can wrongly suggest to students that conventional spelling is never important. So to avoid this misunderstanding, we tell students, "Inventive spellings are OK in a First Dare, but we will replace them with the correct spellings during the Repair stage as a courtesy to our readers." That's why I make Franklin Spelling Aces available to students at the Editors' Table for round 1 (self-repair).

Grammar

Grammar issues are also difficult for struggling writers—and their teachers. We all agree that grammar is an important convention that makes communication (both oral and written) possible, that it has not been mastered by many of our students, and that incorrect grammar reflects badly on the person using it.

Despite the general agreement on these points, there is widespread disagreement on what to do about it. I do not have a solution to this problem, but I can suggest some reactions to it.

Recognize student language proficiency. Native speakers of American English are experts in our language's grammar. I know that this statement has caused immediate and profoundly arched eyebrows. It seems that many students are far from expert grammarians. (Some even persist in spelling it *grammer,* but since that is not a high-frequency writing word, I refuse to get bent out of shape over it.) I am not suggesting that our students are flawless speakers of English, but rather that after speaking it for thirteen to eighteen years, they have most of it down. And if they can speak the language, they are well on the way to writing the language.

Connect written language to oral language. You can take advantage of the students' speaking ability. Writing in school can be connected to speaking. For example, many teachers use discussions in the prewriting stage. They use discussions for content acquisition of literature, science, history, the arts. Point out to students that although speaking is easier than writing, both are communication modes, and speaking can lead to writing. The National Council of Teachers of English (NCTE) recommends this in their *Guide for Creating an English Curriculum in the Eighties:* "Written language is closely related to oral language. Teaching should emphasize and exploit the close connection between written and oral language" (accessed November 9, 2002).

Practice grammar orally. For example, you can conduct grammar practice with "Daily Oral Language" (Great Source Education Group, 2000), which helps students drill on grammar for five to ten minutes out loud instead of on paper. This reinforces the oral language–written language connection, plus it comes as a relief to struggling writers to leave the pencil on the desk occasionally. Great Source produces teacher guides and student materials for grades 1–12. I used Level 8 when I taught eighth-grade language arts. Each lesson presents a set of sentences containing grammatical errors for the students to identify and correct. Options are available: use the overhead transparencies to beam the lesson onto the white screen as students are entering the classroom. Train them to preview the lesson, so that when the bell rings to start the period, they are ready to go. Or sometimes have them do the lesson in writing, or with a partner. Add variety, so that they do not get sick of it.

Consider other programs. Great Source offers another product that is available to purchase to assist in teaching grammar. "Daily Language Workouts," according to the publisher, "provide a daily, high-impact language workout to develop students' editing and proofreading skills. . . . Daily MUG (Mechanics, Usage, and Grammar) Shot Sentences (and Weekly MUG Paragraphs) contain language blunders for students to identify and fix—a daily jump-start for quick, efficient review and practice." Sandy Becker, a teacher in Minnesota, wrote on the NCTE Web site teacher exchange, "The MUG Shot sentences are much more interesting, centered around a theme. Most have interesting trivia. There are also paragraphs that can be used as tests, reviewing the skills of a particular themed set of sentences. I also think the MUG sentences have more practice on the kinds of mistakes kids actually make and have more practice on useful skills."

Avoid spending much class time on grammar drill. Even though many of *our* teachers relied heavily on grammar drills out of an English textbook, research does not defend this practice. Quoting again from the NCTE Positions and Guidelines: "Watch out for 'the *grammar trap.*' Some people may try to persuade you that a full understanding of English grammar is needed before students can express themselves well. Some knowledge of grammar is useful, but too much time spent on study of grammar *steals time* from the study of writing. Time is much better spent in writing and conferring with the teacher or other students about each attempt to communicate in writing" (NCTE, italics mine; accessed November 9, 2002).

Connect grammar instruction to the students' own writing. The problem with skill drill (and kill) exercises is that even if they are brief (like DOL or MUG Shots), they are disconnected from actual writing. And there is no evidence that practicing with sentences or paragraphs in isolation from one's own writing triggers any reduction of grammatical errors in one's own writing. Many of us have struggled with frustration when students successfully proofread practice drills only to make the exact same errors in their own writing. No transfer of practice into action. That's where tools like the Sentence Opening Sheet, the Stack the Deck four-column self-repair sheet, come in handy—they help guide students into analyzing their own grammar, usage, and mechanics in the context of their own writing assignments. Or you can use the Daily Oral Language or MUG Shots technique but with sentences and paragraphs from real students. Anyone have a source of student sentences with mistakes in them? (Removing the student's name before projecting a sentence containing an error would be required, of course.)

Deputize word processors. As time and equipment allow, let students write with a computer word processor. The built-in grammar checker indicates potential grammatical errors. Though not foolproof, a grammar checker sends an alert to the student-author that something needs double-checking for a possible grammar mistake.

Deputize the Web. Speaking of using computers, you can enlist other people's computers to help you teach grammar rules. Some of my favorite Web sites are listed under "Other Instructional Support Sites" in the Appendix.

Connect the study of grammar to the study of literature. Let the very best writers tutor your students in the fine art of grammar. While reading a piece of fiction, either a short story or a novel, instruct your students to fill in a Sentence Opening Sheet (SOS) on a passage. Then have them conduct an analysis of the professional author's writing just as they would analyze their own writing. Now they get to dissect a passage from the professional's work to discover what a pro does that makes the writing so good—including bending the rules to make the sound come out right. (I gained this idea from the College Board, creator and administrator of the SAT. They suggest, "The SOS Sheet is a useful tool that allows students to contrast the writing of two authors, [or] to study the style of a single author. . . ." (Stack the Deck Writing Program Catalogue and Web Site, 2002).

Finally, make up your own grammar-enhancing activities and send the idea to me, so that I can post it on my Web site for other teachers to Share. I will credit you.

TEACHING RESEARCH TACTICS

Modern lesson plans often delegate some of the responsibility for content learning directly to the students. Instead of the teacher providing all the materials to study, the students are instructed to find their own resources.

This entails researching skills, which have been part of our curriculum forever but never so intensely promoted. It has never been easy to teach students how to conduct independent (or even semi-independent) research, but today it is both easier and more difficult with the arrival of the Internet's World Wide Web.

The Web as a Resource Library

Face it: The Web is here to stay. It is not a technical fad, a distracting toy, just a bunch of dumb games, a flash in the pan. It is a bona fide educational tool that already has had a major influence on teaching and learning. My projection: The Web will increase in importance, usefulness, and frequency in our classrooms. If you don't believe this, then you need to hang on and hope your retirement is soon. However, I also believe that the Web will not replace libraries with their traditional resources. Rather, I see the Web joining these resources, a new and welcome addition to researching tools.

The Web is marvelous for locating information. Now, it is true that lots of that information is accessible from other sources (books, magazines, encyclopedias—hardcopy references available in libraries). But the Web saves gas! And time! It delivers (at varying speeds) the resources right to me at my computer. It is great. I love it.

OK, enough. You get my point. It is a research tool worthy of use in school. But as teachers we must pave the way for our students on the Web. Dangers lurk out there.

First, the issue of garbage. Whatever your definition of garbage, you—and your students—can find it somewhere on the Web. Two choices for blocking inappropriate sites: Your district installs a software filter that obstructs the flow from known objectionable sites or sites with objectionable words. Or you, the teacher, monitor student use of the Web.

I vote for the second option because the filter technique doesn't work well enough; filters tend to militantly block perfectly good sites while missing objectionable ones. Why? The filters are software programmed to do the librarian's job of selecting resources, but they don't have real judgment and therefore tend to apply very simple rules very strictly. For example, a high school literature teacher told me that when he tried to Pre-Search the Web for sites to supplement his unit on Macbeth, the software filter blocked everything and notified the System Network Administrator that he was misusing a school computer! Why? Because in the play, Lady Macbeth utters, "Out, damned spot!" The vigilant filter caught this no-no word and prevented the teacher from accessing the Web sites. Dumb.

Things have improved, but software isn't smart enough (yet), and districts are hard-pressed to hire enough humans to keep one step ahead of the kids on the Web. Plus, to qualify for the federally subsidized e-rate, law requires installation of a filter.

Teacher monitoring is not foolproof either, of course, but we are human, and we are smarter than the kids. If you agree, and you would like to learn more about teacher-monitoring techniques, ask your building or district's technology coordinator for advice.

Evaluating Content Information on a Web Site

The second issue is "information garbage." That's what Jamie McKenzie, editor of the online technology journal *From Now On,* calls misinformation on the Web (McKenzie, 1996, 1997).

A former student of mine once assured me, "Of course all the information on the Web is accurate! Otherwise the Internet Librarian would not allow it!" But you know how untrue that is. In fact, the Web has plenty of misinformation, distortions, inaccuracies, and biased material available. So when students use the Web for researching a topic, they need to be trained to be on the lookout for erroneous, biased, or missing information.

And, by the way, should they not also be on guard when using traditional resources like textbooks, articles, videotapes, teacher lectures? Yes, they should. It's just that the Web has less quality control built in. In fact, it has no quality control—anyone who knows how to construct a Web page using HTML programming (or how to use software that does the programming), has a registered URL (Web address), and a way to store it on a Web server (a computer connected to the Internet with a host address) can post anything at all on a Web site.

No one evaluates the resulting flood of information for approval or disapproval. The Web is unadministered, it is totally open and therefore completely democratic. Well, not completely democratic because it takes financial resources to create and post a Web site, and certainly the money needed is not equally distributed across the globe. As a result, the wealthier countries with established and expanding telecommunication infrastructures, plenty of computers, and cash for software have a far greater presence on the Web than less developed countries—but it's as close to completely democratic as anything the world has ever seen, and rather more chaotic than most human institutions.

Recognizing this, we move to student evaluation of Web resources. Because there is no Internet Librarian, it is the user's responsibility to evaluate Web information. This is difficult for our struggling students. They are so thrilled to be allowed on the Web, and doubly thrilled when they find a site on their topic, that the last thing on their mind is to evaluate it. So here are three ways to help them—three ways to "pave the information superhighway" for them.

First, the teacher does it for the students. That is, the teacher locates Web sites on a topic and evaluates them for content usefulness, accuracy, readability, and layout. If the site is deemed accurate and considerately written and displayed, the teacher directs the students there. In my Internet book I coined the term "Pre-Search" for this approach (Lewin, 2001). Teachers take the time to Pre-Search the Web for useful sites and then screen them and select them for student use. This handles the quality control issue, but it requires that all students use the same Web resources. But what if the assignment is for independent research on individually selected topics?

So a second evaluation strategy is needed. Students need to be trained to do this appraisal independently. I show students how to "take the elevator to the basement of a site," meaning to scroll down the home page to the very bottom to see who created the site. Reputable sites post the name of a person or organization there and often include an e-mail address for getting in touch. This adds credibility— so much credibility that without it, I get suspicious. Sites without identification are like books printed with no author, no publisher, no identification of any kind. Suspicious. . . .

Third, students can learn to evaluate content by being coached on what aspects to scrutinize. Beyond the owner's name and e-mail address, students can look for a host of other considerations, including date of posting, cited sources used, author or organization's credentials, and domain (.com, .org, .edu, .gov), and consider whether this information could be gleaned from another source. In the "Internet Usage: Site Evaluation" section of the Appendix I have listed several Web sites that address this issue and can help you teach your students how to do their own analysis, including media specialist Kathy Schrock's "Critical Evaluation Surveys" and an advanced technique, Professor Nissen's link evaluation.

Digital Plagiarism

Not only do we teachers worry about misinformation from the Web making its way into our students' papers (and minds), we fear that they may use the Web to cheat. And it is very easy to cheat with this electronic medium: words on a Web site can be highlighted with the mouse, copied, and then pasted into a word-processed paper. Students have surely discovered this oh-so-easy way to digitally plagiarize information. In a sense, I am jealous of these kids. When I was in school, I had to *copy by hand* the words from a book, magazine, or encyclopedia that I wanted to steal (er, use) for my term papers. It took forever! Kids today have it so easy....

And the amazing thing is, many of our students do not realize this method is wrong. They think copying and pasting equals conducting quality research. So we'd better teach them how to avoid plagiarism. Here are some nifty antiplagiarism techniques:

Change the assignment. Too often we make an assignment that begs for cheating. For example, a literature research assignment: "Select a Romantic poet and explain his contribution to the movement" is asking for plagiarism because it is so factual. The Web is a perfect environment for fishing for facts—that is, finding them, highlighting them, copying them, and pasting them into a paper. Why not revise the assignment to force students to think about the topic instead of merely regurgitating the information they read: "Select a Romantic poet and explain why or why not this poet's work is a better example of the genre than the work of Keats, whom we have studied." Much tougher to copy and paste on this because it requires analysis, deeper content processing, and evaluation.

Teach students how to use quotation marks. I know this sounds ridiculous to teachers of secondary students, but I have met any number of secondary students who do not really know how to use quote marks to correctly quote a source. Instead of assuming that they know, it's better to review for them exactly how to quote.

Teach students how to paraphrase. Again, it might be easy to assume they have been taught this skill, but why take the chance? It is far safer to review the difference between paraphrasing and plagiarizing. Using terms like "translating," "putting it into your own words," and "restating the information in easier student friendly language" can help as you demonstrate paraphrasing to your class.

Teach students how to cite sources in a bibliography. By "giving credit when credit is due," they are moving away from plagiarism. The Web can be an ally here: I know of three Web sites that have handy bibliographic templates for students to use to create citations. (See "Internet Usage: Online Citation Assistance" in the Appendix.)

Require students to attach a printout of any Web page they cite in their bibliography. This technique comes from Canadian teacher Jason Shea. His students realize that by including the Web resources with their papers, they are providing him with evidence needed to convict them if they plagiarize. (Teachers are smarter than kids.)

Tell students that you have taught long enough to be able to notice a change in their writing. When one of their papers shows up at seven ability levels above where they were yesterday, you'll know it's not a sudden blossoming of genius.

Tell students you have spent a bit of time on the Web, and you have familiarized yourself with most of the Web sites. Of course, that is a lie (estimates put the Web at over *three billion* sites), so get some help. There are subscription services available for schools to electronically submit student papers to be compared to Web resources. That's right, these services match student words to Web site words, and if those student words appear on a Web site, you get the site's address to use when you show your shocked student this "coincidence." TurnItIn.com is a popular paid service. To check it out, along with other antiplagiarism services, see "Internet Usage: Plagiarism Sniffers" in the Appendix.

Get smart and use a free service. When you suspect that a student has "borrowed" someone else's work off the Web, highlight that portion of the paper, copy it, and then go to a search engine. What's a search engine? It is a Web site that will hunt for sites on your topic. A search engine such as Google, AltaVista, or AlltheWeb (listed under "Internet Usage: Search Engines" in the Appendix) matches any words you type in to Web sites that have those same words. Nice device, and free. So instead of using a search engine to locate Web sites to help you teach Shakespeare, environmental disasters, or first aid methods, use it to detect cheating. The search engine doesn't care. How could it? It is software programmed to match whatever words you give it. So if you give it, by pasting in, the words from the fifth paragraph of a student essay on states' rights versus federal centralism that just happens to be written far better than the kid has ever done before, the search engine will provide you with any sites that also have those very same words. Bad news for the budding plagiarist. Good news for you because now your students will believe you when you say, "I've spent a bit of time on the Web. . . ." For a review of this procedure, visit my Web site.

All this implies that the student has written the paper with a computer word processor and you have a copy on disk. If all you have is paper, then you have to type the words into a search engine—but it needn't be too much work, as even a brief memorable phrase in quotes may be enough to get you to the same site the student found.

Finally, why not help nip this problem in the bud by having an honest discussion about plagiarism with your class. Angela Andréa Hernandez, a teacher in Monterey, Mexico, did, and she even supplied her students with a form to define plagiarism and commit to not using it. She has given me permission to post it on my Web site for you to consider.

And the Web offers other resources on the topic. For example, see Jamie McKenzie's useful discussion of "The New Plagiarism" and antidotes for it, in *From Now On* (1998).

CONCLUSION: SMOOTHING THE ROAD

This chapter has been devoted to the details of making writing work in the classroom. It covered the mechanics of classroom management and the three rounds of Repair, the advantages and disadvantages of using computers for writing assignments, and three special writing skills: spelling, grammar, and research. These three skills are so important to student writing that it's useful to review them in detail.

Spelling, always a bone of contention, was addressed in three ways: reviewing half a dozen simple English spelling rules, teaching the high-frequency writing words, and providing students with a set of spelling tools, including my favorite, the Franklin Spelling Ace electronic dictionary.

Grammar, too, has been tough for teachers to teach and students to learn. I suggested a series of instructional options for teaching this difficult but essential skill.

Finally, I looked at student researching skills, focusing in on the new technology, the World Wide Web. I discussed the Web as a resource library, evaluating content information for accuracy, and presented a set of antiplagiarism techniques.

That winds up the basic discussion, but read on. The Epilogue returns to the question of what it is we need to do, and why.

Epilogue: The Work Ahead

I once asked a skillful adolescent reader, "How do you read so well?" The student shrugged and replied, "I don't know, really. I just read it, and it comes alive in my mind."

Alive in my mind.

If I were King for the Day, I would proclaim for every reader the ability to make words on the printed page "become alive in the mind."

As king, I would also proclaim equalized funding for all schools, mandatory Wednesday afternoon early release for students so their teachers could have three hours a week for professional reading, discussion, and planning time, and smaller class sizes.

If that list was impossible even for a king, I would go with "alive in my mind."

I would. Think what this would do for all readers, and for all writers, too.

Meanwhile, while we are waiting for my dream proclamations to materialize, we'd better do something.

And we are. Many of our students do read and write successfully.

According to our nation's report card, the National Assessment of Educational Progress (NAEP), in 1998, the most recent year secondary grade levels were assessed and identified in three levels of reading ability, Basic, Proficient, Advanced:

- At grade 8, a *greater percentage* of students performed at or above the Basic level and the Proficient level of reading achievement in 1998, compared to 1994 and 1992.

- At grade 12, a *greater percentage* of students performed at or above the Proficient level and the Advanced level of reading achievement in 1998, compared to 1994. The percentage of students at Advanced was also greater in 1998 than in 1992. Although the 1998 percentage at or above Basic was greater than that in 1994, it remained lower than the 1992 percentage [italics mine].

But we still have work to do:

Proficient level: fourth graders 31 percent; eighth graders 33 percent; and twelfth graders 40 percent.

Advanced level: fourth graders 7 percent; eighth graders 3 percent; and twelfth graders 6 percent.

Given the realities of our new century, I would assume that Proficient reading is the bare minimum standard for citizenship responsibilities and economic survival, and that Advanced reading ability is probably going to be an important indicator for one's success in the world.

We have our work to do.

Similar news for writing on the 1998 NAEP:

At grades 4, 8, and 12, the percentages of students performing at or above Basic level of writing achievement were 84, 84, and 78 percent. Those at or above Proficient level were 23, 27, and 22 percent, and those at or above Advanced level were 1 percent, 1 percent, and 1 percent.

Looks like we have the basics covered, at any rate. (But the NAEP further breaks down the data by subgroups, including gender, race or ethnicity, parent education level, and free or reduced-price lunch program. You can find this data at their Web site.)

But is basic proficiency good enough for any child? I do not think so.

For those students who still struggle at a basic or near-proficient level, we face the challenge of inventing ways to reach out to them, to connect with them, to convince them to give us a try. That is, to pave the way for them. Until they can read and write successfully without our intervention, it is our job to figure out how best to help them become fully literate.

I have advocated in this book that teachers, all of us, can help. Further, that teachers, all of us, in all grades, in all subjects, in all districts, *must* help. "It takes a village" to teach literacy skills.

Throughout this book I have endorsed reading and writing practices that will bump up student ability to comprehend text and compose text. I examined

- Assigning reading and writing in every classroom
- Providing "training wheels" to support developing readers and writers
- Offering a general problem-solving process approach
- Connecting reading to writing
- Implicitly teaching and modeling strategies to apply while reading and writing
- Structuring writing with scaffolded events that facilitate written communication
- Providing assignments that transcend simple recall as their purpose and move to the higher-order targets of analysis, critique, and persuasion
- Surprising struggling students with new, different, and engaging activities

My suggestions surely are not revolutionary or controversial, nor do they appear to be wildly idealistic. This book has advocated positions that we can all agree on. They seem pretty obvious to me.

According to findings in "School and Home Factors Related to Reading Performance" from the 1998 National Assessment of Educational Progress (NAEP):

- Pages read for school and homework
  In 1998, at all three grades assessed [fourth, eighth, twelfth], students who *reported reading more pages daily in school* and for homework had higher average scale scores than students who reported reading fewer pages daily.

- Explain understanding/discuss interpretations
  Eighth- and twelfth-grade students reported on how often they were asked to *explain their understanding and discuss interpretations of their reading.* At both grades, a positive relationship was observed between these instructional activities and student reading performance. Students who reported being asked by their teachers to explain their understanding or discuss interpretations at least once a week had higher average scores in 1998 than their classmates who reported doing so less than weekly.

- Writing long answers in response to reading

    At all three grades, a positive relationship *between writing long answers to questions on tests and assignments that involved reading* and student reading performance is generally supported by findings from the 1998 NAEP assessment. Students who reported engaging in this activity on a weekly or a monthly basis had higher average scores than students who reported doing so only once or twice a year, or hardly ever. At the twelfth grade, students who reported doing such writing at least once a week demonstrated the highest reading performance [italics mine].

The good news is that many students are succeeding in becoming literate adults due to the wise practices of their literacy coaches.

And for those young adults in grades six through twelve who are still struggling in reading and writing, the good news is that we, their teachers, recognize their struggles, we understand how difficult those struggles are, and we are standing in solidarity with them as they struggle mightily toward literacy.

Author's note: This data comes from only one source, the NAEP. But even with my concerns and criticisms of the overabundance of politically mandated standardized testing, the NAEP is the measure I have the most confidence in. It is, as the organization states, the "only nationally representative and continuing assessment of what America's students know and can do in various subject areas. Since 1969, assessments have been conducted periodically in reading, mathematics, science, writing, U.S. history, civics, geography, and the arts."

Appendix: Web-Based Instructional Resources

The range of online resources available to content area and English/language arts teachers is mind-boggling, and their number and variety increase daily. This Appendix lists those I've set up for your use, found exceptionally helpful in my own work, or otherwise mentioned in the book. They're presented in the following categories:

- Items on the Lewin Web site
- Other Instructional Support Sites
- Reading and Writing Standards
- Online Content-Area and Literature Selections
- Software and Equipment
- Internet Usage

  Site Evaluation

  Search Engines

  Plagiarism Sniffers

  Online Citation Assistance

- Outlets for Student Work
- General Information

Items on the Lewin Web Site

Home page: http://www.larrylewin.com

Larry's Tech Tips for Teachers Web site, Pre-Search, We Search, and Free Search http://www.larrylewin.com/TeachTechTips/techtip%231.htm

Anti-Plagiarism Tips: http://www.larrylewin.com/TeachTechTips/techtip%235_answer4.htm

Anti-Plagiarism Contract by Angela Andréa Hernandez Sepulveda: http://www.larrylewin.com/TeachTechTips/techtip%235_answer4.htm

Letter to surrogate adult editor: http://www.larrylewin.com/Struggling/surrogateletter.htm

"Bandennammen" short story in printable .pdf format: http://www.larrylewin.com/Struggling/Bandennammen/bandennammen.htm

"Bandennammen" short story with embedded First Dare reading strategies in printable .pdf format http://www.larrylewin.com/Struggling/Bandennammen/bandennammen.htm

Other Instructional Support Sites

Bangkok Post Educational Services' explanation of schema theory: http://www.bangkokpost.net/education/schema.htm

Collins Writing Program—"Peer Evaluation Sheets": http://www.thenetworkinc.org/dssbhdpcboss6.htm

Corrective Reading (Engelmann & Becker, SRA) provides assistance with "decoding": http://www.sra-4kids.com/product_info/direct/standard.phtml?CoreProductID=16&navid=6

"Daily Oral Language," Great source Education Group http://www.greatsource.com

Dyslexia.org Web site Spelling Rules: http://www.dyslexia.org/spelling_rules.shtml

Herman Method for Reversing Reading Failure—Dyslexia, reading, remedial reading, learning disabilities, multisensory methods. This site describes Rene

Herman's method of assisting with "decoding" problems: http://www.herman-method.com/index.html

Learning Strategies Database—Muskingum College Center for Advancement of Learning: http://muskingum.edu/~cal/database/ReadingComp.htm#Strategies

Muskegon, Michigan, School District—samples of student editors working with "focused correction areas" (FCAs): http://www.muskegonisd.k12.mi.us/language/writing_strategies/five_types_writing4.htm

Reading strategies for ESL students (likely to work for native speakers as well)—Vietnamese Language Homepage maintained by Lê Pham Thuy-Kim at Arizona State University: http://www.public.asu.edu/~ickpl/Reading_Strategies.htm.

Reading strategies from Valerie Gray Hardcastle at the Department of Philosophy/Center for Interdisciplinary Studies at Virginia Tech: http://mind.phil.vt.edu/www/1204crs.html

Reading strategies from Kathleen King at Idaho State University (drawing on the work of Lee Haugen, a Reading Specialist at ISU Academic Skills Center): http://www.isu.edu/~kingkath/readstrt.html

Rebecca Sitton's Spelling Sourcebook Series: http://www.sittonspelling.com

REWARDS (Reading Excellence: Word Attack and Rate Development Strategies) Student Book (set of ten). The Multisyllabic Word Reading Program method of "decoding" words by segmenting their parts is key to the creatively designed exercises in this program. http://www.sopriswest.com

Schwab Learning Web Site, Electronic Spellers: http://www.schwablearning.org/articles.asp?r=444&g=4

Stack the Deck Writing Program—Karen Antikajian's Synonyms for Said: http://www.stackthedeck.com; at the bottom, click on "Teaching Tips," then click on "*Said* Synonyms from *Check*"

Stack the Deck Writing Program—Partner Checklist Sheet (versions available for all Stack the Deck writing assignments): http://www.stackthedeck.com/labor.html

Stack the Deck Writing Program—Sentence Opening Sheet: http://www.stack-thedeck.com; at the bottom, click on "Teaching Tips," then click on Great Strategy to Help Students Revise Using Our Sentence Opening Sheet (SOS) and Revision Strategy with a Word Processor (Based on SOS Sheet)

Susan Jones's "Complete List of Spelling Rules for Nouns and Verbs" at Georgia State University: http://www.gsu.edu/~wwwesl/egw/susan.htm

University of Arizona's Instructional Support Group Web site: http://www.u.arizona.edu/ic./wrightr/other/sq3r.html

University of St. Thomas Instructional Support Services (ISS) Web site: http://www.iss.stthomas.edu/studyguides/texred2.htm

Reading and Writing Standards

Four Traits of Reading Scoring Guide, Secondary Grades 6–12, Oregon Department of Education: http://www.ode.state.or.us/asmt/scoring/guides/student/6-12rdg.pdf

National Council of Teachers of English, Commission on Composition, Teaching Composition: A Position Statement: http://www.ncte.org/positions/teaching_composition.shtml

Northwest Regional Educational Lab, The Traits of an Effective Reader: http://www.nwrel.org/assessment/scoring.asp?odelay=3&d=2

Oregon's Six Traits of Writing Scoring Guide, Oregon Department of Education Web Site: http://www.ode.state.or.us/asmt/resource/scorguides; click on "Writing"

Texas Essential Knowledge and Skills (TEKS), 6th grade level, English Language Arts and Reading: http://www.tea.state.tx.us/rules/tac/chapter110/ch110b.html#110.22

Washington, Office of the Superintendent of Public Instruction, Reading BENCHMARK 3—GRADE 10: http://www.k12.wa.us/curriculumInstruct/ealrs/default.asp?iSubjectID=5

Online Content-Area and Literature Selections

David K. Brown's "Children's and Young Adult Literature Web Guide" which features a page on Story Collections: http://www.acs.ucalgary.ca/~dkbrown/storcoll.html.

John McPhee, skilled personal essayist: http://www.johnmcphee.com.

Project Bartleby, Columbia University's archive, offers links to key texts in hypertext editions of classic literature. http://www.bartleby.com

The Moonlit Road: http://www.themoonlitroad.com/index.html; I found this via David Brown's site, which routed me to "Ghost stories and strange folktales of the American South, told by the region's most celebrated storytellers." Students can "read it," "listen to it," and "discuss it."

Tom Cantwell, my friend and colleague from the Eugene, Oregon, School District, writes great stories for young adult readers. Check him out at his Web site: http://www.cantwellbooks.com

Software and Equipment

AppleWorks: http://www.lowendmac.com/tech/trifold.html

ClickBook: http://www.bluesquirrel.com/clickbook

Electronic Graphic Organizers, Inspiration Software: http://www.inspiration.com

Franklin Spelling Ace: http://www.franklin.com/estore/platform/bookman/category.asp?category=2 (Spelling Ace is at the bottom of the page)

Making a Tri-fold Brochure Using AppleWorks 6.0 on a Mac, Low End Mac's On-Line Tech Journal: http://www.lowendmac.com/tech/trifold.html

Microsoft Publisher: http://www.microsoft.com/office/publisher

Microsoft Word: my version, Word 98, has a "Brochure 1" template when I open a "New" file and select "Old Word Templates"

Schwab Learning Web Site, Electronic Spellers: http://www.schwablearning.org/articles.asp?r=444&g=4

Internet Usage: Site Evaluation

Classroom Connect's ED's Oasis Speed O'Light: http://www.classroom.com/edsoasis/evaluation.html

Kathy Schrock's Evaluation Survey: http://school.discovery.com/schrockguide/eval.html

Prof. Nissen's Web Site Validator: http://www.indiana.edu/~latino/325/nissen/validation.html

Internet Usage: Search Engines

Google: http://www.google.com

AltaVista: http://www/altavista.com

AlltheWeb: http://www.alltheweb.com

Internet Usage: Plagiarism Sniffers

TurnItIn.com

Glatt Plagiarism Services: http://www.plagiarism.com

Internet Usage: Online Citation Assistance

EasyBib: http://www.easybib.com

NoodleTools' Quick Cite: http://www.noodletools.com/quickcite

Oregon School Library Information System (OSLIS) Web site: http://www.oslis.k12.or.us/tutorials/cited/index.html; click on "Cite Works Form"

Outlets for Student Work

Gail M. Szeliga, "K12 sites that publish student's writing," Nov. 1997: http://scout.cs.wisc.edu/addserv/NH/97–08/97–08–19/0005.html

Karen Kellaher at *Adventures in Writing*

Merlyn's Pen: http://www.merlynspen.com

MidLink Magazine: http://www.cs.ucf.edu/~MidLink/mission.htm

Stone Soup: http://www.stonesoup.com

The National Council of Teachers of English (NCTE) Writing Contests: http://www.ncte.org/solutions/publishstudentwriting.shtml

The Write Source "Publish It": http://www.thewritesource.com/publish.htm

General Information

Adina Marcus, Churchill Junior High School, East Brunswick, N.J., Distance Learning article: http://www.njsba.org/members_only/publications/school_leader/sept-oct-2001/spotlight_on_learning.htm

Stack the Deck's SOS Praise—College Board Quote on Sentence Opening Sheet: http://www.stackthedeck.com/tips-college.html

U.S. Network for Global Economic Justice, "50 Years is Enough": http://www.50years.org

William O. Beeman's article "Understanding Osama bin Laden," Pacific News Service, Alternet: http://www.alternet.org/story.html?StoryID=11487

I am always interested in learning about additional educational Web resources, so please e-mail me with your favorite sites: larry@larrylewin.com. Also, be sure to check out my Web Site for links to all the sites listed on these pages. This will save you from typing the URL addresses: www.larrylewin.com.

Bibliography

"A Little Theory." Bangkok Post Educational Services. Available online: http://www. bangkokpost.net/education/schema.htm. Access date: Aug. 2002.

Anderson, R. C., and Pearson, P. D. "A Schema-Theoretic View of Basic Processes in Reading Comprehension." In P. D. Pearson (ed.), *Handbook of Reading Research*. New York: Longman, 1984.

Beatty, P. *Lupita Mañana*. New York: Beech Tree, 1981.

Beeman, W. O., "Understanding Osama bin Laden," Pacific News Service, 2001. Available online: http://www.alternet.org/story.html?StoryID=11487. Access date: July 2002.

Bennett, J., Donahue, M., Schneider, N., and Voit, M. *The Essential Cosmic Perspective* (2nd ed.). Menlo Park, Calif.: Addison-Wesley, 2003.

Burke, J. *Reading Reminders: Tools, Tips, and Techniques,* Portsmouth, N.H.: Heinemann, 2000.

College Board's Review of the Sentence Opening Sheet. Available online: http://www. stackthedeck.com/tips-college.html. Access date: Oct. 2002.

Great Source Education Group. "Daily Oral Language," 2000. Available online: http://www. greatsource.com. Access date: July 2002.

Hillocks, G., Jr. *Research on Written Composition: New Directions for Teaching*. Urbana, Ill.: National Conference of Research in English/ERIC Clearinghouse on Reading and Communication Skills, 1986.

Hillocks, G., Jr. *Teaching Writing as Reflective Practice*. New York: Teachers College Press, 1995.

Hrebic, H., and Cahill, R. *Stack the Deck,* 2001. Available through the "Stack the Deck Writing Program," P.O. Box 429, Tinley Park IL 60477. Program and catalogue available online: http://www.stackthedeck.com/. Access date: Oct. 2002.

Inspiration Software. "Inspiration, version 7." Available online: http://www.inspiration.com/. Access date: Oct. 2002. Company address: 7412 SW Beaverton Hillsdale Hwy., Portland OR 97225.

Lewin, L. *Using the Internet to Strengthen Curriculum.* Alexandria, Va.: Association for Curriculum and School Development, 2001. Available online: http://www.ascd.org/readingroom/books/100042.html. Access date: Dec. 2002.

Lewin, L., and Shoemaker, B. J. *Great Performances: Creating Classroom-Based Performance Assessments.* Alexandria, Va.: Association for Curriculum and School Development, 1998.

LeWine, L. *Bandennammen.* Eugene, Oreg.: Damp Dog Press, 2002.

LeWine, L. *The First Time.* Damp Dog Press, 1983.

Lowery, L. *Number the Stars.* Boston: Houghton Mifflin, 1989.

McKenzie, J. "Info-Glut, Info-Garbage, and Info-Treasure." *From Now On,* 1996, *5*(6). Available online: http://www.fno.org/may96/infoglut.html. Access date: Aug. 2002.

McKenzie, J. "Deep Thinking and Deep Reading in an Age of Info-Glut, Info-Garbage, Info-Glitz and Info-Glimmer." *From Now On,* 1997, *6*(6). Available online: http://www.fno.org/mar97/deep.html. Access date: Nov. 2002.

McKenzie, J. "The New Plagiarism: Seven Antidotes to Prevent Highway Robbery in an Electronic Age." *From Now On,* 1998, *7*(8). Available online: http://www.fno.org/may98/cov98may.html. Access date: Nov. 2002.

McTigue, J. "Maryland Assessment Consortium," 2000. Available online: http://mac.cl.k12.md.us:2000. Access date: Oct. 2002.

Murray, D. M. "Teaching Writing as a Process Not Product." *Leaflet,* 1972, *81*(4), 11–14.

Myers, W. D. *Fallen Angels.* New York: Scholastic Paperbacks, 1991.

National Center for Education Statistics. "The Nation's Report Card (home)," 2002. Available online: http://nces.ed.gov/nationsreportcard/about/. Access date: Nov. 2002.

National Center for Education Statistics. "The National Assessment of Educational Progress 1998 Reading Report Card for the Nation and the States," Mar. 1999. Available online: http://nces.ed.gov/nationsreportcard//pubs/main1998/1999500.asp. Access date: Nov. 2002.

National Center for Education Statistics. "The National Assessment of Educational Progress 1998 Writing Report Card for the Nation and the States," Sept. 1999. Available online: http://nces.ed.gov/nationsreportcard//pubs/main1998/1999462.asp. Access date: Nov. 2002.

National Council of Teachers of English. *Guide for Creating an English Curriculum in the Eighties.* Urbana, Ill.: National Council of Teachers of English. "Positions and Guidelines." Available online: http://www.ncte.org/positions/how-to-help.shtml. Access date: Aug. 2002.

National Council of Teachers of English, Commission on Composition. *Teaching Composition: A Position Statement.* Urbana, Ill.: National Council of Teachers of English. Available online: http://www.ncte.org/positions/teaching_composition.shtml. Access date: July 2002.

Northwest Regional Educational Laboratory. "Six Traits of an Effective Reader." Available online: http://www.nwrel.org/assessment/scoring.asp?odelay=3&d=2. Access date: Oct. 2002.

Odell, S. *Sarah Bishop*. New York: Scholastic Books, 1988.

Ogle, D. "KWL." *Reading Teacher,* 1984, *39,* 564.

Oregon Department of Education. "Reading Traits." Available online: http://www.ode.state.or.us/asmt/reading/readingscoringguide4–12.pdf. Access date: Oct. 2002.

Oregon Department of Education. "Six Traits of Writing Scoring Guide." Available online: http://www.ode.state.or.us/asmt/resource/scorguides. Access date: Oct. 2002.

Patterson, K. *Lyddie*. New York: Dutton, 1991.

Pearson, P. D., and Johnson, D. D. *Teaching Reading Comprehension*. Austin, Tex.: Holt, Rinehart and Winston, 1978.

Robinson, A. "Kelfala's Secret Something." In A. Applebee (ed.), *The Language of Literature*. Evanston, Ill.: McDougal Littel, 2001.

Shoemaker, B. J., and Lewin, L., *Creating the Future Through Innovative Instruction*. Norwood, Mass.: Christopher-Gordon, forthcoming.

Soto, G. "Fear." In *Living Up the Street*. New York: Bantam, 1992.

Soto, G. "The Challenge." In *Local News*. New York: Scholastic Paperback, 1993.

Soto, G. "Born Worker." In A. Applebee (ed.), *The Language of Literature*. Evanston, Ill.: McDougal Littell, 2001.

"Survey Routine," University of Kansas Center for Research on Learning, 3061 Dole Center, Lawrence, KS 66045.

Tierney, R. J., and Pearson, P. D. "Toward a Composing Model of Reading." *Language Arts,* 1983, *60,* 568–580. (Reprinted in J. Jensen (Ed.), *Composing and Comprehending*. Urbana Ill.: ERIC/RCS & National Conference on Research in English, 1984).

Twain, M. "The Californian's Tale." In A. Applebee (ed.), *The Interactive Reader*. Evanston, Ill.: McDougal Littell, 2000.

Yep, L. "The Great Rat Hunt." In A. Erlich (ed.), *When I Was Your Age*. Cambridge, Mass.: Candlewick Press, 1996.

"Why Do They Hate Us?" *Teen Newsweek,* 2001, *3*(4), 9.

Index

A

Adult editing (one-on-one conference) Repair: classroom management of, 196–202; described, 141

Advanced writing skills: brochure assignments for developing, 178–179, 180*e*–181*e*, 182; essay assignments for developing, 177–178; final thoughts on share stage of, 182–183; informational/emotional content and, 173–177; Study Guides for developing, 153–173. *See also* Writing

Adventures in Writing (magazine), 182

Alternet Web site, 40

Analyzing strategy, 49

Anderson, R. C., 23

"Anticipatory set," 18

Atwell, N., 6

Author feedback memo: additional preparation possibilities for giving, 133–134; content area memo for, 131–132; early repairs for, 134–136; literature class, 136–137; paving the way for student, 132–133; sample template for, 135*e*; text structure of, 133; using, 129, 130

Author/text evaluation, 41–42, 43*e*, 44

B

"Bandennammen" Critique Memo, 113*e*–114*e*

"Bandennammen" (LeWine), 82, 83*e*

"Bandennammen" (LeWine) lesson: E.G.O. (electronic graphic organizer), 102, 103*fig*; Embedded First Dare Reading Strategies, 104*e*–105; First Dare step for, 102, 104–105; practical Interpretative Cards for, 107–110; Prepare step for, 102, 103*fig*; Repair step for, 105–110; Share step for, 110–114*e*; Sticky Stories activity for, 102, 104; Strategy Prompts: "Bandennammen," 149*e*

Bangkok Post Educational Services, 24, 25

Barnett, G., 28

Becker, S., 213

Beeman, W. O., 40

Bennett, J., 53

Blum, J., 171

Bonar, J., 168

Book review persuasive e-mail, 171–172

Borkon, S., 151

"Born Worker" (Soto), 73

Bo's Open Mind, 37*fig*

Bradford, J., 63

Brochure writing assignments, 178–179, 180e–181e, 182
Burke, J., 153

C

Caffeine, Sugar, and Bone Loss Web site, 1688
Cahill, B., 148
"The Californian's Tale" (Twain), 155
Calkins, L., 6
"The Challenge" (Soto): ChecBric: "The Challenge," 94e–95e; Clip Art for SnapShots, 96fig; Complex Photo Album: "The Challenge," 92fig–93fig; final draft on, 89, 91, 93, 95, 98; Simple Photo Album: "The Challenge," 90fig; using SnapShots to understand, 87, 172
Character Analysis Sheet: "Bandennammen" lesson using, 83e, 106–107; description/example of using, 82, 84–85
Character Emotional Scenes activity, 69, 73, 74fig
ChecBric: Memo Writing, 130e
ChecBric: "The Challenge," 94e–95e
ChecBric: Translation Exercise, 52e
ChecBric: assessing student writing using, 129, 130e; comic strip activity and, 63; description/use of, 50–51, 54; Reading ChecBric: "The Californian's Tale" Study Guide, 158e–159e; Student Sample Study Guide: "The California's Tale," 161e; Study Guides and, 156; Writing ChecBric: "The California's Tale" Study Guide, 160e
Chemistry review booklets, 159, 161–162
Chemistry Study Guide: Jessica, 162e
Chemistry Study Guide: Ryan, 163e
Circle Version, 39fig
Classroom one-on-one conference: classroom management during, 201–202; decision time during, 199–200; described, 196–197; loaded teacher questions during, 199; on "Sky Eyes" (student assignment), 197–200; using surrogate teachers during, 200–201
Classroom Repair rounds: one-on-one conference, 196–202; peer partner editors, 194–196; self-editing, 189–194, 190fig
Classroom self-editing management: Editors' Table, 189–191, 190fig; logistics of, 193–194; procedures for table editing, 191–193
Classroom writing management: building special writing skills and, 206–215; completing First Dare homework, 186–189; Repair rounds of, 189–202, 190fig; researching skills and, 215–220; technical tools for writing and, 203–206. See also Writing
CliffNotes, 154–155, 159. See also Study Guides
Clip Art for SnapShots, 96fig
"Coke Loses Its Fizz" (newspaper editorial), 168
Comic strip activity, 61–64fig, 62fig
Comic Strip Panel: Columbus Reaches the New World, 62fig
Comic Strip Panel: Human Digestion, 64fig
"Complete List of Spelling Rules for Nouns and Verbs" (Jones), 208
Complex Photo Album: "The Challenge," 92fig–93fig
Comprehension. See Reading Comprehension
Computer skills, 205–206
Creative writing, 118

Literary text: comprehension of information text versus, 67; connecting grammar to study of, 214–215; Prepare and First Dare activities for, 67–79; Repair step activities for, 79–87; sample lesson for "Bandennammen," 101–114; Sharing step activities for, 87–101. *See also* High School literature class

Lupita Man[=]ana (Beatty), 69

Lyddie (Patterson), 146

M

McCormick, Marge, 151, 152

McDougald, P., 159

McKenzie, J., 220

McTigue, J., 129

Madras High School (Oregon), 38

Mansell, M., 143

Mappes, R., 34

Marcus, A., 171

May, E. L., 131

Meaning, 48

"Meeting of the minds" activity, 41–42, 43*e*, 44

Memo. *See* Author feedback memo

Memories: past knowledge stored in, 23; schemata categories of stored, 24

Menu of Content Reading Repair Strategies, 49*e*

Menu of Literature Reading Repair Strategies, 80*e*

Menu of Reading First Dare Strategies, 22*e*

Menu of Reading Prepare Strategies, 19*e*

Merlyn's Pen (magazine), 182

MUG (Mechanics, Usage, and Grammar), 213

Murray, D., 8

"My Personal Dictionary" technique, 210

Myers, W. D., 142

N

NAEP (National Assessment of Educational Progress), 223–224, 225–226

Narrative writing mode, 126

National-Louis University, 32

NCTE Positions and Guidelines, 214

NCTE Web site, 213

New England Association of Teachers of English, 6

Newman, J., 36

News Article: "The Revolutionary War," 146*fig*

News article assignment, 144–146*fig*

Number the Stars (Lowery), 101

NWREL (Northwest Regional Educational Lab) Web site, 11, 13*e*

O

Ohio State, 7

OM (Open Mind) activity: literary text, 69, 72*fig*; text comprehension, 36, 37*fig*, 38

One-on-one conference Repair: classroom management of, 196–202; described, 141

"Opener" (mini-writing assignment), 172–173

Oregon Department of Education, 11, 12*e*, 172

P

Partner editing (peer review) repair: classroom management of, 194–196; described, 141

Past knowledge, 23–25, 25–32

Patterns in the Sky activity, 53–55

Patterson, K., 146

Paulsen, G., 120

Pearson, P. D., 7, 23

Perspective-taking strategy, 49

The Self-Directed Learning Handbook

Challenging Adolescent Students to Excel

MAURICE GIBBONS

$19.95 • Paperback
ISBN: 0-7879-5955-3

"When Maurice Gibbons introduced his Walkabout model a few years ago, he opened exciting new possibilities for relevant, meaningful, and challenging learning to take place in high schools. In this new book he provides teachers with a comprehensive, step-by-step process for realizing these possibilities in their classrooms."

—Ron Miller, executive editor, *Paths of Learning*

School reform advocates have called for more personalized approaches to teaching, both to promote independent and high-level thinking and to honor the diverse ways that students learn. *The Self-Directed Learning Handbook* offers teachers, principals, and even parent home schoolers an innovative program for customizing schooling to the learning needs of individual students and for motivating them to take increasing responsibility for deciding what and how they should learn.

A student's individualized learning plan may involve community field projects as well as academics and can be designed to develop particular skills or abilities. Advanced students welcome the special challenges; the less advanced discover new strengths and abilities, bolstering their confidence and motivation. The book includes abundant examples of lesson units, student contracts, and assessment instruments, and offers guidance on motivating students, on negotiating student learning agreements, as well as on managing independent learning in the classroom.

Books of Interest

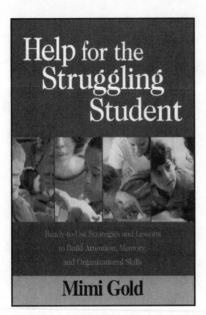

Help for the Struggling Student

Ready-to-Use Strategies and Lessons to Build Attention, Memory, and Organizational Skills

MIMI GOLD

$29.95 • Paperback
ISBN: 0-7879-6588-X

"Mimi Gold approaches teaching with insight and imagination. All parents, teachers and students will benefit from her creative approaches for the struggling student."

—Dr. Barbara M. Weissman, associate professor of pediatrics,
Emory University School of Medicine

Written by an experienced educator who works with at-risk students of all ages, *Help for the Struggling Student* is a unique picture book of learning solutions for teachers and parents who are trying to help students struggling in three main areas of learning—attention, memory, and organization. For each area, it identifies specific problems such as difficulties with left to right scanning (an attention problem), presents an observed student behavior, explains the problem, and provides strategies and visuals to correct it, including illustrated worksheets.

Help for the Struggling Student also provides information about how to identify a student's personal learning style, select strategies for the individual student based on his or her learning style and needs, and tailor these strategies to help students become more effective, independent, and successful learners.

Prices subject to change.

Reading Workshop Survival Kit

Gary Robert Muschla

$29.95 • Paperback

ISBN: 0-87628-592-2

Here is a complete, step-by-step guide to setting-up and running a successful reading workshop in grades 5–12.

Part I, "Management of the Reading Workshop," offers a host of specific strategies, techniques and reproducible materials for classroom management and student evaluation, including communication techniques, building a positive atmosphere, organizing discussion groups, and using portfolios, student logs, and conferencing to assess progress.

Part II, "Using Mini-lessons in the Reading Workshop," provides 100 different ready-to-use mini-lessons focusing on specific reading topics and skills. Each lesson stands alone, can be used in any order you wish and is accompanied by reproducibles. The lessons cover various types of reading (from mysteries, to mythology, to poetry); story elements (including leads, symbolism, motivation, foreshadowing, etc.); and 25 specific reading skills such as cause and effect, fact vs. opinion, detail recall, and other strategies to enhance comprehension. In short, the *Reading Workshop Survival Kit* gives you all the guidelines and tools you need to use the workshop approach effectively.

Prices subject to change.

Books of Interest

Real-Life Reading Activities for Grades 6–12

Over 200 Ready-to-Use Lessons to Help Students Master Practical Reading Skills

JAMES F. SILVER

$29.50 • Paperback
ISBN: 0-13-044460-X

Help your students experience greater school success and give them confidence in mastering reading challenges across the curriculum! For reading specialists and English teachers, here are over 200 ready-to-use lessons and exercises to teach and reinforce basic reading skills with students of all abilities.

Organized in seven convenient sections followed by a complete answer key, each lesson includes an instructor's page with background information and teaching suggestions followed by one or more Student Skillsheets for sequential development of skills. Some of the topics covered include vocabulary development; reading diagrams and charts; interpreting maps, tables and graphs; building study skills; and connecting to writing and research.

These lessons and activities are completely flexible and can be used with individual students or an entire class to meet particular corrective or remedial reading skill needs.